To Sue
and
Pat, Jr., and Missy
and Brett and Wanda

To Pat,
War Eagle
Pat Dye

Whatsoever thy hand findeth to do,
do it with all thy might.
Ecclesiastes 9:10
(Quoted in the 1957 Richmond
Academy *Rainbow*.)

IN THE ARENA

IN THE
Arena

By Pat Dye
With John Logue

The Black Belt Press

Montgomery

The Black Belt Press
P.O. Box 551
Montgomery, AL 36101

Printed in the United States of America
by Arcata Graphics, Fairfield, Pennsylvania.

LIBRARY OF CONGRESS CATALOGING-IN-PUBLICATION DATA

Dye, Pat (Patrick Fain), 1939-
    In the Arena / Pat Dye, with John Logue.
    p.   cm.
    ISBN 1- 881320-00-6: $21.95
    1. Dye, Pat (Patrick Fain), 1939-   . 2. Football–United States–
    Coaches–Biography. 3. Auburn University–Football–History.
    I. Logue, John, 1933-   . II. Title
    GV939.D94A3 1992
    796.332'092–dc20
    [B]
                                    92-27625
                                    CIP

All photographs courtesy of the Auburn University Athletic Department, Auburn University Sports Information Office, Auburn University Photographic Services, and the Dye family.

Contents

IN THE ARENA

WINNING

Well, you know my race is not run in coaching.

Not yet. It's no fun to lose. I hate losing. But I don't hate losing to the point that I'm gonna do anything stupid, or anything drastic, or immoral, or illegal. I'm just gonna find a way to win.

My basic philosophy is: if you are losing, you've got to find a way to be a little more productive, work a little harder, make sure that you are doing the right things, and doing them with all your might.

A COACH'S FOREWORD

I didn't get into coaching football to make money. I have to laugh when I read critics who say coaches make too much money. Anybody who got into coaching when I did knows there was no money to be made in 1965. I stayed an assistant coach at the University of Alabama for nine seasons. Coach Bryant started me out making $6,000 a year. After taking out social security, and taxes, and insurance, and teacher retirement, I took home about $350 a month. It didn't go up a whole heck of a lot from there the next nine seasons. But I don't guess I worked more than about a hundred hours a week. I kept food on the table for my family by staying active in the National Guard. I enjoyed that too. I didn't just show up. I gave 'em their money's worth and met one of the best friends of my life.

I tell you what I didn't do. I didn't sit on my butt and complain because somebody else worked for what he got. I didn't do that.

I got into coaching because I was called to coach. I knew what my coaches in high school and in college meant to me. I believed I could be a positive influence in the lives of young men. I wasn't wrong about that. I don't claim I helped every kid I ever coached. I wish I could say I did. But I believe 98 percent of the kids who played in our programs are better for it. I believe that. You can get their names at Alabama and East Carolina and Wyoming and from the last 11 years at Auburn. You can ask 'em yourself. Ask 'em what they learned about sacrifice and discipline and being responsible for their own lives. What they learned about gettin' knocked down and stepped on and gettin' up and puttin' their guts on the line. What they learned about what it takes to be a champion. Winning is not the main thing. Paying the price to be able to win is what matters. I guarantee you they learned that.

When I took the job at Auburn, there's no doubt I was the lowest paid coach in the Southeastern Conference. My contract was for $50,000 and another $50,000 for radio and TV, but I was gonna have to sell those broadcast programs myself. And I did. I didn't come here for money. I came here for an opportunity. And Auburn has provided me with an opportunity to fulfill my ambition: to compete at the highest level and grow in my profession and to have a positive influence on a thousand kids in the last 11 years.

It would take a near-sighted guy to come in here and not see the progress Auburn has made in its athletic program in those years. When I got here, we were a million dollars in the red. And we were getting a million dollars a year from the university administration just to keep the athletic department doors open. Just to have men's golf teams and baseball teams and track teams and women's basketball and track and golf and all the other non-revenue sports that are important to the kids and to the University. But football has to take in enough money to support everything else except men's basketball.

And football had to make more money at Auburn. You have to win to sell tickets. And we won, including four Southeastern Conference championships.

The important word here is "we" won. And most important among the "we" have been the players, who have paid the price in blood and sweat and sacrifice. And with that payment has come self-discipline and confidence that will help sustain them the rest of their lives. But they couldn't have won without a smart, dedicated staff of assistant coaches that never got outworked and that taught the schemes and techniques that put the kids in a position to have a chance to win almost every game we have played. All the folks in the athletic department, and the university administration, and the board of trustees, and the students and faculty, and the Auburn fans who are there rain or shine, have been important to our winning.

The one thing that's bothersome about writing your autobiography, besides all the things you wish you'd done better, is you have to use the word "I" so often. And if you are a football coach, you know it's not an "I" game.

Our teams and our university have been on television 67 times. We've been to nine bowls. We enlarged the stadium to 85,000 seats. We set records for season ticket sales almost every year. We brought our home game with Alabama to Auburn where it belongs.

Today we don't get a dime from the administration to run the athletic department. We've put a million dollars in the university library, and we're proud to do it. I've personally helped raise thousands of dollars for academics, and I believe in what the faculty does, and in this university.

I would be a damn fool to still be the lowest-paid football coach in the Southeastern Conference. All those years I was also athletic director—not a job I sought but one that sought me when we were in debt and needed the leadership.

I'm not the only member of the Auburn University faculty who has significant outside income. And I'm proud of that. One of my dearest friends teaches design at Auburn. He designed the house we live in. He did a good job. I was pleased to pay his design fee. And if he makes good money on his own initiative, on his own time, and sharpens his own design skills, then I couldn't be happier for him. We have plenty of other faculty members who are designers or consultants or who have written books that became motion pictures, and I wish it were true for every faculty member. As for those people who want to sit on their butts because they are too damn lazy to get out and do something on their own, and who criticize others for being successful, they get no sympathy from me. They have their reward, their own bitterness.

Let me be clear about this: Auburn has been wonderful to me and to my family, and we love it here, and I look forward to ending my career right here. Auburn has enjoyed the greatest growth in its history in the last decade. But the Auburn Spirit is not in its buildings or even its budget, but in its people. Auburn people have a love for this school that goes beyond anything I have seen at any university, and it is the secret of the greatness of Auburn. Now, there ain't a damn one of 'em that hasn't complained about something dumb the football coach has done, including my wife, Sue. But that's okay. I don't mind it. I even enjoy it. I like it down in the arena, even when the noise isn't flattering. And I would rather you dislike me for something I am, than like me for something I am not.

Let me say this about criticism: it comes with the territory if you are a football coach, and if it tears you up, you better get in another profession because you are gonna be miserable. As for criticism within the university, I believe in the First Amendment. I believe in free expression within a university. I believe in honest, positive dissent. I encourage it within our coaching staff; we fuss and argue about what we're going to do, but once we settle on a game plan, we all pull together. Anything as complex as a university is going to have plenty of shortcomings. No thinking person can help finding honest objections, and by overcoming problems you build a greater university.

But let me also express myself openly. There's been a small crowd at Auburn which has criticized athletics, criticized the administration, criticized the board of trustees, constantly, and the individual names in that crowd haven't changed much in 11 years. They don't seem to like much of anything about the way the university is run. They are in the small minority of faculty members and administrators.

I'm not talking about those people with positive objections. I'm talking about full-time, unhappy people who bellyache about *everything* the university tries to do. I can only offer my own experience as advice. I became unhappy with a new administration at East Carolina, after I had been coaching there and winning there for seven years. And we loved the community and had dear friends there. But I quit without a job. And got another job. At Wyoming. It's not an easy thing to do. But if you are truly unhappy and out of joint with a university, leaving can be a positive thing for both parties. But anybody who had rather stay and make a profession of complaint, it's okay with me. It comes with the territory if you are a football coach.

Let's go back a minute to my income. I've talked about the money I earn as much as I have at the beginning of this book to make this point: I didn't cheat to get it. And I didn't cheat to keep it. And anybody who says, or implies, that I did is a liar.

If I was a cheater, I would have left a paper trail from Tuscaloosa in 1965 to East Carolina to Wyoming to 11 years at Auburn. It's not only that I have never been found guilty of cheating, I had *never been accused* of cheating until this late stage of my coaching life. And I still haven't been accused by Auburn or the SEC or the NCAA. And I don't expect to be, because I'm not a cheater. I decided not to cross that bridge a long time ago. Actually, I never had to make a decision not to cheat the rules. I just wasn't going to do it. From the time I turned down $10,000 to be a college football player, I wasn't going to be for sale, and I wasn't going to buy any football players who were. I can't tell you how much $10,000 would have meant to me and my family when I came out of high school in 1956. Until you chop cotton all day in the south Georgia sun for $5, you won't know what I mean. Those were looser times in the college game, to say the least.

All you got to use is one ounce of logic to realize a head coach who is thinking at all, even if he is not an honest man, is risking too much to cheat. The only way he can lose everything at once is by getting caught cheating. Most head coaches have it in their contract, they can be fired for cheating. I have it in mine. I'm proud to have it there. Now a head coach can get beat every Saturday, and he can lose his job that way. But he won't lose it all at once; it'll take a few seasons. There is more pressure on an assistant coach to cheat to try to earn a reputation, to try to be a head coach.

But the truth is: cheaters are gonna cheat. It's a character flaw. It's not what a man stands to gain or to lose. There are plenty of faults about Pat Dye. But I'm at peace with myself; I'm not a cheater, and I never have been.

The truth is, college football itself is cleaner today than it has ever been. I don't think it. I KNOW it. Those folks on the President's Commission of the NCAA ought to go out and talk to some of the old timers...from Michigan and Notre Dame and Georgia and Auburn and Alabama and Texas and Oklahoma and Southern California. I'm talking about with old players who are now 55 or 60 years old, or 65...and ask them what it was like, what was going on when they played college football?

And the truth would stun them. Not only what was being paid to some players. But the way it was, how tough it was. I know. I was there. I was a boy growing up with pain and in a tough life. I went to Georgia in the mid-fifties, and it was survival of the fittest in the classroom and on the field and, believe me, off the field. Before I got to Georgia, in the postwar days of the forties and early fifties, schools would bring in over a hundred kids every year. The strong would survive. And if you tore up a knee, or flunked out of school, too damn bad. And the weekend fights and the barroom brawls and the hazing with wooden paddles. Ask the old timers, even of my generation, what it was like. But I will tell you this, and it's a hard truth: Those guys who did survive, most of 'em are tremendous success stories today, running corporations or their own businesses or maybe they are doctors and lawyers. I guess it was more like the Marine Corps than anything, or like the Rangers—you were trained for skilled combat, what your body was put through was torturous, and the iron discipline on the field and, too often, the absence of any discipline off the field. Only the fittest survived, believe me.

And there were an awful lot of casualties. Uncounted kids fell by the wayside. Nobody remembers their names. You won't find 'em in anybody's Hall of Fame. Not that plenty of 'em, I'm sure, didn't find a way without football, or even without college.

There are an awful lot of good things about the college game today. Things we can be thankful for. And plenty of things we can improve.

But the world of college football has gone full circle. Today, we live in the age of rules and regulations. A time of too many committees. And every time there is a new committee formed, then they've got to come up with a new rule or a new regulation to justify their existence. And plenty of people making the rules never put on a headgear or knew the love and pain of the game and what it can teach you about yourself.

I don't think there is any doubt that the same things still win football games that won them 60 years ago. You've got to have ability, a certain amount of ability; you've got to be well trained and well disciplined, well taught in the fundamentals, the techniques of the game; you've got to have good speed, offensively and defensively. I still think that there can be a relationship among coaches and players that is very special and powerful. But the time allotment they give you now to be with the players...you are always conscious of the 20-hours-a-week limit. I guess over the years my talks with our athletes have been more about becoming men than about becoming football players...what they can learn about themselves, how to be responsible for their own lives. These things help you win football games, but they are a helluva lot more important to the rest of your life. But you have to be careful as a coach today how much time you burn teaching the values of life rather than the techniques of football. It seems a strange turn of events to me. I always thought what the game taught you was more important than the game itself.

But this last year has taught me something else I've not had much experience with: fear. As a responsible head coach, or athletic director, you live clean, you do your best to stick to the rules, but you live in constant fear that somebody, somewhere is going to do something for a kid, maybe a kid in need, that shouldn't be done. Because as head coach, you are responsible for all of it, everything that happens. Just like this tragic thing with Eric Ramsey. And that's probably the name you have been waiting to read in this book.

Before we go a sentence further, you might imagine I hate Eric Ramsey. No, I don't. I hate what he said, the unfairness of it, and what it did to our kids and to our coaching staff and to our program and to our 1991 season, and I hate what it did to Auburn. I don't worry that much about myself. I've been looking after myself since I was about 10 or 11 years old, and I've got a lot of scars. I can live with one more, even if it was a painful one. And I've also learned something in life, and I hope it shows up in this book: Life is short, and you don't want to waste any of it carrying around a load of bitterness. In the first place, your bitterness is only going to sour your own life; it's only going to make you miserable; the world won't pay any attention. Eric Ramsey is a young man, and I hope he can come to learn that lesson, too.

It's strange how something can jump out of the dark to threaten your career. Or your life.

I guess I was lying up in the hospital after a major operation when Eric Ramsey first told the world we were running a racist program at Auburn, treating football players like galley slaves. He said one true thing. He said football practice was hell at Auburn. If it's not, it's meant to be. And when you get out there across the line of scrimmage from the big, tough, fast, smart, angry boys from Florida, and Georgia, and Alabama, where there is no quality of mercy on the ground and no place to hide, you know why practice is hell at Auburn. And it always will be, as long as I'm here, and I intend to coach here until I get ready to retire.

I was in the hospital to be sure I would still be around at all. If you ever wonder if the good times in this life are worth the pain we all suffer, I can tell you what will reassure you: a look at the other side of life—death. I got up out of bed one night two years ago, in the middle of a difficult football season, and vomited up solid blood. There aren't any good things that happen to you that cause you to vomit up solid blood. What happened to me was hemochromatosis, and we'll talk more about that when this book gets to the year 1990. Simply put, your blood retains too much iron and deposits it in your organs, especially in your liver. Damage in the liver makes it difficult for blood to pass through it and causes a buildup of blood pressure and the danger of a major vein bursting, and you hemorrhage to death in a few minutes. It's more terminal than a blown assignment on the goal line, even against Alabama. (I can hear an alumnus saying, "But not by much.")

As you probably know, I chose to have a major operation, to shunt some of the blood away from my liver. Thanks to the wonderful doctors at Emory University in Atlanta, where the operation was perfected, I have my health back. And with it came a greater appreciation for my life. All the things I love...my family; puttin' my beagles down in the winter woods, listenin' to 'em, their separate voices, on the scent of a rabbit; a good song from the fifties on the radio (every generation has its own music, but mine was the luckiest, we had the best); old friends I grew up with and played ball with and hunt with...and, of course, football, too: Tuesday afternoons when we snap on the chin straps and everybody tries to get better, and seeing a kid grow up and get his confidence, and become a man among men.

Close as I came to maybe losing my life, I learned again how much I loved it. And the knowledge came at a lucky time for me because it helped sustain me among all the lies the public circus trotted out, not just in local newspapers, but on TV around the damn world, to bring down a college football program that a decade of Auburn kids fought and bled to establish. And one I put my own heart and guts into building. I've had friends call from as far away as Hawaii and California, and kids who played for me at North Carolina and even at Alabama, who saw the charges against us on TV and were upset. Auburn people everywhere have been upset and embarrassed and frustrated.

The University investigation has been long underway to separate the lies from the truth. I will be a happy man when it's over. I can tell you, as much as I love football, as much as it has been a part of my life since I was a boy, all of the joy went out of the game for me in 1991. I hid the pain every way I could. And I know our players did, too. I'll always respect the kids on that team for sticking together despite the turmoil and the losses and pulling for one another and fighting every day to try to get better.

Maybe you have been in a country that doesn't carry CNN, if there is one. But Eric Ramsey, a fifth-year senior from Birmingham, first said we were running a racist football program at Auburn in early 1991. The charge came in an essay Eric allegedly wrote in a sociology class at Auburn. Why he wrote it, or if he had help on it, I don't know. It's something Eric's got to live with, and, I hope, learn from. I do know an alumnus says Eric tried to sell the essay to him before he turned it over to the *Montgomery Advertiser*. It hurts me to think that might be true. In any event, the *Advertiser* was pleased to publicize the essay without first asking our black athletes how much truth there was to it. And the man who wrote the story for the *Advertiser* had been fired in recent years by the *Opelika-Auburn News*. It has not been a newspaper to fire its reporters on a whim. Of course, Eric's essay was untrue. The *Advertiser* and the *Birmingham News* were quick to quote the essay without bothering to authenticate what it said. There have been hundreds of athletes— and a majority of those on scholarship have been black—who have been a part of our football program at Auburn the last 11 years. I believe the overwhelming majority of them would have been pleased to identify Eric's claims of racism against Auburn football as being untrue, but these kids don't own newspapers. Some of them volunteered their opinions to radio talk shows and to newspapers, who published a precious few of them.

When our own black athletes, past and present, challenged Eric, and pretty much laughed at his false charges of racism, Eric decided to release to the public tape recordings that he said he had made over the past couple of years at Auburn. Eric claims the tapes were made of conversations with Auburn coaches and with at least one booster. Eric claims the conversations reveal his asking for and getting illegal financial help. Eric and his lawyer have refused to release the tapes to Auburn or to the NCAA, which asked for them, so that they can be authenticated.

They did place alleged excerpts of the tapes in the *Birmingham News*, and Ramsey and his lawyer were interviewed on the national TV show, "60 Minutes," and a few seconds of alleged conversations were played on that show.

One of the newspaper reporters—I won't say which one—who listened to the tapes told me that he heard several alleged conversations, with *different* individuals at *different* locations, all played on the *same* strip of tape. Now how could that be done without selective editing or taping over or cutting and splicing? And why would the reporter go on and report them as authentic? If the *Advertiser* and the *News* had wanted to serve college football, they could simply have insisted that Eric and his lawyer turn the tapes over to the NCAA, which asked that they be turned over and not be made public.

It's been frustrating not being able to answer back during all this time the Auburn investigation has been going on, and I still have to be careful what I say in this book.

But I can tell you something that happened between me and the advance man for "60 Minutes." His name is Bob Anderson. He came in here before they put together all of the show. They had already talked to Eric Ramsey and his lawyer, of course. They knew the spin they were going to put on the story, and it wasn't going to be favorable to Auburn. They sent Anderson in here to talk to me and soften me up and get me to say something that could be turned around so that I would sure as hell regret having said it. Except it didn't work out that way. No one from Auburn University appeared on the show. Anderson sat up here in my office and told me how his daddy had recruited football players in the Ivy League. And how he, Bob Anderson, knew all about what went on in recruiting. And he talked about illegal things that recruiters did. He kept saying he knew all about it, because his daddy had recruited in the Ivy League. I let him keep talking. I just listened to him. And when he finished, I leaned toward him and said, "You mean your daddy cheated recruiting?" Oh, now he began to backpedal. Oh, hell yes. I don't know if Bob Anderson's daddy cheated or not. Maybe the Ivy League ought to look into it. But I know Pat Dye never cheated for Auburn.

The "60 Minutes" tapes had a sentence or two that are supposed to be from me, and they probably are. I'm telling Eric and his wife, Twilitta, that I will talk to the bank. He wanted to get a loan. I told investigators a long time before the TV broadcast that I did talk to the bank. I'm a director of the Colonial Bank out of Montgomery. I told the bank to be careful in talking with Eric and Twilitta Ramsey, to be careful to treat them like they would any other customers, to give them no special consideration because he was an Auburn football player, but not to be prejudiced against them either. If that's helping him, I helped him.

It's a tragic thing to me that Eric has gotten himself so turned around he's not sure what he's said. He went on a talk show up in Birmingham, the "Paul Finebaum Show," back when Eric was charging us with racism. When Paul asked him to name one real example of racism that was practiced against him in his five years at Auburn, Eric said that I *kept him* from getting a loan from the bank. Of course, he later claimed I *got* him a loan at the bank. Neither is true. I didn't get Eric a loan, and I didn't keep him from getting a loan. College football players and college seniors who aren't football players have gotten loans from banks for as long as anybody can remember. Later on in this book I'll tell you about having to get a loan from the bank myself to finish school at the University of Georgia. (I'd like to make it clear I paid back the loan myself.)

I wish Colonial Bank had permission to reveal exactly what happened between it and the Ramseys. The bank is bound by law to keep in confidence all records of its customers.

I've spoken of Eric's lawyer, Donald Watkins. He lives in Montgomery and maybe Birmingham, too. I understand Birmingham paid him more than a million dollars in legal fees in 1991 alone. And in this recent recession, Birmingham's been as broke as every other city. So you'd have to say Watkins is a clever lawyer. You have to give him that. He apparently likes to see his picture in the newspaper and on TV, and he damn sure knows how to get it there. Maybe that's why Donald Watkins took on Eric Ramsey as a non-paying client. I don't know. I can't look in a man's heart and know why he does something. I do realize that Watkins has been one of several lawyers suing the state's colleges and universities the last ten years for racial discrimination, and I noticed where they submitted a legal bill this spring for *twenty million dollars*. Sounds like big business to me. I don't know if Watkins thought Eric's charges would help publicize his own case. I don't believe for a minute that Watkins got involved in order to, quote, *clean up college football*. All he and Eric had to do to advance the truth was to turn over to the NCAA *all* of the tapes.

It's ironic the pain this man's actions have caused innocent kids at Auburn, and most of them black kids. Donald Watkins is a black man. But he grew up in a privileged family. His daddy is Levi Watkins, who was president of Alabama State University in Montgomery for years. And as far as I know, he was a good one. It would be interesting to know how his daddy, Levi, grew up in his time, which was a cruel time for a young black man. I expect he worked for everything he got. I expect he cared for all the kids at Alabama State University. Donald Watkins doesn't give one damn for the kids, black or white, on our football team. And I can tell you not one of the football players at Auburn grew up as the son of a college president. College football ain't a country club game played by privileged kids. It's hard. It's tough. It takes tremendous sacrifice. Most kids can find an easier way to get a college degree. And, yet, it's the greatest game ever invented to teach you about yourself. And the kids who play it have to love it. And those who play it the best have a hunger for it and what it can mean to their lives. Donald Watkins wants to "save" these kids from the "inequities" of the college game that they love and that is their chance for an education and a better life. Donald Watkins is full of hogwash.

These kids come to Auburn, mostly from tough circumstances, and it's astonishing to see them grow in confidence, on the field and in the classroom and in their lives. And when they do make it, they have a strength of character they carry with them that can help change the community they came from.

God, the four and five years of blood effort the seniors had given toward their last season at Auburn... And Donald Watkins dangled them and our program in the newspapers and on the television for no purpose except to humiliate them and Auburn and myself.

Let me say right here, I don't worry about me. I'm full grown. I can hurt, but I've hurt before. Donald Watkins doesn't keep me up at night. I never gave Eric Ramsey a dime, and I never knew of anybody who did. And I didn't get him a loan or deny him one. Nor have I illegally given any player money or a loan. I love and honor the game of college football, and I'm going to be right here, coaching football at Auburn until I get ready to retire. Or until I get whipped often enough on Saturday afternoon that they'll throw me out for losing, which is an honorable way to go.

Why? Why did it all happen? That's a priceless question I can't answer.

But one thing's for sure. Eric Ramsey was not bought out of Homewood High School to play football at Auburn. We were the only major school that offered him a scholarship. I don't think I ever saw anybody happier to get one. We needed defensive backs. He was not big or especially fast. He was a project. But, with work, we thought he could be a decent player. He even became a starter. But never an outstanding player. But it takes some guts to stick it out five years, and you wouldn't think a guy would stay five years in "pure hell," as he described it, if he was miserable.

You'd have to look into the hearts of Eric Ramsey and his wife, Twilitta, to know what they were about. I can remember the first time I met Twilitta. And I have wondered how much that encounter influenced their later actions.

Twilitta was not then married to Eric. She got an appointment with me and came to my office. She was there, I found out to my shock, to demand that I drop an athlete from the football team. He was not a starter. He rarely got to play at all in his career. I later learned that he and Eric had competed for Twilitta's affection.

Now I don't know of but one more serious charge than the one she made. I have daughters, and I come from a family that honors women, and so do I. But I do not know any football coach who is capable of sitting as judge and jury on so complex and serious a charge. I could only advise that she would have to take her accusation to the authorities...that so serious a charge was far beyond the breaking of football training rules. It was her business to take her charges to the authorities. She chose not to do that.

Eric decided to marry Twilitta. I tried to talk him out of it. My opposition had nothing to do with his wife's charges against another athlete. I didn't believe Eric Ramsey could afford to get married. How tragically right I was. He came from a broken home; he had no support from his family; he had almost no family. Twilitta's own mother opposed the marriage, I understand, and even called me about it.

Eric was sure they could get by on his Pell Grant and his scholarship, and his wife would work. Of course, he was wrong. Something happened to his wife's job.

It's hard for me, even now, after being a year-long victim of character assassination...it's hard for me to take out after a former player at Auburn. When I say we are family, I mean it. And you don't throw somebody out of your family because he makes an ass of himself. The double tragedy, to me, is what the controversy has done to Auburn and what it has done to Eric himself. I doubt you'll see Eric Ramsey walk into Sewell Hall among his old teammates.

You know this is the hundredth anniversary of college football at Auburn. Old players will be coming back to the campus all year, and especially in the fall, and they'll hug one another and see who has gotten fat or bald or who has the most grandchildren, and the gigantic lies they'll tell about the old days under Shug Jordan or

Jack Meagher or Mike Donahue, or even Pat Dye, "and what a tyrant he was." And I don't imagine Eric Ramsey will feel a part of the players and the program he bled for for five years. He won't be among the guys he practiced with and played with, and on some Saturday afternoons he led on the field as their captain, and there were even times when he came down and led devotionals among the [Fellowship of] Christian Athletes. I find it infinitely sad that Eric Ramsey won't be a part of the Auburn family because I know how little of his own family he has.

I can't say I'm surprised Eric Ramsey doesn't like me. Most of his career I stayed on his ass. He was the kind of kid you had to keep after to do what he was supposed to do. And the years after he was married, he was rarely on time for any meeting or anything. I stayed on him about that. When I was a younger coach I would have run him back to Birmingham. If you can't count on a guy to care enough to be on time, if he always has some problem to keep him from being where he is supposed to be, you can't count on him on Saturday afternoon. But as you get older, you get more reluctant to give up on a kid. If you give up on him, and he quits school, it's such a waste of a life.

Eric may hate me, and I may hate what he has become. But I have said before, I will be the only college coach he will ever have...forever. And he will have been one of my players, whether I like it or not.

Eric came by my office after his last season and asked my honest opinion of his chances of making it in the pros. I told him I didn't believe he would make it. That he had been an ordinary player at Auburn. And the competition up there was so intense among so many great athletes. I told him he should get his degree and prepare to make his living another way. It wasn't what he wanted to hear. It happened to be the truth. He was drafted by Kansas City. But he didn't make the team. On that Kansas City team were two former Auburn football players who believed in our system, linebacker Chris Martin, who had been captain of our defense, and defensive back Kevin Porter. It takes tremendous talent and desire, such as Chris and Kevin showed at Auburn, to make it as a defensive player in the NFL.

I had tried to get Eric a spot in the Senior Bowl in Mobile after his final season so that he could compare his ability among the top seniors in the country, and so that the NFL coaches in the game could see what he could do. But his play at Auburn just hadn't been strong enough for him to be invited. I tried. But I could also understand the Senior Bowl's position. They attempt to pick only the best pro prospects in the country for the game. Eric has said he resented my not recommending him for the game, but, of course, I did everything I could.

Eric has also said if he had made the Kansas City team, he would never have made his charges against Auburn. I can't begin to understand that reasoning. But I don't understand very much about the Eric Ramsey I once thought I knew.

I do understand what it's like to be broke and have a family. I know what it's like to have to borrow money from the bank to finish college. But I had the good luck to be raised in such a way that I knew, even when I was broke, that my good name was worth more than the money I needed. A *Sports Illustrated* editor has said repeatedly that Eric's wife, using her maiden name, called and offered the tapes to the magazine for $25,000. I don't think the man would lie about it. And friends of mine had an even more startling experience.

They were called and offered the Eric Ramsey tapes, and the tapes were offered to my friends for $10 million, if you can believe that insane amount of money. I don't know who the people were who made the offer. I don't know if Eric and his wife knew they called. But I found out later a series of calls followed, and the price dropped to $750,000, and finally to $360,000. At that point, my friends called me. I told them, absolutely not. No way would I pay one penny for the tapes. I hadn't done anything wrong, and I was not ashamed of anything I might have said on one of them.

I have been amazed to learn how many people Eric Ramsey called to beg money from in his years at Auburn. I'm amazed, and I'm embarrassed. I'm embarrassed for him. And I'm embarrassed for myself for not being more aware of what was happening and not being stronger and insisting that Eric live up to his responsibilities as a student-athlete or go home and go to work. He's not the first guy to get married and have a child while playing college football. As I told him and Twilitta before they were married: it's tough to play football and go to school; it takes sacrifice; it's tough to be married under the best of circumstances; it takes sacrifice; it's damn tough to play football, go to school, and be married.

I've learned that Eric called some individuals as many as 150 times asking for money. He even called our team chaplain, Reverend Baggett. And all the time he was taping certain conversations to use later against the person he was asking to help him. How could Eric wake up ten years from now and be proud of that? I honestly don't think he will be.

I said, I believe 98 percent of the kids who have been through our program are better people for it. I stand by that belief. I also worry about the other kids and what I might have done differently to reach them.

Now what's going to happen to the Auburn football program? We're cooperating with our own internal investigation. We want only the truth of what happened...for all the parties involved. We can live with the truth. I know our program was not built on buying football players. If it had been, we wouldn't have lost so many great ones along the way, some of whom over the years committed to me in my office. We do our best to sell kids on the many strengths of Auburn University and our football program. We've had good luck doing that. If some kid, or his family, wants more than a legal scholarship, we have just gone to the next kid.

We run an honest program, and nobody knows it more than our own players, many of whom struggle to get by with little family support. I often hurt for them. But I also believe that struggle makes men strong. And I am under no illusion that things don't happen in college football: that a kid doesn't find himself in honest need, and somebody within the program or outside it, helps him. I don't condone it. I don't believe any head coach can afford to condone it. Your heart may break for a kid, but it just has to break. I told Eric and his wife, over and over, in the interview I had with them, which will be on the real tape if it's ever released: I said, "I can't help you, Eric." I said several times, "I can't help you." I don't condone, can't afford to condone, even humanitarian acts for athletes in need. But I also know human nature. And I know it has happened at Penn State and at Notre Dame and at Michigan and at Alabama and at Auburn and at Texas and at Southern Cal and at every school that has 95 kids on football scholarship: People have helped kids in need. I wish kids didn't have to be in need. I wish it were a more perfect world. But this world I was born into is flawed. And I learned that at an early age.

I also learned a long time ago that bitterness only hurts the man who carries it with him. I learned it the hard way as you will see in this book. Will I live long enough to lose any sense of bitterness about Eric Ramsey? I don't know. Only time can answer that question.

All of us at Auburn look forward to the day this investigation is behind us. We have a new President taking over the University, Dr. William Muse. I've met him, and I like him. I like the things he stands for. And I look forward to working under his administration. And as for this investigation, I say again, we can live with the truth.

I've also said I was called to be a coach. And that's how I feel. I was not called to be an athletic director. When we were losing a million dollars a year, a lot of people wanted me to take the job. We're on solid ground now. Auburn athletics more than pay their own way. You can fault me for not watching over the athletic department as closely as I might have. Our tennis team and our basketball team are on probation, and I hate it. I don't think you can say either program was wildly out of control, taking unfair advantage of competing schools. But we are committed to sticking to the rules and the spirit of the rules, and we didn't do it.

I couldn't be more pleased with Dr. Muse's choice for our new athletic director. Mike Lude did a remarkable job with the program at the University of Washington. It's a tribute to Dr. Muse and to Auburn to attract a man of his reputation. I like it that he has been a head football coach. He knows what it's like in the arena. He has my absolute support.

There were times this last year when it seemed like our troubles had been going on forever. That's not true. Our program is 11 years old, and most of the memories have been good ones.

My personal memories go back almost a half century. If you are still with me, I invite you back to the beginning of my life. Sometimes it seems like a thousand years ago, and sometimes it seems like yesterday.

IN A MAN'S EYES

It's amazing what you can see in a man's eyes. Fear. Confidence. Determination. I doubt there are many players who aren't afraid. Who don't have some kind of fear. Fear of failure. We deal with fear every day. That's where courage comes in. Nobody says that courage is the absence of fear. Courage is mastering fear.

Myself, I'm terrified playing golf in front of a big crowd. I'm scared I'm gonna miss the damn thing. But I can master fear in football. I can walk out there in that stadium on Saturday afternoon, and I have no more fear than if I'm taking a stroll by myself. Because that's my damn place.

BACK TO THE BEGINNING

I was born at Old Town. A farm on the Ogeechee River in south Georgia. My granddaddy, Louis Wayne Dye, owned the farm. My daddy ran it. My granddaddy was gettin' old and feeble; I guess he probably died of Alzheimer's. Anyhow, his mind began to go. This was November 1939. And sometime in 1940, about three months after I was born, we moved to Blythe, Georgia, about 20 miles from Augusta. We lived first in a little house in downtown Blythe, which was a good country town. It had three general stores, three cotton gins, a railroad, and a depot, a barber shop, and a beer joint. Let's see, it had a Baptist Church, a Methodist Church, and a Presbyterian Church.

My granddaddy and grandmother were Baptists. We called her Mama Dessie. I never knew my grandfather. They called him Daddy Louis. He built—I don't know whether he built the Baptist Church or he gave 'em the land, and they built a church on it. But he built the house I grew up in adjoining the land. When I was a kid, I could lie in my bed in the summertime and listen to the choir singing on Wednesday nights and Sunday nights because there was no air conditioning and the windows were all up. They had the graveyard right there behind the church. I played in it. At night, I'd run by, not walk by. I never remembered Old Town. Never remembered living in the little house in downtown Blythe.

My first memories were of living in our homeplace next to the Baptist Church. It was a four-bedroom house, old country farm house. Had a fireplace in every room, no insulation, a tin roof, a back porch, and a front porch.

My daddy's name was Frank Wayne Dye, and my mama's name is Nell. She was from Athens, Georgia. I grew up with a brother, Wayne, four years older than me, and a brother, Nat, two years older, and my sister, Jane, was one year younger. Daddy Louis died when I was a baby, but Mama Dessie lived in the house with us; her real name was Desma; she was a Foss.

In our backyard lived an old black man, Charlie, and his two sisters, Emma and Henrietta, who was blind. Charlie did what he could, yard chores, milkin' cows, feedin' the stock, but he was an old man, 65 or 70, when I was little. Emma stayed in our house all the time; she was part of the family; she could do one thing better than mama, cook biscuits; she cooked biscuits every day, and I can still taste 'em. I guess the three of them had probably grown up working for Daddy Louis, and when he died, they stayed on with us.

There wasn't a paved street in Blythe, even downtown. I can remember as well as anything going into town Saturday afternoons, and we couldn't walk across the street for the mules and wagons, old cars, and country folks coming into Blythe shopping at the general stores. They'd put on their best clothes. It was a social event, too; black and white together; it was as segregated as it could be, but all of 'em comin' into town. They lived on little farms; their nearest neighbor would be a half-mile or a mile away. That's the setting I grew up in.

My daddy was six feet. Probably a little taller than me now. He was a good looking guy. Dark hair. Strong features. Strong personality. He was raised on the farm and quit school when he was in high school and started farming. They called him Big Wayne. He did cast a long shadow. It was like he was 10 feet tall. Not six feet. He was an athlete. Played semi-pro baseball, basketball. Basketball was his thing. They didn't have football when he came along; he could've played. He was probably as good a fisherman as there was in his time, fishing in rivers and creeks with casting rods and fly rods and cane poles, the way we fished back then. We also set hooks in creeks and rivers and caught catfish. And he was the best natural shot with the shotgun that I ever saw. He shot a 16-gauge. Hunted quail and dove. Also ducks. We always had bird dogs. Good ones.

He had pretty strong rules, my daddy—I always thought he would have been a very difficult man to live with. I would say he was damn hard to live with. He grew up on a farm and quit school, I think, in the tenth grade and started farming. He was raised with four older sisters and had a special respect for women. I never heard him say a cuss word around a woman; he didn't like women to use ugly words. But he also had that mean streak in him; you could call it violent; I don't know what you'd call it. My mama will have a lot of stars in her crown for havin' put up with him over the years.

He was a different kind of a guy; he had a dominating personality, probably an intimidating personality. How much whiskey did he drink? He drank most of his life, which created problems for my mother. But he was a good provider and set a lot of good examples in a lot of ways. He was an alcoholic, because he drank all the time. He wouldn't get drunk and stay drunk three or four days; it wasn't that kind of thing. Just that he had the smell of alcohol on him all the time. And when we were kids growing up, there would be family squabbles. He might quit drinking for a year or two years...which were always, I guess, the most peaceful times...when he wasn't drinking. He smoked. It wasn't unusual for him to smoke five packs of Camels in a day, and I guess that helped kill him finally. But I was close to my daddy. And he, I don't know whether he felt sorry for me being the youngest boy always left behind, or whether it was because of my feelings toward him, I don't know what it was, but I was probably closer to him than any of the children. And it might have been that he needed me. I don't know. We might have needed each other.

I was the only one of the boys who really loved fox hunting. I used to go at night, go early in the morning; I loved to hear the dogs run; I still have a pack of beagles who I enjoy listening to. I loved the dogs; I loved gettin' 'em up and handlin' 'em, and you know...just...sittin' and listenin' to those old fox hunters talk about dogs and tell tales and yarns around the fire, and on those cold nights when we'd stop, and the dogs happened to be runnin' in a particular hollow, I'd always be the one to get up the wood to build a fire, so we could stand around it. It made me, to be able to do that, feel more of a part of it, more important. You can see pictures on the walls of our house today when my daddy and I went to the field trials. Daddy always had good dogs. He always won in field trials, which is the running part of it; he also showed dogs in the bench shows. The fox hounds we kept in pens. The bird dogs were mostly pointers and would run loose around the house.

My father, Frank Wayne Dye, is next to me, second from right. We always had fine dogs. And I never wore shoes.

I'm not sure how old I was. Probably 10 or 12. Daddy took me to Lincolnton, Georgia, to the hotel and rented me a room and left me with two dogs, by myself. Just the two fox dogs, at a field trial. I was that mature. I can remember distinctly I didn't even take a pair of shoes with me. I didn't wear shoes until I started the eighth grade in school. I just didn't wear shoes. How did the dogs do? They won. We had the best fox hounds in the field trials up there for 30 years. The same kind of Runnin' Walkers you see in all those famous fox hunting pictures. We had Walker dogs, but we didn't ride horses. We drove pickup trucks…we weren't as sophisticated as fox hunters who rode. But as far as hearing the dogs run and the thrill of the chase—there is somethin' about that that people don't understand. Ordinary people, when they hear a pack of dogs runnin' a fox, all they hear is a pack of dogs barkin'. But when I hear it, it's more like separate voices; it's more like music. And there's a thrill to it. But you got to appreciate it.

I don't know. The thing about my daddy that stands out in my mind—two things—that I would say were very, very dominant in his personality: he was as tough and ornery, or mean, or however you want to describe it, as anybody that I have ever been close to. And he was the most honest man that I've ever met. He demanded honesty from everybody around him. If you weren't, you had a real problem with my daddy. I hope that I've got many of his traits. I'm not a mean person. But I know I've got the ability to make tough decisions without looking back.

We farmed. We row cropped probably 3,000 acres. We planted everything: peanuts, corn, peas, wheat, oats, soybeans. Daddy had about a hundred acres of watermelons. So in late July and August, we worked watermelons until we started school or started to play football. We'd bring 'em out of the fields and pile 'em under trees. We'd load eight or ten 18-wheelers until they were mostly gone. Then we'd load a ton-and-a-half truck and peddle what was left to Waynesboro, Sardis, Wrens, little communities. Sold 'em anywhere from 25 cents to a dollar. You'd take a load of watermelons and come in with $150 to $200 in a day—that was a big deal in 1952, '53, '54. It always worked better to peddle the watermelons during that time of year because all the families had money because of picking cotton.

The most cotton we ever planted in one year was about 800 acres. That was our money crop, cotton. But most of the land was leased, which was a mistake. Daddy could have bought it for what he was payin' to lease it. He was a lot better farmer than he was a businessman. We lived from one year to the next. We gathered our crop, and he went to the bank and paid off our note. Come spring of the year, he'd go back to the bank and get money to plant, fertilize, and he'd owe that money until cotton picking time. And when cotton was picked, he'd pay the bank again. That's the way we lived. We were big farmers, but we weren't rich farmers. Leasing the land was a mistake. But if we had hindsight, we'd all do things a lot different.

My daddy always had good help. He was tough on his help. They understood that. But he was, just like I said, honest. They knew they could trust him. What he said was the law, and that's what they expected from him.

I'm gonna say there were probably 12, 15 families living on the place. Sharecroppers, blacks and whites. That's the people I grew up with, farm hands. It wasn't like it is today when a man can take one big tractor and farm several thousand acres. Back then we had 12 tractor drivers, drivin' those little John Deere tractors. We still had mules, but I never got involved with the mules; they were just going out. Cotton was picked by hand then. That's the way our farm hands made it, the way they survived. Most of them had big families. The best friend I had growin' up was Major Hardin; he was black; he was a little younger than me. His mama, Patience Hardin, had, I guess, 18 kids, from babies to grown children up in their twenties. Major and I would go to the woods or go to the creek, Briar Creek, and set hooks to catch catfish. When I was 14 years old

I was like a grown man; I'd drive the pickup truck all over the county; we'd fish at night and again in the morning. Lots of times I would go to Major's house instead of goin' home. Most of the time we didn't have a telephone; mama would just know where I'd be. Patience would throw me a pallet and a blanket on the floor; I'd fall in there and go to sleep; Patience Hardin looked on me like one of her own 18 children. She was family, and I was family. She would put that crowd of hers out in the field, once they got to be 12 or 14 years old, and make $100 a day or $150 a day, or whatever it was. Some could pick 300 or 400 pounds of cotton a day, and Major could pick 500 pounds a day: at $2 a hundred, that's $10 a day, $50 a week. You got ten children out there making $40, $50 a week, you made enough during cotton pickin' season to carry you through the year.

Coaching football in the Deep South, I've got a different perspective on blacks and whites than I might have in another occupation, or if I had been raised in a lily white neighborhood, where I didn't associate with blacks. I've got the advantage of having worked, black and white, goin' down the cotton rows together. That's the way I grew up. The blacks were just as important as we were. They were important to our survival, and we were important to their survival.

I said Major was my best friend growing up...until I started in high school, playing football, and we got further and further apart. I believe Major is living in Boston now. The thing that stands out about Major—and will tell you something about my daddy, and as I look back, it made a tremendous impression on me—my daddy bought a brand new tractor, a John Deere. An R John Deere, the biggest tractor they made back then. I'm not sure what horsepower it was. But it was big. It would pull a big plow. A $10,000 tractor was a lot of money. I mean a lot of money. Well, Major was 14 years old. My daddy put Major on that tractor. He did it because of the kind of person Major was, the kind of confidence he had in him, that he would do exactly what daddy told him to do. We had hands, black and white, some 40 years old, been driving tractors all their lives. But they weren't as responsible as this black kid at 14 years old. My daddy put him on that tractor and he had never driven a tractor before. He taught him from scratch, how to check the oil and grease it and do the maintenance on it. Because he had confidence in Major to take care of it. And he had enough insight to do that in 1952 or 1953 in South Georgia. And today, I depend on these black kids playing for Auburn for my livelihood. They depend on us for a chance to get an education. Maybe if I had been raised different, I would feel different. But that's the kind of relationship, mutual respect, mutual survival, I've always known.

I don't know what Major would have been able to do with an education. I think he has done well. We had a family reunion a couple of years ago, and Patience and some of the girls came back, some of her granddaughters. We called Major on the telephone, and I talked to him. He kinda keeps up with our teams on TV. When he left the farm, he went North. He sang in a choir or a quartet for a long time. I never heard him sing on the farm. And then I think he started driving a truck. I'm not sure what he's doing right now. I bet he does it well. Major on that tractor made a great impression on me I carry to this day.

And when they buried my daddy, there were as many blacks in the church as whites. A white man preached his service in the church, and a black man preached his service at the grave. A great black preacher, John Tarver. He was an old man. Both his legs had been amputated. We had to carry him to the church and to the graveyard. It was as segregated as it could get, as I said before. And my daddy was tough and hard-nosed, and it didn't make any difference to him whether you were black or white. He treated everybody the same, tough on all of us, and all his chillun, and he was the most honest man I ever met in my life. I want to say that again.

I experienced a lot of pain growing up. I didn't realize it then. It was just survival to me. But I can see now...kids that grew up in the same kind of situation that I grew up in, and have obstacles to overcome at an early age, they develop a certain toughness about them that I think is beneficial to them as long as they live.

They called me Pat. I was supposed to be a girl. And they were going to name me Patricia. They named me after my baby doctor, and my daddy's baby doctor, who was the most famous baby doctor that ever came through that part of the country: Dr. Andrew J. Kilpatrick. I got to know him after I was growing up; he loved to fox hunt.

My mother, of course, grew up in Athens. I've got a picture of her at home, from 1917. She was in the group of little girls who made the first poppies and sold them for the wounded veterans coming back from the First World War. That bunch of little girls started it in Athens, and it went all over the country, selling poppies for wounded veterans. She grew up right across the street from the old State Normal School, right on Prince Avenue; some of the buildings are used now by the Naval Supply School. She played on the high school basketball team that won the state championship two or three years without losing a game. Very competitive. A lady. But tough as nails. That's her name, remember: Nell.

My daddy was hard to live with. He wasn't no easy guy to please. She went to the University of Georgia. And came to Blythe to teach school. That's where they met and got married. I guess it's true: opposites attract. It wasn't easy for her, having come from the kind of environment she grew up in. She lived in a pretty, blue-blood neighborhood, society; her daddy's family were teetotalers.

My grandmother, Mannie Fain Slaughter—if I had to pick one of my ancestors that I'd like to be most like, it would be her. She was born and raised in Dallas, Georgia. She was a gracious lady, just pure gracious. I spent time as a boy in Athens with my grandmother and grandfather, Dr. Slaughter; he was a dentist. He was a competitive person, loved to play golf. The world in Athens was a long way from the world in Blythe, and as country, as rural as I was, it made me a little different, set me a little apart.

You had to earn the right to fish. Me and Wayne with a nine-pound bass from Richmond Factory Pond.

A Country Boyhood

The Burke County line ran in front of my house. Across the road was Richmond County. If you lived in our house now, you would have to go to a Burke County school. But back then we went to Blythe elementary school and then on to Richmond Academy in Augusta, which was the county high school. When you grow up in a small town like Blythe, the teachers know you long before you get to school. We had a fine grammar school. Great grammar school teachers. Ms. Lucile Wilhite knew me all right; she already had plans for me before I stepped in the door to the first grade. I got it the first day of school, set the tempo right there for who was boss. But I loved all my teachers. Ms. Etta Lovette taught me fourth grade, and Ms. Amy Dozier taught me, I guess, fifth and sixth grades. Ms. Pennington, I can't remember her first name, taught me seventh grade, and Hoyt Williams taught Vocational Agriculture. Funny how you can remember their names, even their voices, after all these years. I think there were nine or ten of us in my seventh grade class.

Was I a good student? I was average. I mean I was a boy, a country boy, just full of life and energy. Studying wasn't the most important thing to me. I did what I had to do. I had so damn much energy it was hard for me to sit still, if you know what I mean. But we never missed a day of school, never played hooky. My mother went to college. She raised us to go to college. My father supported that. There were maybe a half dozen times in my life where there was going to be a big dove shoot, a big hunt, and he'd let us miss a half day of school. I wasn't a bad student. But I always struggled in English. I just never put the English together. Now my sister, Jane, who was the student among us, went on to major in English at Georgia. If there was one thing I could change about my life, I would be a more serious student.

I described our house. It was a country house, cold in the winter time. We had fireplaces we burned coal in. And then we put in space heaters, oil-burning space heaters, and closed up the fireplaces. We ate in the dining room or in the kitchen or on the back porch. We'd put a long table on the back porch, and we ate there a lot—fresh vegetables that we grew, corn and okra and squash and tomatoes; nothin' frozen can ever taste like those vegetables right out of the garden. We milked cows. Made butter. We always had chickens in the yard. Mama'd get biddies, Rhode Island Reds. We'd eat a hundred chickens every three or four months. We'd kill hogs every year. Had a smokehouse full of hams. When I was small I fed the animals, the dogs, chickens, hogs. I never will forget a hog biting the end of my big toe off, the skin on the end. I jumped up on a feeding trough, and he bit it right off.

My room, well, I stayed in a couple of places. I guess the first I remember, we three boys were staying in the same room. But as Wayne and Nat got older, they moved me out. I ended up sleepin' in the hall upstairs. It wasn't anything unusual for me because I always got what was left over. All my clothes were hand-me-downs. Wayne and Nat slept in the same bedroom, across the hall from my grandmother, Mama Dessie's bedroom. My sister Jane slept in the other bedroom upstairs, and mama and daddy's bedroom was downstairs. When Wayne left home for Georgia, I moved back in the bedroom with Nat. I can still hear the rain on the tin roof of that house; we have a tin roof on our farm cabin today outside Auburn; I wouldn't take anything for it. I can also still hear the sound of the rain on the magnolia tree outside my old bedroom, because the window would be up, as I said, in the summertime; I can hear the drops hittin' those wide leaves. Livin' in the hall was one of those things where I didn't get a vote. But I believe that growing up in the environment that I did, with my mother and father both highly competitive and both athletically inclined, and two older brothers who didn't mean to lose at anything—growing up in a struggling situation for everything made me a person who hated to lose. And

A football for Christmas: That's Nat on my left, and Wayne on my right. In the picture below, I'm eight, and I've got on Wayne's old tennis shoes as Jane and I get ready for Sunday School.

it was a long time before I won anything. My little sister was right behind me and my mother naturally protected her and kind of left me to take care of myself.

Well, that's what I did. I was always independent. I tried to compete with my older brothers. They would go downtown to play—we made do; if there was nothin' goin' on, we found something to do, played cops and robbers, or war games through

the trees, until we got old enough to go hunting and fishing. Wherever they went, they meant to leave me behind. I started wanting to fish or hunt when I was eight, nine, ten years old, before I was ready to go. And I didn't understand why they wouldn't take me. And I'd pull fits. I'd follow 'em. They'd tie me to a tree to keep me from following 'em. Wasn't any such thing as winning a fight. How you gonna beat a brother two years older, four years older? And my father worked; he'd be gone in the morning when we got up. He left at daylight, just like we did as we got older, just like I do today.

I don't know if it belongs in this book, but I started defending myself a long time before I caught up with my brothers in size. I wouldn't let 'em pick on me. It didn't make any difference what I had to use: baseball bat, or axe, or shotgun, or kitchen knife, or whatever it took; I wasn't gonna let 'em pick on me. The one thing that stands out in my mind about my personality is that I don't know of anybody it hurts to lose more than it does me. I tell my players today I don't think there is anybody that's ever lost as often as I did when I was little. And I hated every time I ever lost. I didn't win many. And another thing, I never liked being a second class citizen. You know, I'd drive a pickup truck. I was country, rural, like I said, a little on the rank side. But I had that Slaughter side of the family in my background; I didn't mean to be a second class citizen.

There was one day of the week I didn't get left: Saturday. From the time I can remember, mama would give Nat and me a dollar apiece. We would catch the bus from Blythe to Augusta on Saturday morning. I think the bus cost 15 cents. We would ride to Augusta, and first we would go to the Miller Theater where Sanckins Dairy sponsored a talent contest we would watch. Then we'd go to see two double-featured movies and maybe a serial, at either the Majesta Theater, or the Rialto, or the Imperial Theater. Sunset Carson. Gene Autry. Roy Rogers. Johnny Mack Brown. I played football at Georgia with Fred Brown, the nephew of Johnny Mack Brown who once played football at Alabama. The moving pictures cost nine cents or a dime each, that's twenty cents of our dollar. We'd go to Snappy's to eat lunch. Snappy's was like a Krystal. We'd get two hamburgers and an orangeade. Which all cost 25 cents. Now we've got 25 cents to go to Kress's to buy something at the 10 cent store and 15 cents to catch the bus and get back home on. Oh yes, mama would have to write a note for Nat to get in for half price at the moving picture; he was 12 years old and weighed 200 pounds.

I started driving a tractor on the farm, probably, when I was 10, 11 years old. Of course, by then Wayne and Nat were 12 and 14; they'd been working, and I couldn't wait to go to work. I wanted to be with the older boys. By the time I was 14, 15 years old, I would work with any hand on the farm, from daylight to dark; there wasn't a man on that farm who could outwork me. I started off drivin' a little old Allis-Chalmers tractor, pulling a Bushhog, cuttin' weeds off of grain and cleaning up fields, that sort of thing. I believe I started out working for $2 a day. Graduated up to $2.50, and then I believe $5 was as much as I ever made. That's the way daddy operated the farm. He paid us like he did the rest of the hands. If you were a top hand, you got top pay.

I was the kind of kid growing up that old people liked. I don't know why. But they took an interest in me. A grown man, John Bates—I don't know if he felt sorry for me, getting pushed around and left at home by my older brothers or what it was. But John and I fished a lot together. He would just come by and get me. I was 12 or 13 years old, and we happened to be fishing one Sunday afternoon. We worked six-and-a-half days a week on the farm. I was paddling for John Bates. That's the way we fished: one paddled the small creek boat, because it was running water, and one fished. I was paddling us down Briar Creek. I said to John, "What's that floatin' up in the bushes? Looks like a man." He said, "Oh, boy, hush!" We got a little closer. I said, "It looks like somebody." He said, "Boy, hush!" So I paddled right up there where he could see from the front of the boat. And he said, "Man, this don't look like somebody. This IS somebody!"

It was a soldier from Fort Gordon. Still in his uniform. Face down in the creek.

So we were about two or three hundred yards from the landing, below the bridge, an old wooden bridge on a dirt road. One of those country bridges with no rails or no anything. The boy's car had run off the bridge, and he'd gotten out but drowned and floated down the creek. We paddled to the bridge and called Fort Gordon. They came out in an ambulance. A staff sergeant wanted to go get the body. He didn't know anything about paddling a boat. I never will forget he asked me if I would mind paddling the boat down there to get him out. I said I'd do it. I paddled the boat, and the sergeant tied a rope around him, and I paddled us back up the creek, pullin' him, floatin' in the water, right behind the boat. We got to the bank below the bridge, and they put a rubber sheet under him to get him out. It didn't bother me so much until then. He had been lying face down and all you could see was the back of his head. I thought about it a long time afterward: when they put the sheet under him, he turned over and the gas came out of him, and the skin was coming off his hands and his face. Well, it bothered me for a long time.

The strange thing is, about two weeks later John Bates and I went to Walterboro, South Carolina. He had a friend down there, Marion Simmons, and we'd go down there and fish with him on the coast. We left Blythe at midnight and got down there about three in the morning and went into a diner to eat breakfast. The man who ran the diner knew us. We'd been there before. He'd heard that we found this boy in the creek. I can't remember the boy's name. But the man I sat down next to in the diner was his daddy. The man who ran the diner told him we were the people who had found his boy. Of course, he wanted to know about it. He started asking me about it. I was amazed to be sitting next to the boy's daddy. I didn't want to talk about it. I said, "Mr. Bates is over there, and you can talk to him."

I played just sandlot football in grammar school; we didn't have any kind of organized team in Blythe. Both my older brothers had played at the YMCA in Augusta. It was a hardship on my mother to drive me there and back.

We had an unusual situation in Augusta. There was only one public high school, one public *white* high school. Because everything was segregated. And there were three junior highs feeding that one senior high school, which made for a competitive situation. I started playing organized football in the eighth grade at Tubman Junior High. It was in downtown Augusta and had once been a girls' school. I played, and I wasn't very good. Just kind of a pudgy little ole boy. But I went from maybe 115 pounds that year to 150 pounds in the ninth grade. I played, and I was pretty good for a ninth grader. I transferred that year to the new Murphy Junior High that had been built on our side of town where a lot of military kids lived. We weren't what you would call the upper crust of Augusta. That didn't bother me because the way I was raised I could survive in any environment.

In a way I believe the toughest time in a man's life is that time from the eighth grade to the tenth grade. When he is trying to be accepted…beginning to like the girls, and he's scared, scared of rejection. Sue and I went back to Augusta recently, and I saw an old classmate, Wallis Lee Stephens. I can remember she was cute. Nice. Fun. Popular. Brown hair. I had the damnedest crush on her in the ninth grade that anybody ever had. But I had no confidence; I was scared to speak to her. I told her that the other night. She said, "Well, boy, I wish I'd known the way you were going to turn out; I'd have paid you a lot more attention."

I was 13 at Murphy. I started school when I was five, so I was a year younger than most of my classmates. I drove all over the county in our pickup truck, but I couldn't drive legally until I was a senior in high school.

The most popular girl in the ninth grade was Kay Tice. To me, she was damn gorgeous. I did get up the nerve to ask her out. We went to the County Fair. Wayne, my older brother, drove us. Here she was gorgeous, and we're walking around at the fair, and I'm having a great time. We're getting ready to go meet Wayne for our ride back, and we stop, and are standing there, just lookin'— it wasn't a planned thing—and we were outside the tent for the last show of the girlie show. And the guy, the hawker, talkin' up a crowd, points at us and says, "YOU TWO GET IN FREE!" And I looked at Kay, and she looked at me, and I was in shock. Before I know it, we are sitting on these plank seats and then the girls come out there buck naked. And here I am with the prettiest girl in the ninth grade, who I am crazy about, and I don't know whether to look at her or not look at her. I had never seen naked women in the ninth grade. I can't remember that Kay said anything. I was too embarrassed to say anything. I don't know that we ever told anybody. I know good and well we didn't tell her mother; she lived alone with her mother who was divorced. We went on to school together, but I know I never told anybody what we saw at the County Fair.

I didn't date that much anyway. I was too interested in football and fishing and lived 20 miles out of town. I was always hitchhiking back and forth, from Blythe to Augusta. Nobody today can realize what that's like, not to be able to get where you got to go. A lot of times I rode to school with Larry Hildreth. His mother's sister was married to Coach Ralph Jordan of Auburn. It's how my father got to be good friends with Coach Jordan, and how I first got to know him. But I'll talk about that later. The Hildreths ran a dairy farm in Rosier, which is just a settlement between Matthews and Keysville which is right on Briar Creek, about five miles from my house; I doubt Rosier had a post office. Larry drove the milk to town every day and came by the house in his pickup truck at 6:00 or 6:30. When I was in the 11th grade I'd catch a ride with Oliver Russell who lived in Keysville. He was a year ahead of me. Sometimes I could ride home with him because he was playing football or basketball. Part of that time he was ridin' a dang motorcycle. I mean a big old Harley Davidson. Big as a saddle horse. And, man, I was as scared of that thing as I was a rattlesnake. Oliver was a little on the wild side. I know he's still got scars in his back right now from me clawing him to try to make him slow down when we were coming home. I'm not sure what Oliver's doing now; I know he came back and coached in high school a long time.

Most of the years when I was playing football, practice would be over, and it would be dark, and I'd have no ride home. One of my friends would drop me off on Highway 1, 20 miles from Blythe. It would be seven or eight o'clock. I'd hitchhike home. Lots of times I'd catch a ride with a soldier to Fort Gordon, which was halfway to Blythe. Most of the times I had an armful of books and was wearing an ROTC uniform, so local people knew I went to Richmond Academy. Of course, I caught rides with big semis, or with people from the East going to Miami and everywhere else down Highway 1. But the majority of time I'd get out at Fort Gordon and catch a ride to the Corner Store, which is where No. 1 turns and goes to Wrens. It was still two miles to my house. Part of the time, when we had a telephone, I'd call mama, and she'd come pick me up. Or I'd walk home. I'd be dead tired, hitchhiking up and down the road at eight or nine or ten o'clock gettin' home. And that's one reason why I now have a tough time with these people in the NCAA tellin' me we can't work football players but 20 hours a week. As if there weren't enough time for them to do whatever they need to do to play ball and do their school work. I'm sure there's a lot wrong with me, but sometimes I think having it tough growing up ain't too bad.

Football, the hardnosed, physical part of it, has always been easy for me. I also realize that it's not easy for everybody. I don't know that I ever thought of it this way before, but everybody doesn't love the game equally. And I was one of those who loved the game as much as you could love it.

If you played football at one of the three junior high schools in

Augusta, you went to Richmond Academy in the 10th grade. The same was true if you were a cheerleader, or played in the band because 10th graders were not allowed to participate in sports in junior high school. So I started Richmond Academy in the 10th grade. It was the public high school, but a military high school, and we had to wear a uniform. Richmond Academy is an old military school. Not too many years ago, it celebrated its 200th anniversary. I had grown to maybe 165 pounds. I had been working in the fields and the sun all summer, loading watermelons. I was conditioned to the heat. I remember starting practice in August, and there were 13 or 14 guards, and I was the last one. Dead last. By the time we got through two-a-days and early fall practice, I was No. Three. Because of nothing more than conditioning. The rest of them had fallen by the wayside. I ended up playing a lot as a 10th grader. We had good teams all three years I played.

My junior year we got beat in the South Georgia playoffs. In those days, there were just the playoffs in South and North Georgia, and then the State championship game. We lost in 1955 to LaGrange. In LaGrange. They were coached by the great Oliver Hunnicutt. Great guy. And a great coach. We had the best football team. But they beat us. I can remember Dusty Mills doing his heroics for them at quarterback. The writer who wrote the game up for the *Atlanta Journal* was Jim Minter. He later became editor of the newspaper. He wrote that Dusty Mills "was no bigger than a Panama mosquito at 135 pounds." But he threw a 29-yard touchdown pass on us in the first quarter. And then they blocked a punt and were leading us, 14-0, at the half. They intercepted a lateral and scored again in the third quarter. Then we woke up. And made two long drives for touchdowns. We were a stronger team, and they were just like a punchdrunk fighter on the ropes, and we couldn't knock 'em out. Which was a tremendous compliment to the coach and the players.

I saw Oliver Hunnicutt at the Atlanta Touchdown Club, just last year. He's long retired but as feisty as ever. I told him everything I've accomplished is in part because of that whippin' he put on us in 1955.

In the dressing room after the game, I didn't think some of our guys were hurting enough, getting beat in the state playoffs. And I called up all the juniors and sophomores, and we had a little session right there in the dressing room in LaGrange, Georgia. I told 'em,

"Look. Next year, we get in this position, we ain't gonna lose!" And I can remember the hurt today. I mean, I believe things hurt worse when you are young than they do when you get a little older. And it hurt plenty. There was something I was born with, maybe it was a fire burning in me that the only way you could put it out was to win. Over the years it has not always been easy to control that fire. You've got to work at it every day. Do a lot of praying. Soul searching. You want to live the right kind of life, do the right kind of things. Sometimes it's hard.

LaGrange went on to tie Rossville for the state championship. And Coach Hunnicutt told me in Atlanta that little Dusty Mills was a junior high principal in his hometown of LaGrange. He was a competitor.

The year 1956 Coach Harry Milligan—everybody called him Sack—left and went back to McCallie. He was an outstanding person, and an outstanding coach. He won the state championship at Richmond Academy in 1951. His son, David, was our quarterback in 1955, and we ran the T formation. Coach Milligan played at Georgia Tech, and he ran what they ran at Tech.

Anyway, Coach Frank Inman, who was on his staff, got the head job at Richmond Academy. He was truly a great coach, and he hired two of the toughest young assistant coaches the game of football has ever known: Fred McManus and Major Talent. Fred McManus was a little ole scrawny overachiever who played at the University of Georgia. Major Talent was a 180-pound guard, an overachiever who played at the University of Arkansas, and a guy that I grew to love very much. He coached my position. He had a way of turning my motor on and off like nobody I ever knew.

He was raised in the country in Tennessee, I think, and liked to coon hunt and loved his players and could make you play beyond what you thought you could. I played guard on offense and line-backer on defense. Inside linebacker. We played both ways. I played the whole game.

My senior year we went up to Athens Y Camp at Tallulah Falls for preseason practice. Coach Inman was a director of the camp. We took two buses up there, and we barely had a bus load coming back. They either had been hurt or quit and went home. I might have quit myself if I hadn't been captain of the team. I've never run for captain. But I have been captain of every team I ever played on from junior high, to high school, to college, to service ball at Fort Benning.

Except in Canada in pro ball, and I only played up there two years. In all of my football experience, I have never been through anything like the one at Tallulah Falls.

Now I had been to Athens Y Camp as a youngster, seven or eight years old. When you were raised like I was raised, you didn't expect to go to camp, but my granddaddy, Dr. Slaughter, sent us. Believe me, this wasn't the same deal in 1956.

I worked in the fields that summer, helping daddy gather all the grain. Then I went to Athens and helped my brother Wayne who had a service station there at the time. Our Richmond Academy team had worked hard the year before under Coach Milligan. But this was the toughest 10 days of my life. We got up, and we practiced in the morning for three hours without stopping. And we'd go lie on our cots at mid-day, too hot and too tired to eat. I didn't think there was any way I could get up. And then we went back in the heat of the afternoon and practiced for three more hours. How hard you work depends on who's doin' the workin'. The people involved. It wasn't the location. They could have done the same thing in Augusta. But it was harder to quit and go home. And they had 100 percent of your attention. Every day. Twenty-four hours a day. And the people doin' the workin' could work you. I mean it was tough. This was in the days before they gave you a drink of water. But they put a bottom in that football team. Put a heart and soul and guts in it. Got down to the foundation to where whoever played wasn't gonna quit. They just weren't gonna give up because they'd had too many opportunities if there was any give-up in them.

The coaches made champions of the few that stayed. We were a conglomeration of players. Of course, it was before integration, and there just wasn't a lot of talent on the football team. But we didn't know it. We thought we were good. And we were Richmond Academy, and we were supposed to win. They made believers out of us. Nobody was going to out-condition us. Nobody was going to be more perfect in execution. Or play more mistake-free football—all of the intangibles involved around the game. Nobody was going to have more of that going for them than we did. We scratched, fought, and bled, and worked until we got to the South Georgia championship and then the State championship.

A Team

A team is like a man. It's got a heart, physical ability, mental ability, spirit, character. It can grow and improve, or fade and decline. It doesn't live but eleven weeks. That's it. From the time you hold the first practice, it is different from any other team that has ever played the game.

RICHMOND ACADEMY, AND SUE

When I went to Richmond Academy I developed a tremendous group of friends, and we went through high school together. We had all played against each other in junior high. Being tenth graders we had an uphill battle for identity. We kind of bonded together. Tommy Ash remains a close friend of mine. We went on to play together and room together at Georgia for four years. I was close to Mont Miller. Mont and Tony Atkins were two white boys who ran the 100-yard dash in under ten seconds in 1956. They finished 1-2 in the state 100 and 220 dashes—a segregated track meet, mind you. My senior year at Richmond Academy, we won the state championship in four sports and came in second in basketball. We won football, baseball, track, and I believe golf. We finished pretty high in tennis. We were a special class. No doubt about it. And some of us became friends for life. I spent the night with Tommy Ash and Mont Miller a jillion times when I didn't want to go out there and get on that road home. Tom Nichols was also a close friend. And his family was close to my family. His daughter, Bobbie, baby-sat me and then tutored me in English in high school. The Nicholses had a big house in Augusta. If I ever got in a tight, I could always call Mrs. Nichols and go up there and spend the night. As I said, most of the time we didn't have a telephone. No way to contact mama. I just wouldn't show up at home that night. I was mature enough. And that's the way we lived.

Before I ever got to high school, if they played a basketball game, we went to it. I told you basketball was my daddy's thing. We sure didn't watch television. We didn't have one until I was in the ninth grade. I sold six beagles for $150 and bought a black and white TV. I believe it was an Emerson. We did love to sit around and listen to the radio: I can remember those old "Innersanctums," "Boston Blacky," "The Shadow, "Cincinnati 1, Ohio," and the "Grand Old Opry" on Saturday night. But if they played a basketball game at Richmond Academy, we were there. Basketball was big. They would fill up the auditorium. That's how I got to meet Sue Ward's sister, Wanda, before I ever met Sue, whom I married. Wanda was a senior, and she was dating one of the basketball players. She'd sit with Martha Goodwin. And I was a little ol' snotty-nosed, worrisome seventh grader, and I'd go and sit with them at the games. Two seniors. I don't know why they put up with me.

Sue went to Langford Junior High. She didn't come to Richmond Academy until the 11th grade. But the first time I met her was the year before. I was with a bunch of guys, and she was in a crowd of girls, and they were having a party, and we went by the house. That was the first time I ever saw her. I was as country and rural as you could get. And probably brash and arrogant. I'm sure I came on too strong for a quiet, timid city girl. She was a bit on the shy side where boys were concerned. She wasn't the flashiest girl in school. She was just kind of a special little lady. And everybody knew she was special. Sue says that I was cocky. I probably was. But I wasn't bad. And I was drivin' a pickup truck. I didn't see her again until the summer she was to be in the 11th grade. I was working for my brother in Athens and went home for the weekend and a friend of mine and I went by the Augusta Country Club. I can't remember why. I saw Sue and her friends. I spoke to her.

And then all of us who survived at Tallulah Falls came back to play our first football game against Aiken, South Carolina. I saw this friend of mine at school that Friday, Finley Merry. Of the Merry Brothers Brickyard. I didn't have a date for the dance that night. I said, "Hey. Get me a date for tonight." And he did. He got me a date with Sue. We double-dated. And we went in my car.

I forgot to say, when I was 16 years old, I got me a car. Because I had hitchhiked up and down that road, standing out there in the cold, tired after football practice...I just made up my mind, the Good Lord willing, I was going to own a car. I saved my service station money and bought a 1939 Ford. I paid $125 for it. It wasn't the fanciest car. I had to park it on a hill everywhere I went to make sure

Sue was elected Honorary Cadet Colonel at Richmond Academy.

it would crank up when I got ready to leave.

Well, Sue lived on a hill. After the opening game, which we won, 26-0, I wouldn't let her get in the car until I was sure it would crank comin' down the hill. If it didn't, they would have to push. That was automatic. We got it cranked. And went to Julian Smith's Casino, where the high school had its dances. Sock hops, they called 'em. I don't think I knew much about dancing. In fact, I know I didn't. I was also tired. But Sue was an excellent dancer, loved to dance. It was Sue who showed me how. I probably stood around all night talking with a bunch of friends about the game. And Sue was probably bored to death. She did not have the reputation as the No. 1 hot date in town. What do the modern kids say? Cool; she was cool. Nobody ever said a word against Sue Ward. I can tell you that. I know without reservations, she stands for the right things. And if I am doing the right things, then I'm in good shape. If I'm doing the wrong things, I'm in trouble. Let me put it this way, Sue and my daddy were the two most honest people that I ever met in my life. Even when the truth hurts. What did she see in me? I don't know...I was rough. A country boy. Maybe contrasting personalities do attract. You'll have to ask Sue. Her parents? Well, I think they probably tolerated me. Thought she would get over me. I didn't have a bad reputation. I wasn't a drinker or a hell raiser. I was just kind of country. Kind of rural. Football was too important to me to be a trouble maker.

Sue had a unique group of friends in high school, just as I did. The kind of friendships where for 30 years we've gone back, and it's just like we left yesterday. Those roots are deep. I think we were more like brothers and sisters than friends, all the kids that we ran with and played with. When they hurt, we hurt. Those kind of friends.

Did I make the next move with Sue? I made all the moves. She was probably duckin' and dodgin'. We started dating. She was cute, little, big brown eyes and a big smile and as pure as the driven snow. I liked what she stood for, and I liked what she was. She's also tough as nails. I'm not easy to live with. And she's not easy to live with. But we've worked at it. I know she's had a lot to do with the success I've had. Even back then. Because she's always stood for the right things.

Sue was elected Honorary Cadet Colonel, which was THE thing, the top honor a girl could win at Richmond Academy. Elected by the troops as their choice to represent them for the school year. A girl was chosen in her junior year so she could serve her senior year. Every year they have a military ball. Which is the big social event in the high school. That's where she was crowned as the Honorary Cadet Colonel.

My senior year I was company commander of the 10th grade students. Most had never had a uniform on before, never drilled before; you can imagine what a rag-tag outfit it was. But by the end of the year, it was the best company we had.

Sue and I have been a team for a long time. But it wasn't always going to be easy. Not too many things that are worth it are easy. I believe that.

THE TEAM CALLED DESIRE

I can tell you that the fall football season of 1956 wasn't easy. Coach Inman gave me one of the greatest lessons I ever learned. We had to win on conditioning and all the intangibles. Plus being a close-knit family. We weren't good enough to win on talent. I was one of the fastest, best-conditioned players on the team. We were running wind sprints one day after practice. We'd line up, and they'd blow the whistle, and we'd run 10 yards and line up and go again. I'd be three or four yards in front of the rest of them. They weren't running as hard and they weren't running as fast as I was. So it took me longer to get back and get lined up with the others.

Looking back on it, I really wasn't making a special effort to hurry and get back. I was dragging a bit to get a little rest. Coach Inman said, "Dye, get lined up with everybody else." He said it again on the next sprint. I mumbled something under my breath. He said, "Dye, I told you to get lined up with everybody else." I said, "Hell, Coach, make everybody run the same speed I'm running."

Coach Inman said, "I'll see you after practice." And we went around and around that field into the dark. Finally, he said, "I'm gonna tell you something, Dye. As long as I'm the coach here, I don't ever expect any questions or backtalk in practice." He said, "I am running the show."

It was just a good lesson for respecting authority. It's been a valuable lesson for me. Today, whether I'm right, or whether I'm wrong, I'm the football authority at Auburn. Respect for authority is part of discipline, and part of my personality, too. A big part of it. Of course, with authority goes responsibility. There have been a lot of times when I didn't agree with a decision...whether it was made by Coach Bryant, or by one of the college presidents I've worked for, or maybe I didn't agree with a rule or a regulation. But you do the job, the way you are told to do it. That's the way it's got to be. Coach Frank Inman helped teach me that.

We were so beat up and worn out after Tallulah Falls pre-season practice that we struggled to score, and fumbled the ball, and lost our second game to North Augusta, 13-7. We barely won against Glynn Academy, 9-0. That was a typical score for us. We did a helluva job shutting out quarterback Francis Tarkenton and his great Athens High team. Tony Atkins scored our only touchdown from about the seven-yard line. I remember we held Athens to only nine plays the second half. We were never a great offensive team. And probably weren't a great defensive team. We just didn't know it. We beat the Commercial Cobras, 14-2. Another South Carolina team, Camden Academy, beat us, 13-7. We made 35 points against Coffee County; they got six. I remember I blocked a punt for a touchdown. We lived on Bill Lanier's punts to beat Benedictine, 15-6; our quarterback, Larry Willige, didn't have a strong arm and had a hurt knee and couldn't run the hundred from daylight to dark, and he's bald-headed now, but he could stand up under the center like a man and you could win with him; he hit a jump pass—Willige didn't jump too high on that trick knee—to Jack Fountain who lateraled to Buzzy McMillan for about 40 yards and that was as fancy as we got.

Bill Force was our fullback; we called him "Pollywog." He was probably the best back we had; he scored the only touchdown on Savannah, and we made a goal-line stand to win, 8-0. Tony Atkins gained more yards—a hundred—than the whole Catholic High team, but they played their guts out and tied us, 0-0.

But we won the Region 2-AAA championship and played a great team from Macon for the South Georgia championship. The team was called Lanier then; it's called Central High now. Whatever they were called, they were a great high school team.

Lanier had 10 or 11 boys who got college scholarships. Tommy Ashe and I got scholarships to Georgia. Maybe one other player of ours got a scholarship; I'm not sure. Ronnie Evans was a little 145-pound halfback; he's dead now, killed in a car wreck. Atkins and Mont Miller could fly, but we couldn't throw the ball and hit a tree.

Lamar Fleming was our center and a brilliant student and is a doctor and runs a hospital now in Atlanta. None of us was big. But there was no quit in us: Eddie Anderson, Bernard Williams, Paul Inglett, Charles Broome, Jimmy Smalley, Charles Goodwin, Ray Grubs, Milner Lively...We had a player, Jack Fisher, who was a great baseball pitcher, went on to the major leagues and had a good career. You might remember him as the pitcher who threw the ball Roger Maris hit for his 61st home run.

We played the South Georgia championships at Richmond Academy. It was a dead sellout. They kicked off to us. Ray Grubbs caught it and fumbled it but picked it up in time to hand off to Tony Atkins, and nobody was gonna catch him. I made two blocks. My old high school annual called them "bone crushing blocks." I don't know about that, but they were good blocks. Tony ran the kickoff back for a touchdown.

We knocked loose a Lanier fumble after our own kickoff. We scored in two plays. And every minute, every second of the rest of the game, we hung on. If any team ever hung on, we hung on. Defense was all we had to live by. And the heart and soul put in that team at Tallulah Falls. We won a game we had no business winning, 14-7.

There are a lot of coaches who think you can only win in the big time with great athletes at every position; I'm not one of those coaches. You've got to have athletes, but I believe you can win with the intangibles, with heart and soul and guts and boys who won't lose, like the boys from Richmond Academy who wouldn't lose in 1956.

Now we were going to play Northside High School of Atlanta, the No. 1 ranked team in the state. Coached by a great coach, Wayman Creel, who died in 1990, still coaching in Atlanta. His son was on the team at Auburn when I became the head coach. Northside had some big names and some great players. Stan Gann was the quarterback. He was the most famous high school quarterback in Georgia then, even more famous than Francis Tarkenton at Athens. Gann and Northside won the state championship the next year. Ed Nutting, who played at Georgia Tech, was one of their linemen. Ten or twelve of their guys got college scholarships. They were favored to beat us by three touchdowns.

We were supposed to play in Augusta on December 12, a Friday night. A storm or hurricane or something hit, and they

While at Richmond Academy, I learned about paying the price to win.

cancelled the game until the following night. We ended up playing in the rain on a muddy field. Terrible conditions. I'm sure it helped us. The score was 13-7. We won. We scored on two long drives. Willige, with a broken finger on his passing hand, sneaked over the goal on his bad knees for both touchdowns. Stan Gann hit a long touchdown pass in the last quarter, but that's all they got. We dug in the mud and held 'em. Bill Lanier would kick it, and we'd hold 'em again. We just played defense, the kicking game, and won the Georgia State Championship.

I loved 'em all, our players, and all our coaches. They wrote us up as "The Team Called Desire." It was a fancy name, but it was a true one.

Oh, I remember the dressing room after the Northside game. All the boys I grew up with and bled with, shoutin' to hear one another. My brothers there. All my family. Everybody hollerin', everybody excited. Except my father. My father wasn't a man to get excited. He *expected* you to win. Or he expected you to crawl off the field because you couldn't walk because you gave everything you had. But the noise of it. All of us. Coaches and boys. All of us winners. Winners for all of our lives.

Coach Inman went to Georgia and stayed on the staff there for a long time. Then he was athletic director over all the schools in Glynn County in Brunswick, Georgia. I'm not sure where Coach Fred McManus is right now. Major Talent went up to Hargrave Military Academy in Virginia. Ended up having a heart attack and dying. I still hear from Mrs. Talent.

I loved my high school coaches. They were heart and soul to me. I carry lessons they taught me every day of my life.

The championship game was played up in December. I think after the signing date for college scholarships. Coach Butts came down for the game from Georgia. Coach Quinton Lumpkin drove him down in a big Cadillac. They were waitin' outside the dressing room door. Coach McManus's wife had had a baby. A baby and the State Championship on the same day. He had a big box of cigars, and he was handing 'em out in the dressing room. I didn't smoke. Never did smoke. Can't smoke now. But I lit up a big cigar. And went out the dressing room door. Coach Butts was out there, and his eyes got big as dinner plates. I know what he was thinkin', seein' me: he comes all the way down from Athens to try to sign the Lineman of the Year in Georgia, and here he is: a scrawny little old boy, comin' out of the dressin' room smokin' a cigar. What has he got himself into?

Well, my family and friends and Sue and Coach Butts, we all went to the house. Now we didn't go blocks—remember I lived 20 miles away in Blythe.

The big, old country house was full of people. I can still see little Sue…there was a swinging door between the dining room and the kitchen, and she sat, not even turning her head, just watchin' those big, old men, comin' in and out of the door, only movin' her eyes.

Coach Butts got word that Coach Lumpkin had had a wreck in his Cadillac, or he made it up so he could get out of there, and he left. Coach Butts was a strong man, but he didn't really have a personality for recruiting. Coach Lumpkin did most of the recruiting on me. I wasn't ready to sign. I was scared to death of getting in a situation

where we couldn't win. I'd lost enough games in high school to
know how much it hurt, and I wanted a chance to win. Coach Butts's
heyday had been in the 1930s and 1940s. Georgia Tech was winning
big then under Bobby Dodd. Georgia hadn't beaten 'em in eight
years. And Tennessee was winning under Bowden Wyatt. I had
made a date for the next day to see Coach Ken Donahue of
Tennessee for Sunday lunch. At the Ship Ahoy restaurant. I liked
Tennessee. But I wasn't ready to sign. It was going to be hard for me
not to go to Georgia. My family there. One brother playing there.
One coaching the freshman team.

But that night after we won the State Championship lives on in
my head; I carry it with me every day, how it feels to be a winner.

Recruiting. Those were looser times. I was offered some
things. But I didn't take 'em. I wasn't for sale. Most of the men who
recruited me were gentlemen. And treated me that way. I was going
to tell you about Coach Jordan of Auburn and how he and my daddy
were close friends. When Mrs. Jordan would visit her family in
Rosier where she was raised, Coach Jordan would come, too.
Maybe he and my daddy would go fishing. If you want to know the
truth, what he and my daddy really did, they rode up and down the
roads and drank a little liquor together. Coach Jordan was a wonderful story teller, one of the best there ever was. He recruited
Wayne, my oldest brother, and Nat, when he came along. Coach
Jordan was a gentleman, easy going, and a conservative guy. You
wouldn't know he could ever get mad he was so easy going. The
boys who played for him, and played so hard for him, like Cleve
Wester, who has become a close friend of mine, tell me he could get
up a temper. That he was plenty tough. I never saw it. Coach Jordan
told me—I believe it was the summertime, before my senior year—
he said: "I know you are going to be highly recruited. And I want you
to know we would like to have you at Auburn. But I understand your
family ties to Georgia. But if you don't like Georgia, then we'd love
to have you at Auburn." He didn't pressure me. That was the extent
of it. He was always a gentleman.

I never will forget after I signed with Georgia, I saw Coach
Jordan the next summer. He was driving through Blythe. We were
shipping peanuts or something, but I was working for daddy on the
farm; I can remember being just as nasty and dirty and sweaty, and
Coach Jordan was in his big black Cadillac, and I ran over and

stopped him, and I remember his rolling down the window, and I told him, I said, "Coach, when that freshman team of yours comes to Georgia, we're gonna get after their ass."

Of course, we beat 'em, 27 to nothing. But I can remember telling Coach Jordan that. I can still see him. He just laughed. I went on to play three raging varsity games against his teams. Lost two of 'em. I played in the last Auburn-Georgia game played in Columbus, and the first game in Sanford Stadium in Athens, and the first game in Auburn. Every one was tough. Wasn't no chillun in those games.

And before that, I saw some great Auburn-Georgia games in Columbus. Auburn beat Georgia bad in 1955 and 1956. And then Georgia almost beat Auburn in 1957; Red Phillips caught the only touchdown pass; I guess Auburn missed the extra point; Zeke Smith recovered a fumble on the goal line to stop Georgia's best drive.

Well, I played against Coach Jordan's teams for four years. And it was always a warm relationship between his family and our family. The thing I probably remember the most about Coach Jordan was when I went to coach at Alabama, his blood rival, when we played the big game in Birmingham, he always made it a point to find me and speak, talk, spend some time on the field before the game—all that pressure and all those people in the stands, and he'd ask about mama and daddy and the family. We just had tremendous respect for him.

My father and mother never said much about recruiting. They would never come right out and say where they wanted me to go to school. My relatives up in Athens did. But I didn't sign on signing date, as I said. I had been involved in winning the State Championship. I wasn't ready to make a decision.

I liked Coach Donahue, and Coach Skeeter Bailey, and Coach George Cafego, and Head Coach Bowden Wyatt at Tennessee. They were winning. I was used to winning. We played in front of sellout crowds every week at Richmond Academy, four or five thousand people at every game. And I was ready for college ball; I had been trained in all the right techniques; I was as far along as anyone in techniques. I visited Tennessee, Georgia, and Georgia Tech. I would have gone to Tennessee if it hadn't been so far away from home. Not that I didn't like Georgia or Georgia Tech. Because I liked 'em all. But Tennessee was appealing to me because I was a 185-pound guard, and they had all those small guards making All-

America. They were running the single wing, pulling the guards and trapping, and it would have been a perfect situation for me.

Coach Dodd at Tech realized that my family was Georgia. He was also a perfect gentleman in recruiting. And I knew Spec Landrum, who was the freshman coach at Tech. He had coached at Georgia. Coach Dodd didn't come to Augusta. I visited him in his office. At the time, he had the small guards at Tech, too: Ray Beck and Franklin Brooks. And Georgia was looking for bigger linemen because Coach Butts liked the drop-back passing attack. I was more of a finesse football player than I was a power football player. I had to use what the good Lord gave me and that was speed and quickness.

Before we leave Richmond Academy and Blythe, Georgia, let me touch again on my years growing up.

As I said, I was probably the closest of us boys to my daddy. But he was a man's man—his dogs, his hunting; he would leave for work before daylight. It was my older brother Wayne who spent the most time with me when I finally got old enough to go hunting and fishing. Now you had to earn the right to fish. When Wayne and Nat started letting me go, I paddled the boat for two or three years before they let me fish. You take a 10- or 11-year-old kid tryin' to paddle a boat in a swift creek or river, and it's damn tough. There's a lot to it. It takes strength to be able to paddle upstream and an artist to paddle downstream. It's tough to hold a boat back that's going with the current, so that you can fish a particular hole. Wayne was patient with me. And sometimes he was *not* patient with me. But he taught me. At that point in my life, Wayne and I were close. I wasn't any competition for him. Then he went off to college.

Nat and I got closer playing the one year together at Richmond Academy. And he was a senior and captain of the team at Georgia when I was playing as a sophomore in 1958. We really got to be friends when we played together two years up in Canada. He played defensive end, and I played outside linebacker, right behind him. He did a great job of taking out the interference; all I had to do was make the tackle. In two years, we didn't have a long run made around our side.

In later years, Nat and I have become even closer.

I haven't said enough about my sister Jane. She's a year younger, as I mentioned. We played together, grew up together. I was probably mean to Jane as a kid. She probably needed a little

This family portrait was made at Nat's wedding. Jane and mama are in front. In back is daddy, Wayne Jr., me, and Nat.

more attention than I did, and she probably got it. She was getting new clothes to wear, and I was getting hand-me-downs. You don't have to be too old to know the difference. As chillun, you've got to have that love and attention, and nothing is going to take the place of it.

Jane was smart. And still is. She was the real student among us, as I said.

When I was 16 and got my '39 Ford, Jane would ride to school with me. Only she was always late. I'd get up early, like I still do. I was always fighting with Jane to get ready. Finally, I told mama, either get her up, or I'm gonna start leaving her. Which I began to do. Mama would catch me in her car about halfway to Augusta; my '39 Ford wouldn't go too fast. Jane would get up for a few weeks, then I'd leave her again, and mama would pull me off the side of the road again.

Jane was a cheerleader at Richmond Academy. She met Jerry Snell at Georgia. He was a football player from Skipperville, Alabama. He became a high school coach at Toccoa, Georgia, and coached 25 or 30 years. Jane and Jerry come to Auburn often. Their son, Jerry, enrolled at Auburn and came to football practice about every day. Just good people. Jane has always been community minded. Civic minded. And she's a competitor. Her cheerleaders at Toccoa last year won a big award at camp at Furman and went to Texas for the national competition.

One thing about our family: we are all competitive. None of us is ever going to be wrong in a family argument. If we are in the backyard pitchin' horseshoes, we'll be pitchin' to win. We're competitive. Probably too competitive.

6

GEORGIA FOOTBALL

When it came right down to it, it was just too easy, too convenient for me to go to Georgia. My mother grew up in Athens and her family lived there. I spent a lot of time in Athens as a boy; my brothers were still there. Of course, they had been a part of the losing—I'm not sure if they had been a part of the problem or a part of the solution. I'm kidding. They were both competitors. But I decided if I was going to Georgia, I was going with a purpose. For some reason, I don't know why, at that early age, I was a goal-oriented person. I guess I learned it through football, what it took to win the state championship at Richmond Academy, and what it took to survive as a boy growing up. I know I justified going to Georgia by setting three goals for myself:

I made up my mind I was going to do everything I could possibly do to help Georgia have a winning program. And I went there with the intention of doing that as a freshman. It didn't just happen; I intended to help make it happen. My second goal: when they were recruiting me, Tennessee and Georgia Tech both *promised* me I would make All-America if I came to their schools. And that became a selfish goal on my part; I said, well, if I can make All-America at Tennessee or Georgia Tech, then I want to make All-America at Georgia. And my third goal was to graduate. Those goals I set for myself, but not necessarily in that order. I never entirely lost sight of them, although I was disoriented my sophomore year by some things going on on the practice field that I didn't think were right. And I had a bit of a sinking spell my senior year after I had accomplished all of my goals but one. But I eventually accomplished that one too: I graduated.

I worked for John Murray that summer after my senior year of high school, worked in the bakery of the Murray Biscuit Company. Just as a handyman. Helping tear out a big, long oven and build a new one. Working by the hour. I saved and bought a better car for $500, a '53 Ford from Sue's daddy, Amos Ward. I put down half the $500 and financed half and paid it off myself. I drove it to Atlanta to play in the Georgia High School All-Star Game. Then I drove it to Athens.

What was it like, leaving home? You have to remember, I grew up independent. Many times I spent the night with a friend without even calling home. I worked a summer in Athens. I'd been earning all my own money since I was twelve. It wasn't like I had never been away from home. Or that I was afraid to leave home. My home was no easy place to live. It was home, and I loved it. But there were a lot of hard knocks along the way.

My freshman year at Georgia was a fun year. We were a good class. We didn't have a lot of numbers, but we had some talent: the halfback, Fred Brown, remember he was Johnny Mack Brown's nephew; my buddy Bill Godfrey, the fullback, a good country boy who liked to hunt and fish; center Phil Ash, who was strong and talented; and Tarkenton, quarterback Francis Tarkenton, a truly great competitor; I was driving a $500 Ford, and Francis was driving a Thunderbird. I guess that's the distance between guards and quarterbacks. My only roommate all four years was my old team-mate, Tommy Ash; he was an average player, but worked hard, was an overachiever.

I had one disappointment my freshman year. A so-called best friend from Augusta kept me from joining the SAE fraternity. He black-balled me all the time I was trying to pledge. He was just jealous of me, I guess. I never felt like I was better than anybody. But I always felt I was as good as anybody. I went ahead and pledged another fraternity. But I never went over there. I wanted to be an SAE. It tickled me years later when both of my sons pledged SAE at Auburn.

Coach Quinton Lumpkin was Georgia's head freshman coach. My brother Wayne was his assistant. Of course, Nat was playing on the varsity. There comes a time in the lives of brothers when they get over rivalries and become friends. It happened for us when I started to play ball in high school. I knew a good many of the other upperclassmen at Georgia, and I didn't catch the freshman harassment that some of my class might have gotten. I don't believe in hazing. One of the first things I did when I became head coach at Auburn was stop it. I never saw a good football player hazing a good football player. It was always a third-stringer, who was never gonna amount to anything, hazing a high school All-America. I never liked leaning over and letting somebody hit me without cause. I had to lean over enough when I had done something wrong growing up. If somebody whipped me, it was going to be because he was a better man than I was. At Auburn, we bring new kids in, we never treat 'em like freshmen, even if they are walk-ons. And if they have talent, and maturity, and fit in the rotation, we play 'em. If we win a championship, everybody gets a ring; if we don't, nobody gets a ring, senior or freshman.

We had a good freshman class at Georgia in 1956. We had a lot of good days competing with the varsity. We weren't intimidated by them, which made it fun. And that was the year Georgia "broke the drought," beating Georgia Tech for the first time in nine years, 7-0. Fullback Theron Sapp scored the winning touchdown. But the team still had a losing season. They won three, they lost seven.

Our freshman team beat Clemson. And Auburn. And Georgia Tech. Played three games and won 'em all. I never lost to Georgia Tech as a player. I've never lost to them as a coach. But I respect Georgia Tech and its great football tradition.

The biggest thing that happened to that freshman team was playing Auburn. They had their own famous freshman team. There was an NCAA investigation that led to putting Auburn on probation. It involved the quarterback Don Fuell. I didn't know anything about what happened. We were just excited to play them. They had some great athletes, as I said: Fuell, Ed Dyas, Ken Rice, James Pettus, G. W. Clapp. Those guys.

We jumped 'em. In Athens. And whipped 'em good, 27 to nothing. I can remember one play like it happened yesterday.

Don Fuell was carrying the ball—he was a great athlete. He was hurtling somebody on the sideline, and I got up into him, knocked him into the Auburn bench, broke three of his ribs. I didn't know that at the time. Coach Joe Connally, who was on Coach Jordan's staff for years, was standing on the sideline. Coach Connally swears I jumped up and said, "If you're worth $10,000, I'm worth

Here I am chasing Auburn's Ed Dyas in 1959. Games like this introduced me to Auburn's great football tradition.

$50,000." I don't know if I said it. I probably did. We were just kids, full of ourselves. I can tell you this, I was to battle G. W. Clapp for four years. He might not have been famous to the football world, like Zeke Smith and Jackie Burkett and Red Phillips and Cleve Wester, but he was famous to me—how tough he was and how hard he played.

Tarkenton threw two touchdown passes and Godfrey made a big hit on Fuell and I intercepted a pass and ran it 40 yards for a touchdown. Godfrey was the defensive star. He made 13 tackles the first half. Our coaches said it was the best Georgia freshman team in a decade. Some said since Frankie Sinkwich in the 1930s. We had talent. We didn't have the numbers. Don't be fooled by the score. Auburn had a terrific bunch of athletes.

We also beat the Tech freshmen in the big charity game in Atlanta. I couldn't wait to play my first varsity season.

To be entirely honest, I was miserable my sophomore year at Georgia. We should have had a great football team in 1958. We beat almost everybody we played physically and won only four games out of 10. In my opinion, you ought to win all the games you are supposed to win, and some of the games you are not supposed to win. In 1958, we should have won nine. We could have won 'em all.

The problem was not the technical coaching we got on the field...the fundamentals. It was the undisciplined environment we lived in off the field. Coach and Mrs. Lumpkin lived in the dorm and did as good a job as they could. Their resources were limited. The athletic department got by with the bare minimum. The food we ate left a lot to be desired. You could keep from starving by eating down there. After I got to be a junior and senior and had a little money, I ate out. As far as encouragement, or pressure to do well in your schoolwork, Coach Butts more or less had the attitude that the strong are gonna survive. Character prevailed. The weak didn't make it. The same was true on the football field. Coach Butts was a demanding person. He gave you every opportunity. If you had character, or any mental toughness about you, it would have to be displayed. You couldn't just ease through there unnoticed.

To be blunt and frank, the problem wasn't Coach Butts. It was his staff. Again, I don't mean their technical instruction wasn't good. Some were excellent assistants. But Coach Butts was near the end of his career. My last three years were his last three years as a coach. In 1958, he was 53 years old. The end was in sight. Loyalty among some of his staff had begun to break down. It was not a fun year for me because I could see that we had enough ability and talent to win, and we weren't winning. If the 1958 team could have played for the assistant coaches who coached at Georgia in the 1940s—Shug Jordan and Ears Whitworth—we would have gone to a major bowl. It was a disgrace we didn't, with the talent we had; twelve of those boys went on to pro ball. We never had but one close-knit team that achieved more than it should have, and Coach Whitworth had a lot to do with that team.

All college football players quit, at some time. If they don't quit, they all think about quitting. I left for a day. Francis Tarkenton, Fred Brown, Phil Ash, Bill Godfrey, and myself. We were all starters, or all playing. We didn't leave because football was too tough; we didn't leave because we weren't playing; we really left because of turmoil on the field. Coaches arguing, bitching among themselves. The five of us were all highly recruited, all highly competitive. We didn't want to go through four years of griping and complaining. It was hard for me. My brother, Nat, was captain of the team. It reached the point in practice one day when I couldn't see myself going through my whole college career like that.

We didn't just walk off and leave in the night. We were talking about leaving in the dorm one Monday night, the week before the Kentucky game. My brother, Nat, and Theron Sapp, the fullback, came up and told us, "If you are going to quit, you need to go tell

Coach Butts." So we went to see Coach Butts that night. He was sittin' up in his pajamas. And we told him our feelings. We didn't get much sympathy from Coach Butts. If you knew Coach Butts, how competitive, how tough he was, you'd laugh at the idea we would get any sympathy. He told us to go on back to the dorm and go to bed. So we packed up and left and went to Atlanta and spent the night at Phil Ash's house. I called my folks. Daddy asked where we were going. He said, "You ain't comin' home."

The next morning we were eating breakfast, trying to decide where we *were* going when Coach Lumpkin and my brother Wayne walked in the house. Herding up the lost sheep. We went on back to Athens.

It was homecoming. I ended up playing probably as good a football game as I ever played. I know it was the best I played as a sophomore. I stole the ball from Calvin Bird on the kickoff; I was the first one to hit him, and he tried to spin away, and when he was spinning somebody else hit him, and the ball came loose in my hands. I never broke stride, 28 yards for a touchdown. I also intercepted a pass. And recovered a fumble. I believe I started the next week and started from then on. I had been alternating with Billy Roland.

But the episode didn't help me. It didn't help Georgia. It might have created a situation where Coach Butts ultimately made a change the next year. I don't know. But things didn't change until Coach Butts hired Coach Whitworth in 1959. He brought stability to our team.

Coach Whitworth had played at Alabama in 1930-31. He came back as head coach in the 1950s. His last Alabama team in 1957 lost every game. He went up to coach Canadian ball for a year. And came back to Georgia, where he had been an assistant, to coach the line in 1959. He was a great assistant coach. He had such a settling effect on our football team; I guess because of his powers of maturity, his awareness. He was an old-timer, kinda short, with a ruddy face, a square-jawed guy. He knew how to pull your string, when to hug you and when to kick you. I tell you what he did: he taught me one of the great lessons I ever learned in my life. And I carry it with me every day. It was a lesson about fear. There are times when things happen to you, and maybe you have an anxiety attack, and you don't know what it is when it isn't anything but *fear*. Fear, maybe, of rejection. Fear of failure. Whatever.

We were getting ready to open the season with Alabama in 1959. Coach Whitworth called us linemen together one day on the practice field. He had a way of sitting there and talking to you, just like you were in a philosophy class. He said, "I want to tell you something about this ball game that we're fixin' to play against Alabama. You know Coach Bryant is a great football coach. One of the things that makes him great is the fact his players are scared of him, and his coaches are scared of him, but, most important, his opponents are scared of him." Coach Whitworth said, "That's where we're gonna have an advantage. Because we ain't gonna be afraid of him." He said, "They won't be any better conditioned than we are; they won't be any better prepared; and they won't be any better than we are. All you got to do is go out and play your game and not fear 'em."

We had lost to them the year before, although we gained 400 yards; they quick-kicked about 12 times and upset us. But we dominated the ball game in 1959.

We gave Coach Whitworth the game ball after we whipped them. Coach Whitworth died that winter in Athens. I believe enough of his spirit carried over to the 1960 season for us to have a winning year. But no more than that. And we no longer had as many athletes as most of the teams we played. The next year Alabama beat us, 21 to 6 in Birmingham.

I think having played against Bryant-coached teams for three years and seeing a very, very inferior Alabama team beat our superior team in 1958, then seeing Coach Whitworth's respect for Bryant as a coach in 1959, and playing against them again in 1960 made me want to coach at Alabama.

I went to New York at the end of the '59 season for the *Look* All-America team. We were on the Perry Como TV show. We stayed up there a week in those days. Man, you talk about having fun. You talk about country-come-to-town.

I'd never been out of Georgia much. I hadn't eaten in fancy restaurants like they took us to in New York. I roomed with Billy Cannon. He was the Bo Jackson of his day at LSU. He won the 100-yard dash and the shot put in the Southeastern Conference. And he won the Heisman Trophy. He'd signed a big pro contract. I was just a little ol' nothin' guard from Georgia. But, to me, he was a nice guy. We got along fine. When we left New York, he gave me his jersey. I kept it for a long time. I don't know where it is today. Don Meredith of SMU was up there. Carroll Dale of VPI. Dean Look of Michigan State. And the guard, Marvin Terrell, and the fullback, Charlie Flowers, from Ole Miss.

Marvin and Charlie and I ran together in New York. The bowl queens were hostesses for the players. Somehow we hooked up with three of them. We didn't exactly date 'em; we just had a lot of fun together. Marvin went with the Sugar Bowl queen, and Charlie the Orange Bowl queen, and I went with the Cotton Bowl queen, Dianne Lander. It was the year Syracuse won the National Championship. We finished No. 5 at Georgia with a 10-1 record.

A funny thing happened later to me and the Orange Bowl queen, Nancy Wakefield. It wasn't so funny at the time. As I said, Flowers was going with her in New York; but I was going to play against Missouri *in* the Orange Bowl. So I made a date with her for the night after the Orange Bowl game. Well, when I got down to the game, I never could catch up with her. She was modeling in fashion shows and doing all the things a queen has to do. I was practicing football. I tried to get up with her, but I couldn't. Sue Ward had friends in Miami and had come down to visit them. So I made a date with her for the game.

We were at the official party when the game was over and a doorman comes in and asks me, "Are you Pat Dye?" I said, "Yes." He said, "The Orange Bowl queen is here and her court. She says she has a date with you."

I'm sitting with Sue. So I said, "Well, well." I went outside and told Nancy I had tried to contact her and never could. And in the meantime, I made a date with a girl I had been dating for three or four years. I said, "We've got plenty of guys here who don't have dates." And she said: "I can handle it." Well, she could handle it by herself, believe me. She was a terrific young woman.

Look magazine took good care of us in New York, and we ended up on the Perry Como show. Me from Blythe, Georgia.

The thing I remember most about the trip is when I got back how hard Coach Whitworth rode me in practice in front of the other players, to make sure I had my feet on the ground. I'd been back a couple of days, and we were practicing, getting ready for Missouri in the Orange Bowl. I made a good play. I can remember just as well as if it happened 30 minutes ago; Coach Whitworth fell down on his knees like he was praising the Lord—that's what he said, "Praise the Lord, Praise the Lord, Pat's finally come home from New York."

He was a fun coach and tough. And I loved him.

We had graduated all those good players in 1958. We were picked seventh or eighth in the conference in 1959. Our middle linebacker, Dave Lloyd, left after his junior year. He became a great pro. He was a great college player, too. But he was a controversial figure on the team. Two things rallied our football team: when Lloyd left and when Coach Butts hired Coach Whitworth. I learned again my whole philosophy of football. You ain't got to have the biggest and the best and fastest people to win. But you better have them playing hard and the best they can be, and you better pay attention to all the intangibles around the game. Those things are far, far more important than anybody realizes. I first realized it at Richmond Academy in 1956.

Coach Butts. Coach Wallace Butts. He was tough. He was a great offensive coach long before his time, the way he handled the passing game. We all had tremendous respect for him. Whether you liked him or not, you respected him. He demanded that. And I liked him. During my time we played both ways, one-platoon football. I'm not so sure Coach Butts wouldn't have been an even better coach in two-platoon football. He would have been a natural just handling the offense, with a top coach to handle the defense. But still he was one of the great coaches of all time. Don't doubt that. He was a very emotional coach. I would put him in the same emotional category with Coach Bryant and Coach Lombardi. He was no quiet, meek individual. Coach Butts had a presence about him that gave you confidence. That's one of the things Coach Bryant had, his presence on the sideline.

One thing nobody ever questioned about Coach Butts, if you played for him, or if you knew him as a man: he was a fighter and a competitor. He had the heart, I guess you could say, of a bulldog. Just a tough, competitive guy. A small, but powerful man. I guess he couldn't have been more than five-feet, six-inches. Maybe his stature had a lot to do with his competitiveness. I expect he grew up, pushed around a bit in his younger days, and when he got big enough to defend himself, he didn't care what size you were. Or what size your team was. I regret I never heard him speak except at squad meetings. I hear he was a great speaker.

You couldn't say Coach Butts was quiet-spoken on the practice field. I doubt it belongs in this book, but his favorite expression—

when he thought a player made a less than courageous effort Coach Butts would call him a "yellow-bellied, titty-pullin', piss-ant." A lot of good men who played for him got called one. I never will forget Coach Frank Howard of Clemson came in our dressing room once after we played them. I always liked Coach Howard because he's like he is: a country boy. He yelled, "Hey, Dye! Damn, y'all take all this stuff from Coach Butts. Come over there to Clemson," he said, "I'll treat you royally, and I ain't gonna call you every kind of sonofabitch in the world."

The second year I was coaching at Alabama, after the 1966 season, Coach Howard offered me a job. I went in and talked to Coach Bryant. I said I really wasn't ready to go anywhere; I didn't know enough about coaching; I just wanted him to know I was talking to Coach Howard. Coach Bryant said, "Hell, you're not going to Clemson. I'm gonna give you a $1,500 raise." I called Coach Howard and told him I was staying at Alabama. The next day I got a letter from him: "Dear Pat: You owe me $500 for getting you a $1,500 raise. Coach Howard."

Well, Coach Butts could cuss a bit. Except somehow he got away with it, the way he said things. He also had a wonderful wit and could cut you with that. I remember after we lost to Alabama in Birmingham my senior year, we came back to Athens, and on Monday we got our scouting report for the next game. But Coach Butts started talking about the Alabama game. I played about 50 minutes in the game, or 55. But he jumped me and he jumped Francis about the way we played. He imitated me, walkin', hobblin' off the field. He said, "I look out there and there's an All-America guard. I have to substitute for him." And Coach Butts staggers across the stage, mimicking me coming off the field. He said, "I think he's dyin'." I look back on it, and I know he jumps Francis and myself because he knows we are the two strongest ones who can take it, and he can get a point across. But he was funny to see, limpin' on that stage.

I still smile thinking about Coach Butts, about standing with him on the sideline at the end of our game with Georgia Tech in 1960. It was my last game at Georgia and Francis's last game. We never lost to Georgia Tech. We didn't know it was also Coach Butts's last game as head coach. I played the whole ball game and blocked a field goal and an extra point. We were ahead, 7-6. I was give slam out. So he took me out of the game with a few seconds left

Senior Captains. Me and Francis Tarkenton with Coach Butts.

to play. I was standing beside Coach Butts. Stan Gann, my old Northside opponent from high school, was the Georgia Tech quarterback. He throws a pass downfield, and Francis is playing free safety and intercepts it and runs up the sideline, right in front of Coach Butts. All he's got to do is stay in bounds, and the clock runs out, and the game is over. He runs out of bounds and stops the clock. Coach Butts jumps in the air and hollers, "Goddamn you, Francis, you've been here four years, and you ain't made contact yet!" Oh goodness, that was Coach Butts.

Francis Tarkenton. I met Francis growing up because my family lived in Athens. I met him in the summers. We played him twice at Richmond Academy. We played against his great 1955 Athens team that beat everybody so bad, including national power Valdosta. We played that Athens team in Augusta. That was the first night George Geisler ran the ball for Athens. He'd been playing linebacker or something and the running back got hurt. They gave Geisler the ball. He ran for a hundred and something yards, and they beat us, 14-7. Geisler went on to play with us at Georgia. It was a hard-fought game. A close game. Next year, in 1956, we played them in Athens and beat them, seven to nothing.

In my opinion, Francis was a great athlete. I think about him now and try to compare him to the great athletes of today. He was not as big and strong and fast. But he would still be a great athlete. He was a refined athlete. Great shooter playing basketball. Great hand–eye coordination. But I think the thing that Francis had...I don't believe Francis Tarkenton ever had a negative thought in his mind about losing. If he did, he never let it surface. He figured if there was any time left, there was enough time to win. He could focus all his mental and physical and spiritual ability into winning the ball game. If you played with Francis, you might not like him, but you respected him. I mean you respected the fact he was a great competitor.

Did I imagine Francis would go to the pros and pass for over 40,000 yards and make the NFL Hall of Fame? No. But I knew he had that mental toughness about him. It's hard for me to express what Francis could do...but he could RISE above his ability, above the team's ability. He could take an ordinary football team and beat somebody it had no business being on the field with. Those Minnesota teams he took to the Super Bowl, they lacked that little something that would have allowed them to win. It wasn't necessarily the quarterback. Lots of talented quarterbacks never get to the Super Bowl. One thing anybody who ever played with Francis could agree on: he was a great competitor. He could get it done under pressure. In the clutch. With the game on the line. That's what set him apart.

I said that every one of the three varsity games we played at Georgia against Auburn were tough. For men only. When I came to Auburn to coach, Auburn was down, and hadn't won a conference game the year before. But I remembered the days when I played, when those blue jerseys put the fear of God in many a team. I have a vivid memory of Coach Sterling Dupree, who played at Auburn years before, giving us a scouting report on the 1959 Auburn team. He went down the list: calling off the All-America players: Zeke Smith, Jackie Burkett, Ken Rice, Ed Dyas, Dave Edwards. All those great athletes. I added G. W. Clapp to the list in my mind. Coach Dupree talked about those players and how we had no chance to win. And we *had* to win to be certain we won the Southeastern Conference championship. And our Orange Bowl bid probably depended on it.

I also remember the preacher who talked to us. Coach Butts always had one speak to the squad. I don't remember his name. I remember him talking about a little cork on a string hitting against a steel ball. The cork kept hitting on that old steel ball and would bounce off it, kept bouncing off it, kept bouncing off it...but eventually it got the steel ball to move, just a bit, and then it kept hitting against it until finally it got that steel ball to swinging. I remember that image. Just that. Because against Auburn, I was a little cork. And I had to hit a lot of steel balls that day.

Auburn was a physical team. Oh Lord, yes. Big, good athletes. Well coached. Who played hard. Who knew how to win. They beat us, 21 to 6, the year before in Columbus. They had substitutes who could play. In 1959, every snap of the ball was emotional. It was that kind of game. And I played every snap.

Auburn had the ugliest helmets. I don't know what make they were. We wore Riddell helmets. Theirs fit so tight they made their faces look bigger than their heads. I'd look up and there was that big face of G. W. Clapp. Let me say again how tough he was, how hard he played. Zeke Smith played the other guard; I didn't block on Zeke, except to trap him once in a while, or try to.

The last drive we made, I recovered a fumble by Bryant Harvard, the Auburn quarterback. And when Francis's bunch came in, I stayed in the game. We had 35 yards to go. And six minutes and 30 seconds to get there. Francis made three or four key plays coming down the stretch, throwing the ball to our fullback Don Soberdash, to keep the drive alive. Short passes right over the middle.

Then the last play, fourth down on the Auburn 13, Francis basically made the play up in the huddle. He was as calm in that huddle when he described the play as I am sitting right here at this table. He might not have said exactly this, but it was close: He said: "Now y'all hold 'em out." He told Bobby Townsend: "Bobby, you hook up over the inside against the cornerback." He told Bill Herron: "Bill, you block down inside, and run the deep corner route. I'll hit you in the end zone for the touchdown."

And that's what he did. Kinda play-actioned away, rolled back, and hit Bill Herron for the touchdown and the championship. Cool as that. Athens went slightly crazy. We hadn't won the Southeastern Conference championship since 1948. Hadn't beaten Auburn since 1952. And 1959 was the first time Georgia had played Auburn in

Sanford Stadium, the game having been moved from Columbus.

I remember just as clear, blocking G. W. Clapp on that last play. I remember being up against him all afternoon. I was standing right beside him when Francis threw the pass. I told him, "We gotch-yore ass now." There wasn't time left for them to score. We kicked the extra point to win, 14-13. I just took myself out of the game. I didn't cover the last kickoff.

Our last game of 1959, we led Georgia Tech at the half, 21 to nothing. It meant we had clinched the SEC championship, would go to the Orange Bowl. Coach Butts got so emotional at the half—he was so wound up—he'd taken that abuse for eight years of losing to Tech, for 11 years of not winning the SEC...he couldn't function. We almost got in trouble in the second half but won, 21-14. We did go to the Orange Bowl, of course, and Francis threw two touchdown passes, and we beat Missouri, 14-0.

It's true Coach Butts had taken plenty of abuse and maybe I'm wrong, but I don't think there was as much animosity in that era between Georgia and Auburn, or Georgia and Alabama, or even Auburn and Alabama. In fact, there wasn't. I have to laugh, of course; Georgia fought every game, had a fist-fight with somebody. But it wasn't personal, especially so much with the fans, I think. Years later, when I was the coach at East Carolina, I became friends with Cleve Wester, who was a great player for Auburn in my time. I met him through Frank Orgle who grew up with Cleve in Albany, Georgia. Cleve came up to East Carolina, and we talked football, and we visited, and hunted and fished. We just got closer and closer after that and are still close. Cleve helped get me to Auburn, but we'll come to that later.

I had one more game against Auburn in 1960. It was the first time Georgia played in Cliff Hare Stadium (now Jordan-Hare Stadium). Coach Paul Davis, who came out of retirement to coach the special teams for us at Auburn in 1988 and 1989 and did a helluva job, he coached us on defense at Georgia in 1960. He put in the 5-3 for the Auburn game. The line took down the blockers, and my job was to make the tackle. It was one of the best games I ever played. I don't know how many times I ran head-on into Ed Dyas. He was a great football player. And has made a name for himself in medicine in Mobile. He kicked three field goals to our Durwood Pennington's two and beat us, nine to six. It was a helluva game.

Then we had the last win over Georgia Tech, 7-6. I respected the great coaches I played against at Georgia: Bobby Dodd, Ralph Jordan, Paul Bryant. They were legends. I was lucky to play against such men, all in the Hall of Fame. I was lucky to play for Coach Butts and Coach Whitworth and my high school coaches. All of them made me want to be a coach myself.

Looking back through the years, two things stand out in my mind about Coach Butts. Three things. All of them favor me and not him. Which tells you something about the man. More about him than many of us who played for him realized at the time. Years after I was gone, he was quoted in the paper saying I was the best defensive lineman who ever played for him. And when Coach Bryant called him and asked if I could coach for him, Coach Butts told him, "I don't know if he can coach for you, but he could have damn sure played for you." He couldn't have paid me a bigger compliment, and Coach Bryant knew it. The other thing I remember about Coach Butts was a day I walked in my office at Alabama. It was a Monday. I guess it was December 19, 1973. I had already accepted the job at East Carolina as head coach. In the mailbox was a letter from Coach Butts, congratulating me on getting the job. I was walking back to my desk. Mal Moore stopped me and asked, "Did you hear Coach Butts died this weekend?" I stopped, and I couldn't speak.

I was holding a letter from him—and he was thinking about one of his old boys getting an opportunity, and he was glad for him—and he mailed it before he died.

Regardless of how tough he was, or what you thought when you played for him, Coach Butts cared about you. He wanted to be known as a mean, tough, hard-nosed sonofagun, and that's what he wanted you to be on the field. But he had a heart as big as all out-of-doors, and he cared about his people.

I loved it all: Sanford Stadium. The crowds. Playing between the hedges was everything that college football ought to be. We would come down the steps by the railroad tracks. We would carry our helmets and our shoulder pads and put 'em on in the little shack of a dressing room behind the end zone. And when I played, they had an arch in the hedge, and we ran under it onto the field. I loved everything about it. And when I came to Georgia and played the game, I did everything in my body and soul to help Georgia win. I never dreamed I would ever coach at Alabama. Or Auburn. I thought I would always be a Bulldog. But time passes and life changes. I'll never forget those days or my teammates.

I would be less than truthful if I didn't tell you I didn't always feel that way. A few years later, when I was playing pro ball in Canada, I still needed two quarters to get my degree from Georgia. I went to see Coach Butts. He wasn't the coach anymore, but he was the athletic director. I told him I needed some help my last two quarters. I was married. I didn't have any money. Coach Butts said he could help me one quarter. But he couldn't help me two. I didn't ask him if he just didn't have the money. I turned around and left. I'd been supporting myself since I was 12 or 14 anyhow. I went to the bank and borrowed the money. It taught me a great lesson. It was worth more than the $500 or $1,000 I had to borrow. It taught me a lesson about who I could count on...myself.

I didn't blame Coach Butts so much as my Athens relatives. Everybody had been so full of enthusiasm for me to go to Georgia. It's where my blood was. But when I needed the money to finish, everybody had disappeared. All I had done was everything I humanly could to help Georgia win. Helped beat Georgia Tech four times, blocked an extra point and a field goal in a 7-6 game. Helped win the first SEC championship since 1948. Tried my best—Francis and I—to help Georgia recruit Billy Lotheridge and Billy Martin of Gainesville, but it didn't work out; they went to Tech. I was bitter. I was bitter for seven or eight years. And then one day, I got up and said, this is crazy, being bitter all the time. You aren't hurting anybody but yourself. I was never bitter again.

I loved Georgia. I gave everything I had. I loved my teammates. I still love them: fixed in my heart in that place and that time.

CANADA AND MARRIAGE

Of course, when I left for the University of Georgia in 1956, Sue Ward stayed at Richmond Academy for her senior year. We kept dating. She'd come up for ball games. That sort of thing. Then she came to Georgia my sophomore year. All the time we had our fusses and our fights; we'd break up and go back together. I can't remember a lot about my sophomore year; I was having such a frustrating time on the football field.

Sue's father, Amos Ward, died her sophomore year. He got sick that spring. A brain tumor. They operated. But they couldn't do anything. He just lay there for four months and finally died. Sue dropped out of school when he got sick. She went to work for Weathers Transfer Company. Patricia Weathers was her best friend. And Patricia's father was a second daddy to Sue.

Sue and I had broken up at Christmas time my junior year. We were practicing, getting ready to play Missouri in the Orange Bowl. A friend of mine, Mike Castronis, was coaching the girls basketball team at Athens High School. I went over to watch his team play, and he introduced me to a little ole blonde-headed girl, diving all over the court, Edwina Chastain. She was his baby sitter. We went together for the rest of the year. Her family couldn't have been nicer to me. You know I still love her and her family, just like I did when we were dating.

But there was something else with Sue and me. It was different. That something between men and women that nobody can explain.

When I finished football my senior year, seven of us moved out of the dorm into a house on Lumpkin Street. I can't remember the address, but I could take you straight to it. I lost my goals. I could have lost everything I had worked for up until that time in my life. It was a learning experience for me, and the memory of it helps me now in dealing with young people. I had accomplished all of my goals except graduating. I helped Georgia win. I made All-America. We beat Georgia Tech four years in a row. But I had missed a lot of college life, as far as parties, and dating, and drinking. The party scene had just never been a big thing with me. And all of a sudden, there was no football, and I had done everything I came to do; there was just school and all that time on my hands. I signed a pro contract to go to the Canadian League. I made $600 playing in the Senior Bowl. I was making $28 a month in Advanced ROTC. I had a brand new car I'd bought and was paying for myself. I was full of life and energy.

I'd fish on weekends. Date though the week. Sue and I weren't going together. I was living what you might consider a great life. But I could have destroyed everything I had been working for. I didn't have my priorities in the right place. It was a situation where I stayed in trouble. I'd broken up with Edwina, too. To be honest with you, I probably wasn't good enough for either one of them at that particular time in my life. They weren't gonna put up with my being sorry.

I got into a couple of fights. I believe one was at a Pizza Hut one night. Another time a guy ran me off the road. I got into a fight one night at a dance during the Masters Golf Tournament in Augusta. Just ridiculous things. I look back on it now as stupidity.

I had a date with a girl one afternoon in Athens, and I went by to pick her up. She came to the door, and she was wringing wet. A bunch of fraternity guys had had a water fight. They'd gone in the house, pulled her out in the yard, and wet her down. So four or five of us went on to have our little social party, and the longer the party went on, the more often we said, "Let's have some fun." So we went to the fraternity house—I think the Phi Delta Theta house; there were three of them in a row. We took the fire hose, and we wet down everybody in the house, including the house mother. We weren't bad. We were just having a good time. But it could have been bad.

So Dean Tate came over to Lumpkin Street. Looking for the seven of us: Bobby Walden; Jimmy Vickers, he was actually a graduate assistant; Sonny Lowry, Dr. Lowry now—he's a vet and still a friend of mine who got me the job at East Carolina; Lee Cummings; myself. Tommy Ash, I guess was one of us. And one more. I forget who. Anyway, Dean Tate said that Walden and Cummings and Vickers and myself had to come by his office the next morning before we went to class.

Dean Tate had this high-pitched voice. He said, "You fellows know there must be 60 or 70 boys living in those three fraternity houses. If just one of 'em had had the guts to stand up to you, you'd have had a pretty tough time with that many." He said, "What do you think of that, Mr. Walden?"

Walden said, "I guess you're right, Dean Tate."

Dean Tate said, "What do you say, Mr. Vickers?"

"It would have been pretty rough," said Vickers.

"And how about you, Mr. Cummings?"

Lee said, "Well, Dean Tate, the way I figure it, if we coulda got back-to-back, it woulda been a helluva fight."

That's how we all moved back into a boy's dormitory: Dean Tate moved us back. It was in the spring of the year, so we lived there another month or six weeks. I don't know what I failed and what I passed. I wasn't setting the world on fire; I know that. I was having a helluva time. Or I thought I was.

When the spring quarter was over, I went up to Buffalo, New York, and played in the College All-America Game. I played for the East. We got beat by the West. Our coach was Rip Engle of Penn State. We played in old War Memorial Stadium, where they shot the movie, *The Natural*. UCLA receiver Marv Luster had a great game catching passes from Billy Kilmer. Tarkenton was one of our quarterbacks. He didn't have much time to throw. I played offensive guard. I only had to block Bob Lilly—if you don't think he didn't snatch me around. I became friends with Billy Shaw, the great lineman from Georgia Tech. And I caught up again with my buddy, Charlie Flowers, of Ole Miss, who I'd had so much fun with during the *Look* All-America week in New York.

When the game was over, I flew on up to Edmonton in Canada. Edmonton is in Alberta, about 500 miles *north* of Montana. I think my old teammate Bobby Walden drove my car up there. Bobby stayed in Edmonton three seasons and wound up punting for Pittsburgh on those great Super Bowl teams. Jimmy Vickers also joined us in Edmonton. Of course, my brother Nat was already on the Eskimo team. And Dan Edwards, who had been an All-America end at Georgia with Charley Trippi, in the 1940s, was an assistant coach at Edmonton. Maybe that explained some of the team's Georgia connection.

My salary was $9,000. I got a bonus to sign. Maybe $1,000. Or $2,000. I remember when I was leaving the hotel in Mobile after the Senior Bowl, Al Davis of the Oakland Raiders stopped me. He said, "Pat, I know you are going to the Canadian League. But if you don't make it, or if something happens up there, I'd like to have you play in my organization." You wonder what might have happened if I had taken him up on it.

I got to Edmonton about three in the morning, but I didn't realize it. It was broad daylight. I found a hotel room. I called my brother but couldn't get an answer. I remembered a guy named Ted Tullis whom my brother had often talked about. So I looked up his number and called him.

Ted said, "What the hell are you doing calling this time of morning?"

It was 5 a.m. I hadn't looked at my watch. I was going by the sun; that's how country I was.

Edmonton was an oil town and an agricultural town. It was, I think, a young town. Friends who have seen it in recent years tell me it is now a beautiful city. I liked the people. The football team, the Eskimos, were like the Green Bay Packers in the National Football League. The team was owned by the people in the town. So they supported it. The games were a big deal. And the team had had success. It had won the Grey Cup. Our stadium seated about 35,000 or 40,000. We would draw good crowds.

We could only have twelve American players. The other eighteen players were Canadians. They were not resentful of the American players, most of whom made more money than they did. I think they realized they needed us on the team to win. The Canadian boys would work during the day, maybe in the oil industry. And we would practice at night after they got off work. They made $5,000 or $6,000 playing football. I believe I said my salary was $9,000. And that wasn't bad for those times. Nothing like the millions that star players make today. This was 30 years ago.

To be truthful, the competition to make the Edmonton team wasn't that savage. Our coach was Eagle Keyes. I'm not sure where he played his college ball, but he was from Tennessee; I remember that. He was not the kind of guy to bring in a whole bunch of players; he just brought in athletes who he thought could play. He had a good football team. They had played in the championship Grey Cup the year before, in 1960.

Was the Canadian style of football a big change for me? Not really. Of course, it's a wider, longer field, and you have only three downs to make a first down. It was sideline-to-sideline football. I was small. I could run. It fit whatever strengths I had as a player, the fact I was a full-speed, full-contact player. I always thought I could have played in the old American Football League. I played outside linebacker, as I said, behind my brother Nat at defensive end.

We won big until our quarterback got hurt. Our quarterback was Jackie Parker. An unbelievable football player. An all-time great in Canadian football. He played his last two years of college ball at Mississippi State. It was a tremendous experience being on his team. He could do it all. He could run. He could throw it. He didn't throw it pretty, but he could get it there. And he could play defense. If he had to, he could go play wide receiver with anybody. He broke his collarbone and that killed us as a team. Jackie was in the late stages of his career when I got there. I don't know if he would have been a great NFL quarterback. But he could have been an all-time NFL receiver or defensive back.

Jackie was a great, great competitor. It didn't make any difference what you were playing. He would beat you at football, or playing golf, or shooting pool; he'd beat you playing bridge or playing poker. He was a good guy. He was a helluva guy. He was like Bobby Layne. He was a hard-liver, abused his body. He probably has the body now of a 100-year-old man. Canadians have a different life style. You live up there in the winter time, and there isn't a lot to do indoors that's good for you. Jackie still lives in Edmonton. He's a God up there. After he quit playing, he coached them to a Grey Cup.

I also played against some great ones in Canada. I remember Cookie Gilchrist,. 260 pounds. All man. He played running back, and he played tackle on defense. When he ran the ball, it was like tackling a damn van. When you hit him, you had to hold on to get some help. I couldn't tackle him by myself. And nobody else could. I played against the quarterback, Joe Kapp. He was a tough guy, never ran out of bounds in his life. He went down to Minnesota and took them to the Super Bowl.

When I got to Canada, Walden and Vickers and I got us an apartment. I was still kinda wild and sewing oats. I got up there and made the football team. We practiced at 5:30 in the afternoon so the Canadian boys could hold down jobs. I was playing around all night and sleeping all day.

I didn't like myself, the way I was living. I didn't like where I was headed. My life wasn't a 24-hour commitment, the way I live today. That's the thing I tell these chillun now: get your priorities right, your life right, you don't need alcohol, you don't need drugs, you just wake up every morning excited about that day.

Sue was working in Augusta. I called her and said, "Look. Why don't you come on up here?" She said, "Well, what should I bring?" I said, "Just bring everything you've got." I said, "We're gonna get married when you get here."

Sue said she would talk with her mother. She was living with her mother and grandmother. Sue knew what she wanted. I knew what I wanted. She came on up.

We've been married 29 years. Sue has a strong, strong will; she's a strong person. I'm hard-headed, too. We've had wonderful times; we've had our tough times. We've worked at it. I think probably since we've been at Auburn, both of us have had to work at being married a lot harder than before. Maybe that's pretty typical. I know a lot of people get divorced when they get to be 45 or 50. As I said, most good things take a lot of work. I have a high-profile job. Somebody did a survey; I think 79 percent of the people in Alabama know my face.

I'd say by far the happiest days of our marriage were in Greenville, North Carolina. At East Carolina. The children were growing up. We were young. I was head coach. Working hard. Any success we had was unexpected and appreciated. We didn't have nothin' for money. Anything we got was a bonus. We had a lot of good friends. Good church we were going to. Sue was playing golf, was active. I fished and hunted when I wanted to. It was a great neighborhood, a great place to raise a family. We were just very, very happy.

I quit, and we went to Wyoming. For one year. That was also a great experience. But when you pull chillun up and move 'em, and they're in junior high school and high school, I mean, they have roots and friendships in that stage of their lives. I grew up in a town of Army children, who had to move a lot; that's a tough, tough way to grow up, and I'll always respect them because of it. Anyway, when we moved Missy to Wyoming, she was in her junior year, and we moved again to Auburn in the middle of her senior year. Brett was in junior high school. Wanda was in grammar school, and it wasn't as tough on her. Pat had finished high school. When we moved to Auburn, we stayed in the athletic dorm for a year and a half, and that was tough on the kids and on Sue. It was great for our football program. Forced us to get close to the players. We were constantly with them. I think it brought about a unity and a family atmosphere that we probably couldn't have gotten any other way.

All the time we were married, Sue never had any help. We have help now because we have a big house and a lot of entertaining to do. But our children have never wanted for their share of attention, and Sue has been there to give it. People don't fully understand the hours that football coaches put in. You start in August, and you don't finish until recruiting is over in February. Then you're into spring training. It's seven days a week. Because you've got to go to some kind of function on weekends: alumni deals, scholarship weekends, coaching clinics, something.

Sue's allowed me to do my job. She never complains, never gripes. Maybe a little more now than she used to. The kids are gone. Brett and Wanda still are home a good bit. But Sue, understandably, gets irritated when I have three or four alumni meetings in one week. She might say, "You don't have to do this now." I say, that's not the way I got here. When my race is run, I want to be running full speed until I stop.

THE ARMY, AND ALABAMA

I played that first year in Canada. Then after Christmas I went back to school at Georgia. I had to borrow money, remember, to do it. I needed 15 hours and my practice teaching. That spring quarter I taught at the Athens Y. I graduated, completing my last college goal, and took my officer's commission from Army ROTC. But I was deferred from service until January 1962 so I could go back to Canada and play a second season. It was a so-so year. We got in the playoffs, but we didn't win the championship.

I reported to Fort Benning in Columbus, Georgia, for my Basic Officers Training. When my training was over, they found out I played football and pulled my orders and kept me at Fort Benning. I think I had as much fun playing football in the service as I did anywhere in my career. We had a bunch of guys who loved the game. There were about 25 of us who had played at four-year colleges. The rest were non-commissioned officers or enlisted men. Maybe they played in high school or on other service teams. Pretty good football players, most of them.

I enjoyed it. I loved it. There were us officers, and there were the enlisted men, but we all played together as a team. My closest friends turned out to be Harold Ericksen and Billy Williamson of Georgia Tech. My old Georgia teammate Bobby Towns played. Bill Rice, Bobby Boylston, and Elliott Moseley from Alabama were on the team and later helped me get a job at their old school.

We played Camp Lejeune, Quantico, Fort Campbell, Fort

Bragg, Fort Eustis, Fort Sill, and Pensacola Naval Air Station. But the best football team we played, the team with the most athletes, was Jackson State of Mississippi, a team that sent 12 players to the NFL.

Well, we won all of our games and the military service championship. I played offensive guard and linebacker. It was on defense that I won the Timmy Award that goes to the best player in the military service. I guess I was lucky, to intercept some passes and block some field goals and punts. I even scored a few touchdowns. Just doing things to help us win. I have to say again I had fun playing the game.

The Washington Touchdown Club presented the Timmy Award at its season-ending, black-tie party. Ara Parseghian of Notre Dame was the Coach of the Year. And Coach Paul Bryant was there to accept the 1964 National Championship trophy for Alabama. I guess his being there helped change my life and my career.

Of course, I had played against his teams three years. And in 1963, his old players Rice and Moseley and Boylston and I drove over to Athens from Fort Benning to see Alabama play Georgia. I remember I told them: y'all get the refreshments, and I'll get the tickets. So we got up there, and, hell, I couldn't get the tickets from Georgia, my own school. Coach Bryant ended up giving us the tickets to the ball game.

Well, at the Washington, D.C., banquet, I got to speak to Coach Bryant. I never will forget what he said. Alabama had won the National Championship in the regular season, but had lost to Texas in the Orange Bowl.

I told Coach Bryant, "It looked like Joe Namath scored on the quarterback sneak."

He said, "Shit! If you're that close, and you can't make it look convincing, you don't need to win."

Of course, at that time, I didn't have any idea I would ever be working for Coach Bryant. But I had on my dress blues and wore a crew-cut. I think I made a decent impression on him.

I was already an Alabama fan because of the way they played. They played the way I liked to play...all out. They were the best prepared teams we faced at Georgia.

When I was getting out of the Army in 1965, Bebes Stallings was leaving the Alabama staff to become head coach at Texas A&M. I wrote Coach Bryant a letter and told him I had a job playing

The first time I met Coach Bryant was at the Washington Touchdown Club. Also in the picture are Roger Staubach, Lenny Moore, and Ara Parseghian.

football and planned to go back to Canada, but if I had the opportunity to go to Tuscaloosa and work for him, I would give up playing.

I know that Rice and Boylston and Moseley all told Coach Bryant that I would fit in at Alabama. I'm not sure if they spoke to him or wrote him. And I don't know who else Coach Bryant talked to except Coach Butts.

I got a letter back from Coach Bryant in just a few days. He said he didn't know what kind of coach he was going to hire. He hadn't decided. But if he decided to hire a young, inexperienced coach, he would give me consideration.

Well, I didn't hear from him until I got out of the service the first of June 1965. I was home getting ready to go back to Canada. And Coach Bryant called. On a Friday. He said, "If you're still interested in this job, I can talk to you Sunday morning or Monday morning."

Sue and the two kids were at home in Blythe. I said it would really suit me better if I could come over Monday. If I didn't get the job with him, my family would wait in Atlanta to see if I made the team in Canada. We went to Atlanta, and I went over to Tuscaloosa

Monday morning.

I had heard how early Coach Bryant went to work. I got up at 2 a.m. so I could get to Tuscaloosa before six. When I got there it was still dark. So I rode around for two hours, waiting for him to get to the office.

I was visiting with assistant coaches Richard Williamson and Jimmy Sharpe and Dude Hennessey when Coach Bryant stuck his head in the door and said, "Let me open my mail. Y'all go down to the Supe Store and have a cup of coffee. I'll see you when you get back."

Getting out of the service, I didn't have many civilian clothes. I'd gone to Bremen, Georgia, to Mr. Roy Sewell's (our Auburn athletic dorm is named after him), and I bought two or three suits. When I got up in Atlanta, I was half asleep, and I put on one of the suits that still had tags all over it.

We were walking back from the Supe Store, and Richard Williamson went to laughing and asked me, "Boy, how long have you had that suit?"

I said, "Well, it's the first time I ever had it on."

He said, "I figured it was. Cause you got them tags all over it."

We got back to the athletic offices, and Richard cut the tags off.

I went in to visit Coach Bryant. I said, "Coach, I don't know anything about coaching. I never coached in my life. All I know is what I've learned playing. The only thing I can tell you is I know how to work. And I feel like I can communicate with anybody."

Coach Bryant said, "If we hire you, we can't pay you much."

I said I had a wife and two kids; I had to be able to feed them.

He said, "Well, if we couldn't feed you, we wouldn't try to hire you."

He asked *no* football questions. Not *one*. Coach Bryant was an intimidating man. But to be honest, he didn't frighten me. I mean, I was excited. But I wasn't scared. Could he tell that? I don't know. Probably, knowing him and how he could read people. He knew what I was. He knew I was a highly-motivated player, and that I was willing to give up playing to coach. And I was willing to come to Alabama for $500 a month. That's what he offered me.

You take out social security, and federal and state income taxes, and teacher's retirement, and Blue Cross/Blue Shield, and my pay was down to about $350 a month. The only way I survived early on...my brother and I had bought three houses in Athens, and we sold them and made a little money. I forget how much. I had enough to make a down payment on a house. The house cost $15,000. Payments were $106 a month. It was in Southwood. I went by there the last time I was in Tuscaloosa. It's still there. We added on to it three times in the eight years we lived in it.

Also, I stayed in the National Guard. And every time we had about stretched our finances to the limit—Sue says she wouldn't buy a tube of lipstick; I know the chillun got tired of biscuits and gravy; there wasn't a lot of meat—every time we were about broke, we would get a National Guard check. It paid $1,600 a year, $400 a quarter, for drills. I was a first lieutenant, actually ended up making captain. And Coach Bryant gave me a little raise every year. I stayed eight-and-a-half years. I went from $6,000 to about $21,000.

It was in the National Guard I met my closest friend in Tuscaloosa, Rufus Deal. Of course, he was the great old Auburn halfback. He was a full-time warrant officer in the Guard. He still has some records at Auburn; he once punted the football 87 yards against Georgia Tech. I can tell you he was the toughest individual I ever met in my life.

He and Catherine kind of took our whole family under their wing. Their own children were grown or nearly grown. We became good friends. Rufus Deal was also a great high school football official. He should have been a Southeastern Conference official. He was an Auburn man, but he had a good relationship with Coach Bryant. His brother, Dwight, played for Alabama. Rufus officiated most of our scrimmages. He was good as I have ever seen on the field as a referee. You talk about a guy who could control a game. Rufus was also a real outdoorsman. He had a cabin on the banks of the Tombigbee River. We spent many a good day and night there. He was like a combination brother and daddy to me. And he treated our chillun just like his own. And he's still as strong as a bull today.

Coach Bryant, when he hired me, said, "I'm gonna let you WATCH the linebackers." He didn't say COACH.

By the time I got to Tuscaloosa in the summer of 1965, they'd already had spring training. I was trying to feel my way around. Nobody told me a damn thing about what I was supposed to do. I looked at film in my little old inside office. In my nine seasons at Alabama, I never had an office with a window. I tried to study the play book...that is, study what the linebackers did. Because our defensive coordinator, Ken Donahue, who had once tried to recruit me to Tennessee, wouldn't let me see the entire defensive scheme. He didn't trust me. He was afraid I might leave and go to Georgia or Tennessee or somewhere and take his defense with me. So I had to learn what the linebackers were supposed to do and try to figure out for myself what the rest of the defense was doing. I looked at the faces of the players in the programs and the press guides to learn their names.

We had some talented linebackers. Paul Crane and Tim Bates started; Jackie Sherrill started when Crane went to offense full time. Jackie was a good player, good on pass defense. Very smart. Shrewd. That's the right word to describe him, shrewd. He wasn't going to make a mistake. And Bates was one of the smartest players in the Southeastern Conference. As the season went on, did the two of them come to trust my judgment? I doubt it. Well, I got on the same page with Tim Bates. Jackie probably thought he knew more than I did all year long. And he probably did. It doesn't surprise me that Jackie turned out to be a winning coach. We talk occasionally. Football talk. Mostly swapping film, discussing a coach. We aren't close. I sure remember playing against his Texas A&M team in the 1986 Cotton Bowl. They beat the hell out of us. I remember their scoring with no time left on the clock. I haven't forgotten that.

I didn't see much of Coach Bryant that summer. He was coming and going. He was already a legend. He'd gone undefeated in the regular 1964 season and won his second National Championship.

But were we a talented football team at Alabama in 1965? Hell, no! I didn't know much. But I quickly learned enough to know that.

I was flying by the seat of my pants. You can imagine going into staff meetings, never having coached a day and not knowing our own defensive schemes. We had a knowledgeable staff: Donahue, coaching the defense; Kenny Meyer, coaching the offense. Howard Schnellenberger, coaching the offensive line. Howard lived right across the street from me, and we rode to work together every day. There were Sam Bailey and Carney Laslie, who are now both dead. And Clem Gryska, Dude Hennessey, Ralph Genito. And my buddies Jimmy Sharpe and Richard Williamson and Bill Oliver, who were my age. I would come to realize it was a heckuva staff.

Hell, I was lost. Totally. But I was pushing full speed ahead. I didn't know a damn thing, but I didn't know it.

We started recruiting in August in those days. They gave me

Georgia. The whole state. I didn't know what to do. I didn't know how you were supposed to do it. I went on the road to find the best high school players in Georgia, and I didn't call home for two weeks. I can't remember if I signed somebody that year or not. Probably signed some.

The question comes up, was Coach Bryant a good recruiter? As I said, he was intimidating. And he'd reached such a stature by the time I got there, winning two National Championships—and we were to win another one in 1965, as improbable as it seemed after we lost the first game.

Recruiting at Alabama, everything, was easier because of Coach Bryant's reputation.

To tell you the truth, I did not use him on the road recruiting. Now he went to their homes to sign some players for me after they had been recruited. But I didn't use him to recruit them. Of course, there was a mystique about playing for Coach Bryant. But I could sell him on the road a helluva lot better than he could sell himself. You have to remember, by the time I got to the University of Alabama, Coach Bryant had been a head coach since 1945. And he didn't care a helluva lot about recruiting. The amazing thing is, he was to coach another eighteen years and have his greatest success in the last ten. The two times I used Coach Bryant on the road recruiting, the two kids went somewhere else. Of course, that's probably the reason I used him, I thought we were losing both kids, and we did.

One of the kids was Dennis Chadwick of Atlanta, a quarterback who went to Tennessee. And the other player who really broke me of using Coach Bryant was a linebacker from Columbus, Carl Hubbard.

I had been kind of led to believe that all Coach Bryant had to do was visit and Carl would commit to Alabama. But that was not the case. In fact, I think Carl might have committed to Auburn before we got there. I've been told that Auburn Coach Sam Mitchell was upstairs in the Hubbard house while Coach Bryant was visiting. I don't know; I've never asked Sam. But I do know Carl committed to Auburn the *next day*. I hated losing him. I coached the linebackers, and I thought Carl could be a great player. And maybe he was. Never again did I take Coach Bryant into a home recruiting. Because sometimes he was good and sometimes he was awful. What kind of thing did he say? Oh, we just sat around a table, made small talk. When it came to Coach Bryant, he said, "Boy, if you're good enough, you'll play, and have a chance to be on a great team, win a championship." Something like that.

Now Coach Bryant was at his best as a recruiter sitting behind his desk, an intimidating presence. High school boys would come into his office like they were in God's presence.

We were winning, and we could recruit to Alabama. I got to where I'd tell kids: "*I'm* gonna recruit you. Coach Bryant ain't coming to visit you. If you want to talk to Coach Bryant about coming to Alabama, you'll go to *his* office on *his* time. You tell me right now if I can't recruit you." I'd say, "If you know you want to come to Alabama, and you're ready to sign, then Coach Bryant will come sign you." That's the way I handled it. I guess I cut off at the pass a lot of superficial interest.

I believe, I really believe, the worst thing you can do as a head football coach is get too obligated to a kid when you are recruiting. The time will come when maybe he feels you owe it to him to play him, and you have to play the best football player you've got, no matter who recruited him.

You take Bo Jackson—when we recruited him to Auburn in 1982. I didn't have to promise him anything. Bo looked at our people and knew he could come over and play. We were sitting there playing Mike Edwards and Lionel James at halfbacks. Mike was a 6-5 split end with a lot of heart, and Lionel was a midget. A talented midget. I didn't have to convince Bo he could play.

The Alabama staff didn't give me any instructions on what to look for in a player; they just put me out there. They never said a damn word as to what I should do. I called all my old coaching friends in Georgia. And traveled the whole state. I worked my butt off on some good players who went to other places: Charlie Dudish, the quarterback from Atlanta, who went to Georgia Tech and didn't pan out; Chadwick, the other Atlanta quarterback, who became a part-time starter at Tennessee, and Dennis Scott, who became a fine quarterback at Tennessee.

I finally told Coach Bryant we weren't going to be able to recruit Chadwick *and* Dudish. They were hot commodities and knew it. I said, "I've got to make a choice." He said, "Which one are you gonna recruit?" I said, "I really think over time Chadwick will be the best one." I believe time proved me right about that. And Coach Bryant said, "Well, recruit him." He didn't care one way or the other. He never saw either one of them play. But his staff knew ultimately, and then he knew ultimately, who the top players in our area were.

I've been asked if Coach Bryant knew how good Pat Sullivan was when he played quarterback in high school in Birmingham in the late sixties. Yeah, he knew. And he knew if Auburn also got halfback Johnny Musso of Birmingham, Auburn would probably win the National Championship before they graduated. As it was, Auburn beat us two out of three years. Earlier in Coach Bryant's time at Alabama, when he was hungrier, I doubt if Pat Sullivan AND Terry Beasley would have wound up going to Auburn. But that's speculation.

I know that when we went to the Sugar Bowl in 1973, my last year at Alabama, one of my last jobs was to check the players getting on the team plane, be sure they all made it. I also checked off in my mind the ones I'd recruited. Of the 72 players we took down there, I recruited 27 of 'em, either directly or indirectly. And I also helped recruit the first black player that ever signed with Alabama, but that's another story we'll get to later.

While we are talking about recruiting, I've been asked when I made up my mind if I was going to cheat or not. Well, I wasn't going to cheat. Period. Not at Alabama, or when I went to East Carolina or Wyoming or Auburn. Sure wasn't any decision to be made at East Carolina; we didn't have any money to cheat on. I had a pretty easy situation at Alabama, because I had the whole state of Georgia by myself, and the southeast corner of Alabama. So I had enough territory to find out who I could recruit fair and square. Those were looser times. There were more players who had their hands out. But if a player wanted something illegal, I could just go to the next guy. That's what I did. There were enough players out there for me to recruit that I didn't have to cheat. And that's the way it's always been for me. There were also enough players in the state that I could pick up kids Georgia didn't recruit. That we felt could play. It didn't hurt to have that mystique of playing for Coach Bryant. Of course, I got beat, fair and square, on many kids. But I didn't get outworked.

Back then you could outwork people. There was no limit on the number of times you could visit them. You could recruit all year around. Sometimes I'd have the kid recruited before the opposition got there. Recruiting wasn't a matter of life and death to some of the ones I recruited against, the way it was to me.

I remember when Leroy Cook came out. He was a defensive lineman from Abbeville, Alabama, and Abbeville was an Auburn town. He was a great player. When he was a junior he was the best player in the state. So that year I recruited Ronnie Joe Barnes from Abbeville. He was kind of an average talent, but a good kid and everybody liked him. Ronnie Joe's uncle coached the football team, and I knew Lindy Money kind of raised both Ronnie Joe and Leroy. He was in the pulpwood business, and they worked for him. I had the road paved to recruit Leroy by taking Ronnie Joe. You had more scholarships in those days. You could do that. Leroy turned out to be every bit as good as we thought he was.

Probably the biggest name recruit I ever signed for Alabama was Greg Montgomery. He was a 235-pound running back from Southwest Macon. Greg was a helluva player. He was probably headed to Auburn. That was what his mama and daddy thought. Of course, he ended up coming to Alabama. Greg and I and his family just hit it off. Mr. Montgomery told me an interesting story. I'm not saying Georgia Tech cheated—I want to make that plain—but Mr. Montgomery told me a Georgia Tech alumni called him and asked him what it would take to get Greg to come to Georgia Tech. Mr. Montgomery told him, "Oh, that's simple. That ain't no problem at all." He said, "The only thing it will take to get Greg to Georgia Tech is for him to *want to go* to Georgia Tech." I said to myself, well, if he doesn't want to go to Tech, there's nothing in the world that's going to get him over there.

September came around. And the first game I went into in my life as a football coach was against Georgia, my old school. In Athens. And they beat us with the flea-flicker pass.

Kirby Moore of Dothan, Alabama, passed the ball to Pat Hodgson, who, with both knees on the ground, lateralled it to Bob Taylor of Headland, Alabama, who ran the rest of the 72 yards for a touchdown. Then Moore hit Hodgson for a two-point pass to put Georgia ahead, 18-17, with two minutes to play. People don't remember, but we took the ball after they scored and drove it the length of the field and missed a 42-yard field goal. But you also have to remember we were favored, I guess, by two touchdowns. There was a photograph in *Sports Illustrated* of the flea-flicker play that Georgia Coach Vince Dooley kept on his den wall for years. Vince said he hated to see the Alabama series end, that it was just getting exciting. He wasn't wrong about it being exciting.

I can remember going up to the press box in Athens. I can remember going to the dressing room after the game. I can remember *walking* back to the damn hotel. Because when I got ready to leave in a big, rented Oldsmobile, I couldn't find my keys. I looked and looked. And finally realized I'd been so excited to be at Alabama, to be coaching on a team defending the National Championship...I'd locked the keys in the trunk. So, my first game as a coach: to go over to my old school and get our ass whipped, talk about a sickening feeling. And I had to walk to the hotel through the whole happy campus.

We got whipped, and Coach Bryant stood in the dressing room after the game. He said, "Men. It's kinda obvious that we don't have a very good football team." He said, "But if you are the kinda people I think you are, we'll have a good football team before the year's over." He said, "Get on the bus and let's go back home. And be ready to go to work Monday."

Monday, all hell broke loose. I mean, you talk about young coaches, old coaches, and Coach Bryant working—we started, and we built a football team.

Of course, we went on to win the National Championship. But not without a struggle. I think there were eight or nine guys who started against Georgia who never started another game the whole time they were at Alabama.

On Monday—oh, Lord—it was just an all-out war. Scrimmaging. Pickin' 'em up and makin' 'em go when they were exhausted. We had to know who wanted to play for Alabama. Those kind of scrimmages? We don't have 'em so much at Auburn anymore; but you've got to let 'em know it's there, just every once in a while.

The next week we played Tulane. And killed 'em. Ole Miss was coming up. Our quarterback, Steve Sloan, was struggling. Coach Bryant almost put him on the bench for Ken Stabler. We had a bad practice. Coach Bryant got involved in the kicking game. Nothing was going the way he wanted it to go. He ran everybody off the field, players and coaches. In the dressing room, he talked to the players first. Then he talked to us coaches. He said, "We're going to practice in the morning at 5:30. I'm telling y'all like I told the players. Anybody who doesn't want to make it, just pack your damn bags, and I'll mail your damn check."

Dude Hennessey slept in the coliseum he was so scared he'd go home and not wake up in time.

The next morning I got over to the coliseum early. Our center, Billy Johnson, met me. He was about in tears. He said, "Coach, Wayne Cook ain't coming." Wayne was our starting tight end. I said, "The hell he ain't." I jumped in my car and went over to the dorm. Wayne was laying up there in the bed. I said, "Get up. Let's go." He said, "I'm not going, coach." I said, "You're going. Or I'm gonna whip your ass, or you're gonna whip mine. Right here." Then I said, "Wayne, if you are gonna quit, don't lie up here in the bed and quit like a coward. Go on to practice. Don't let the man intimidate you and make you say it's too tough for you. If you want to quit after practice, walk in his office and quit like a man. This ain't the way to do it." He got up, and we went to practice. And, of course, he never did quit.

The players dressed out. Coach Bryant himself loosened them up. He did all the coaching. The rest of us just stood back out of the way. He took the first offense and put 'em against the second defense on the goal line. Ran six or eight plays. He put the second offense against the first defense and ran six or eight plays. He lined up the punting team and protected and covered punts three or four times. We weren't out there over 15 minutes. But damn, they were wild-eyed, flying-through-the-air, bodies-and-snot-flying minutes.

When it was over, Coach Bryant said, "I ain't got you out here this morning to punish you. I could think of a thousand ways to punish you." He said, "I want you to know something. As long as I am the football coach at Alabama, and I let you get by with less than the best you've got, then I'm doing you an injustice." He said, "Now y'all go on in there and get a shower and go to class. Don't go back to the dorm and lay up in the bed. I'll see you at four o'clock." We came back at four. And we worked.

Against Ole Miss, we went deep into the fourth quarter behind, 16-7. We stopped them once on the goal line. We finally got the ball down close enough to kick a field goal. And we got it back again on our own nine-yard line with seven or eight minutes to go. We took it the length of the field, twice it was fourth down, and we made first down by half the length of the ball. Sloan scored on a keeper. And David Ray kicked the extra point, and we won, 17-16.

We still weren't a good football team. We beat Vanderbilt. Then came Tennessee. It was the game everybody remembers for

Stabler, just a sophomore, throwing the ball out of bounds on fourth down. And we tied, 7-7.

What actually happened, we had the ball down on the goal, and we got thrown for a loss on second down. Coach Bryant sent Stabler in the game and told him to throw it once in the end zone for a touchdown, but if the man was covered to throw it away.

Stabler went back to pass and pulled the ball down and ran. I think the ball had been on the 17. He ran it down to about the 5. He thought he'd made a first down. But it had been first and goal. We lined up, and Ken threw the ball out of bounds. The game was over.

That was when Coach Bryant kicked the door down to the dressing room. It was locked and nobody had the key. He just kicked it in. That will get your attention. How did he handle Stabler's mistake? Coach Bryant just shouldered it. He wouldn't put that on a sophomore player.

We beat FSU. But struggle was our middle name. And we struggled against Mississippi State in Jackson. They had the big fullback, Hoyle Granger, and the halfback, Marcus Rhoden. We beat them, 10-7. Creed Gilmer blocked a field goal with no time left in the game to keep them from tying us.

Finally, we played a complete ball game. Down in Baton Rouge. I remember we were warming up before the kickoff, and LSU's quarterback, Nelson Stokley, fell over backwards. His knee just gave way. They had to carry him off the field. They were ranked pretty high, and we whipped 'em, 31 to 7. For the first time, we were a football team. We beat Auburn, 30-3.

At the end of the season we were ranked No. 5. I believe Michigan State and Nebraska and Arkansas were all undefeated. They all lost in the bowls. We played Nebraska in the Orange Bowl at night. We knew if we beat Nebraska we would be No. 1.

A lot of strategy went into our game. Nebraska was good, but slow. It was before they recruited the great speed. Our plan was throw as much as we could and wear them out on defense from rushing the passer. Coach Bryant had a lot to do with that strategy. We built up a 24 to 7 lead in the first half, with Sloan passing. And we ran it on them real well the second half, with Les Kelley and Steve Bowman carrying the ball. We won, 39-28. We'd come a heck of a long way since losing to Georgia on the flea-flicker. It was the greatest coaching job done at Alabama in the years I was there.

COACH BRYANT

The best football player we had at Alabama in my nine seasons was Kenny Stabler. There's not any doubt about that. And the 1966 team was the only one I've ever been with, as coach or as player, that won every game. Two or three things made that a great team. We had Stabler. We had receivers Ray Perkins and Dennis Homan. We had the same offensive line back from the year before. We lost linebackers Jackie Sherrill and Tim Bates. But we replaced them with sophomores Mike Hall and Bob Childs. Better players.

What made Stabler such a tremendous quarterback? Look at a lot of great ones, and you see the same qualities: he was a tremendous athlete, tough mentally. When the game was on the line, he wanted the ball in his hands. Coach Bryant said he could throw the long ball better than anybody he ever coached. He could throw it long and short. Before he hurt his knees he could run. What kind of guy was he? Free spirited. Was he hard to control? I guess so. I mean, Coach Bryant could never control him. He wasn't as much trouble to handle early as he was after his junior season. Stabler is quoted, from time to time, saying if it hadn't been for Coach Bryant, he would never have amounted to anything. I mean, what else is he gonna say?

Everything hinged around Stabler going into 1966. The question was whether he could handle it or not. He could. We played one easy game, and then we played Ole Miss. We won, 17-7. I remember Stabler completed 16 out of 19 passes. We only had one tight game all season, with Tennessee. Nobody else came close to beating us. We only gave up 37 points the entire season.

Some games you are destined to win. It's what happens when you go undefeated. Tennessee missed a point-blank field goal from *inside the three-yard line* at the end of the game. And we won, 11-10. We'd fallen behind, 10-0. In the rain. We finally got the ball down on the goal and scored and went for two. I never will forget we threw the tight end delay to Wayne Cook for the two. The same end who didn't quit the year before. We took it back down to the one-yard line and kicked a field goal. Biggest play in the game: Les Kelley broke a run of eight yards or so, fumbled, and the ball just went right in Ray Perkins's arms. Some games you are meant to win.

Of course, we beat Nebraska again in the Sugar Bowl, 34-7. Stabler hit Perkins for a 45-yard pass on the first play. It was Stabler and Perkins and Homan and quickness on offense and defense. But don't think Nebraska Coach Bob Devaney wasn't paying attention. The next time we saw Nebraska in the 1972 Orange Bowl, they were bigger than we were, stronger than we were, and just as fast as we were. Then it was Coach Bryant paying attention. And that was the end of the "skinny legged boys" era at Alabama.

They split the National Championship in 1966 between Notre Dame and Michigan State, after Notre Dame played for a 10-10 tie against State. But it didn't take any shine off our 11-0 season.

One thing about Coach Bryant, he had a great feel, or knack, for taking a Stabler, or a Johnny Musso, or an Ozzie Newsome, or, before them, a John David Crow at Texas A&M...and building a team around them...around what I call IT. Building a team around, not just a matter of their talent, their athletic ability, but their heart and guts, and when they had it, character. Now he had some great athletes who didn't have IT. They'd eventually wind up quitting, finding an easier way to go to school, or something. Because Coach Bryant was not gonna let 'em coast through on their ability. I think in his later years, he probably was a lot more patient with those talented individuals than he was in his earlier years.

What Coach Bryant could do, and one of the three secrets to his success above everything else...he could take two or three of those great athletes, Stabler and Perkins and Homan in 1966, who all had IT. And he could surround them with a bunch of ITs that didn't have great talent, but had heart and soul and guts. And he could set a fire in them you couldn't put out. I guess what I'm saying is he had the ability to make a great player perform at his mental and physical and emotional peak, and carry lesser players of the same burning desire up with him. And that's not easy. Because the great athlete is different, and capable of such high intensity. All over America there were great athletes playing average. But not for Bryant.

It's also true when a player proved in practice and in games that he had IT he didn't have to prove it every day. You even have to be careful what you ask a heart and soul player to do. He won't quit. I almost killed Wayne Hall once, now my assistant head coach. I was young. He was a linebacker at Alabama. I nearly worked him to death. I didn't realize a good mule will work until he dies. But a sorry one will lay down in his traces and quit before he will die. Bryant wouldn't make Johnny Musso do the same things he made every other halfback do every day. Because he knew on Saturday, Musso was going to have to carry it 30 times. He wanted to be damn sure his horse was ready to run when he opened the gate.

The second secret to Coach Bryant's success, and maybe his greatest asset: he could get more out of his people than you could get out of yours. He grew up hard in the country in Arkansas, and he was naturally a hungry person. He did not want to go back plowing mules at 50 cents a day. And that's the way he coached. That's the reason hungry kids played for him. And I would rate him way above average in hiring hungry, talented assistant coaches. He was also a great fundamental football coach, teaching blocking and tackling. I mean we worked hard at fundamentals. Coach Bryant could watch practice and see who was getting it done, coaches and players. If he thought things weren't going well, he could be...unpredictable. If you were riding too high, he had a way of getting you down. If you were too low, he had a way of getting you up. One thing he didn't want at all, he didn't want you to be comfortable. He wanted your ass on edge all the time. Am I like that? Well, I don't know. I'm probably not nearly as tough. But a head coach has to have a feel for the whole team. The linebacker coach ain't worried about what the damn running backs are doing. He may want head-on tackling all day until he kills off the running backs. A head coach has to have a feel for the team. One thing was pretty consistent at Alabama, and is consistent with us here now at Auburn. When we were playing somebody we were supposed to beat, we would work the heck out of 'em. We tried to improve when we knew we were going to win, put a bottom underneath them, put guts in them, work on fundamentals, techniques. And if we were playing a big game, Tennessee or Auburn, in all probability we would streamline practice, get 'em on and off the field. We didn't want any tired horses running out there Saturday, and we don't at Auburn.

If you were an assistant, Coach Bryant expected *you* to get the job done at your position. He never came up to me in a drill and said, you're doing it wrong; this is the way I want it done. Never! What he would do, was in a staff meeting, or maybe sitting in the locker room, he would say, "Pat, your linebackers are giving us the worst damn pass coverage I ever saw." I mean, that was all he would say. Now it was up to you to correct it. His theory was if you were going to be an assistant coach at Alabama, you better figure out a way to get the job done.

Another thing Coach Bryant was better at than anybody I ever saw, and something I learned from him: he was unbeatable at copying what somebody else was doing well. In football, if you are doing your job, you learn as much, or more, from your opponents as you do from your own people. My first year at Alabama, I thought Steve Kiner and Hacksaw Reynolds and Jackie Walker at Tennessee were the best linebackers in college football, and I wanted our linebackers to play just as well as they did, and I studied them. Coach Bryant once took the belly series from Bobby Dodd at Georgia Tech and put it in at Kentucky and beat him with it. He got the wishbone from his buddy, Darrell Royal at Texas. He wouldn't hesitate to take a play or an idea from a high school coach. I don't know where he got the tackle eligible pass we used for so many big plays in the sixties until they outlawed it; maybe he invented it. I'll tell you what he did. I sent him a play that we ran at East Carolina all the time; I called it my "TV play." It was a fake reverse, fullback flea-flicker to the quarterback off the wishbone. We ran it off an unbalanced line, and made some big plays off of it, and scored some touchdowns. I don't think Coach Bryant ever ran that play until I came to Auburn, and he ran it against us.

I don't know where Coach Bryant got his emphasis on quickness and pursuit that he brought to defense at Alabama. Maybe he developed it on his own over a period of years. But that's the way we practiced. We had a good chemistry of old and young coaches. I was full of damn excitement. I was just like a player. Heck, I could have

Coach Bryant had a way of holding your attention.

still been playing at the time. Everybody got to the football. Everybody on the field got there. I was coaching linebackers, and I'd get to the ball, too. When we came off the field there were very few players who had worked any harder or run any harder than I had. That was the way we practiced, and the way we lived.

Coach Bryant was just plain, old, country smart. He had a way of sitting down and talking to you, and when he got through, he'd know everything you knew, and he hadn't told you a damn thing he knew. He stayed close to his old rival at Tennessee, General Bob Neyland, and to Bobby Dodd at Georgia Tech, and to Bob Devaney at Nebraska, and to Bo Schembechler at Michigan—he had great respect for Bo, and for Woody Hayes at Ohio State—and to plenty of others I don't even know about. There were a lot of his former players and coaches that he communicated with all the time. There wasn't much going on in American football Coach Bryant didn't know about.

I guess in his 38 years as a head coach there wasn't any kind of system, offensive or defensive, he hadn't run or played against. With so many close friends among the coaches, if anybody was doing anything in football better than he was doing it, he made it a point to find out how they did it. His relationships with people allowed him to do that.

Talking about systems, I think Coach Bryant would have told you that he was a better football coach playing one-platoon football than he was playing two-platoon football, even though he probably won more games coaching two-platoon. In one-platoon football, most of your starters were your better defensive players. And the game went more toward speed and quickness instead of size; you had to survive; and he could teach conditioning and survival better than anybody. I remember at Georgia playing 55 minutes in games and covering kickoffs and punts, too. If you asked a kid today to play 55 minutes, he would think you were crazy.

And the third secret of Coach Bryant's success: he knew a winner when he saw one. He didn't get down on his hands and knees and coach any more, as he did as a young man. But don't think he didn't know personnel. He made out the team depth charts *every day*. He insisted on making every substitution in every game. That's how he came to threaten to fire me twice. Well, I don't guess he really would have. But after we had games won with LSU and Duke, about 1972, I sent in a kid who hadn't gotten a chance to play. Once it was David McMakin; it might have been David both times. Coach Bryant just turned around and asked, "Who made the substitution?" I told him it was me. He said, "You've been around here long enough to know nobody makes substitutions but me. I'll fire your ass!" And I said, "Yes, sir." I'm sure that's all I said. No question who was running the show. It was unusual his making all the substitutions. Today, at Auburn, we decide the playing rotations before the game, but I still approve them.

Nothing has changed about what makes a winner. And maybe I'm not very smart, and maybe I'm not much of a coach, but I also know a winner when I see one. I learned, I suppose, from all the kids I ever played with and against, and from all the coaches I ever played for, and coached for, including Coach Bryant. A winner is a kid who works his butt off. And is dependable. He's not always the most talented. But one who is going to give everything he has on every play. Coach Bryant knew a winner because that's the way he practiced every day, and that's the way he lived every day. And he knew how important the game was to a winner. His Alabama players had a confidence, an arrogance about them; they weren't afraid to win. And at Auburn, I still look for all those qualities. I don't necessarily remember just when I was first able to recognize them. But I do, and I know when a football team is playing together and playing hard, and we are getting the most out of our talent. A head football coach has got to have the ability to get them to play together. Hell, you can't win without it.

I had a special kind of relationship with Coach Bryant. We were both born and raised in the country. We both picked cotton, chopped cotton, I peddled watermelons and he peddled vegetables. We had things in common, but I was a baby, and he was a grown man. I was born in 1939, and he was playing football at Alabama in 1934. I could talk to him about things a lot of folks couldn't even understand. And I didn't play for him. I think not having played for him, I studied him closer. I didn't take for granted things about him that his old players knew so well. I studied him closer, paid more attention to details of how he handled players, coaches, discipline, practice organization, game organization. I wasn't so concerned with how he handled the x's and o's. Of course, he was a great fundamental coach. But even today, when I am facing a crisis, I think, I wonder how the Old Man would have handled it. I roll that over in my mind. I don't say, well, if he would have done this, then I'm gonna do this, too. Because he wasn't always right. He did it his way, and I do it my way. But I learned an awful lot from him. When you have a teacher like him, you try to capture the quality and the good things and let the bad go by. Ain't nobody perfect. I had an undergraduate degree from Georgia, but I got a masters degree in football from Coach Bryant.

LOSSES AND LESSONS

W hat happened to the Alabama team in 1967? Several things. And they resemble some of the problems we had during the 1990 season at Auburn. Both Alabama in '67 and Auburn in '90 were picked to be outstanding teams, but never measured up. At Alabama, we'd won the National Championship in 1964 and '65 and gone undefeated in '66. At Auburn, we'd won the Southeastern Conference championship three straight years, or shared it, and beaten Alabama four straight years.

You get to thinking you are invincible. And at Alabama, maybe we thought we were just automatically going to go out there and recruit the top players, who were supposed to come because we were winning. It's just human nature that you lose that urgency in recruitment, and the kids can sense it. Somebody's telling them, "We got to have you." And you walk in there and say, "Here's a scholarship. If you want it, fine. If you don't, we're gonna line up and beat you anyway." And you can find yourself playing inferior people, which won't win for you.

There's a lot of truth to something Coach Bryant once said, after our teams slipped in the late sixties: if you take an axe and hit one lick on a big tree every day, for a long time it will be fine, and look fine, but there'll come a day when it will fall. That's what happened to us, gradually, at Alabama. We, as a coaching staff, didn't get the job done. We might have had one or two coaches working their butts off, but as a staff we weren't working like we should have been in all the areas of recruiting. Well, that was Coach

Bryant's fault. He was still in full control, no doubt about that. And you can say he had long ago earned the right to enjoy himself some, and travel around the country, and play in some celebrity golf tournaments. And to be honest, in the nine seasons I was there, Coach Bryant never stuck his head in the door once to see how an off-season program was going. I mean, he knew who was watching it. But I don't care what you say, when the Big Man ain't around, it ain't the same. It ain't the same for the players. And it ain't the same for the coaches.

That first game in 1967, we gave up as many points against Florida State as we had the entire year before. It was a 37-37 tie. Joe Kelly started the game at quarterback. Stabler had been suspended. But Coach Bryant "unsuspended" him when we got behind, 14-0, in the first two minutes.

We had graduated Perkins and most of the offensive line. We were a one-dimensional football team; we couldn't run the ball. We also struggled in the defensive line. We lost to Tennessee, and barely beat Auburn, 7-3, in the rain, on the run by Stabler when Auburn linebacker Gusty Yearout said he was tackled, and probably he was. We lost in the Cotton Bowl to Gene Stallings's Texas A&M team. We still couldn't run the ball. It was a team that never measured up to pre-season expectations.

About this time, Coach Bryant was going through some decision making of his own. He could have resigned then, or retired then. The one thing he wasn't going to put up with in his later years was a lot of losing. He wasn't going to do it. And along about then, Joe Robbie offered him the job as coach of the Miami Dolphins, and maybe he accepted it, probably he did. But, ultimately, he turned it down to stay at Alabama. We had an 8-2 season in 1968 and lost again to Tennessee and to Colorado in the Gator Bowl.

No question but that 1969 and 1970 were low water marks. We only won six games and lost to Auburn both years. I got to see first hand what kind of competitor Pat Sullivan was. He kept Auburn up there as a national power. He beat us both years, passing to Terry Beasley. When I took the Auburn job, I tried to hire Pat right off. But he was in business. He did a terrific job coaching our quarterbacks from 1986 to 1991, and I can't say I am surprised.

Coach Bryant dominated the Auburn series, but you have to remember Coach Jordan beat him five times, more times than any other head coach except General Neyland at Tennessee. I didn't realize, but I am not surprised to learn, that Coach Jordan actually had a better winning percentage at Auburn during the 15 years after Coach Bryant came to Alabama than he had in the 10 years before Coach Bryant. Coach Jordan did a heckuva job keeping the Auburn program competitive on a national level.

The lowest point of those years for Alabama had to be our loss in 1969 to Vanderbilt, 14-10. Watson Brown was the Vanderbilt quarterback and later coached for me at East Carolina. We left Johnny Musso at home to get well so we could have him to beat Tennessee. And we lost to Vanderbilt, so we wound up the season 6-4 instead of 7-3. Hell, no, we didn't beat Tennessee. They killed us, 41-14. We couldn't have beaten 'em with Herschel Walker or Bo Jackson. They were just better at all positions than we were.

How did the Alabama fans take those disappointing seasons, after three National Championships? As typical fans. It would be the same with Auburn fans now if we went 6-5 two years in a row. They'd say, well, Coach Dye is sick, and he can't get it done any more. And the program is gone, and we got to get rid of him and get somebody else. You know what they'd say. And really and truly, they would have every right to say it. It's the head coach's job to get it done.

It was during those years that Coach Bryant began his string of eight non-winning bowl games. He lost to A&M, Missouri, Colorado, Nebraska, Texas, and Notre Dame, twice, and tied Oklahoma. Overall, Coach Bryant had a winning bowl record. But in his personality, he was like Bo Schembechler of Michigan, who had a poor bowl record. It was their nature to get so much out of their football teams during the regular season, and especially in preparation for the last big game that sometimes it was hard to get the team up for the bowl game.

Now there are people who don't want to hear what I am about to say, but it's the truth: there are no miracles in coaching. My last three years at Alabama, we only lost one regular season football game: to Auburn on the two blocked punts. I'll talk about them in a minute. But we lost each of our last three bowl games. Everything is relative in football, just as it is in business or life. Step out there with somebody who is as good as you are, and you are only gonna win 50 percent of the time. We were playing teams in the early seventies in our own league that were not as good as we were. Then we got into bowl games with teams as good or better than we were. We weren't nearly as good as Nebraska in 1971. The Notre Dame games could have gone either way. Coach Bryant was the master. At coaching. At scheduling. But when you put Alabama in the arena with people that were as good as they were, he was about .500, no better, no worse. Put Pat Dye's team in there with an equal team, and he is about 50-50. Bobby Bowden's gonna beat Cincinnati and East Carolina and Tulane. He's got more speed and more ability, and he can outcoach the hell out of those teams. But you put him against Miami, Florida, Clemson, Auburn, he's gonna be about 50-50.

Of course, the key to Coach Bryant's great record—and to all winning records—is that not many coaches could build a football team as strong as his. The coaches in the Southeastern Conference in the 1970s couldn't get it done, and Coach Bryant had his greatest success. Can you believe he won over 100 games in 10 years? Coach Jordan was at the end of his career, and Auburn was in transition. Johnny Vaught was gone at Ole Miss. Charlie McClendon coached winning teams, but only one championship team at LSU. Florida was firing Doug Dickey and hiring Charlie Pell and going through that trauma. Bill Battle was going, and Johnny Majors was getting his feet on the ground at Tennessee. Vince Dooley had the only other stable, championship program in the SEC, and Alabama and Georgia didn't play regularly. Coach Bryant won three of the four games they did play in the seventies. And what's been happening in the SEC since I've been at Auburn? They've had four coaches at Alabama, four at Florida, four at LSU, three at Mississippi State, three at Vanderbilt, and two at Georgia, Kentucky, and Ole Miss. Bowden is a great coach at Florida State. He's a helluva coach. But Florida having trouble has helped him. If you get down to it, if you study it, it ain't that complicated: the most stable programs, with sound coaches, produce the best teams which win the most games. There aren't any miracles on Saturday afternoon in the arena.

I suffered a much deeper loss in these years than the loss of a football game. My father died. I guess Nat was living in Augusta. He or my mother called and said Daddy was sick in the hospital, that it didn't look good.

He suffered from emphysema, and with the wear and tear on his body over the years, he was just not strong enough to fight off the virus or whatever he had. He became dehydrated, and his kidneys failed. He actually died of uremic poisoning.

I spent five or six days with him in the hospital. He was coming and going. At times he would be talking out of his head, other times he would be perfectly normal. I wouldn't take anything in the world for spending those days with him in the hospital.

The last five years of his life, daddy quit smoking, and he quit drinking. There were other years when he quit drinking for a while. But he was a heavy smoker. I know the smoking must have been a big part of causing his emphysema. I don't say it was the only cause. He worked all his life in so much dust. Harvesting peanuts. All the dusty jobs a farmer has to do. When daddy made up his mind to quit smoking, and to quit drinking, he didn't get any help, or go through any programs, he just quit. That was very typical of him. He thought you were in control of your own life, and what you wanted to do, you did it.

What did he think about my becoming a coach? I don't guess I ever asked him. He raised us all to think for ourselves. But he liked sports. My mother has always liked football. She'd rather see it now on television than go to the games. Daddy enjoyed the years I coached at Alabama. He enjoyed the games he and mama came to. They went to the two Nebraska bowl games. He enjoyed those. But he was mighty weak.

The owners of the land we farmed sold it to a paper mill about the time I went off to college. My father just grew too ill to farm. I know he hated to see the land he'd worked and slaved over all those years go back to pine trees. It hurt me. I can only imagine how much it hurt him. But his health was such that he couldn't farm. And things had changed; help was harder to get on the farm.

I'll never forget my father's funeral. I've mentioned the great black preacher in Blythe. His name was Tarver, John Tarver. John was a very, very strong character, a great human being. He was respected by everybody, a long time before integration. John Tarver taught my daddy how to bird hunt. I guess he kind of raised him; daddy had three sisters, and I guess John Tarver spent a lot of time with him when he was a kid coming along. John was always close to our family, and particularly to my daddy. John had to be somewhere in his seventies. He had had both his legs amputated because of diabetes.

Goodness, I can't even remember the name of the white preacher who preached the sermon in the church. I had been gone a long time. I didn't know him. I guess he was just the local minister of the Blythe Baptist Church. I can remember our lifting John Tarver out of the car and carrying him up the church steps for the first service. And carrying him back down those steps to the graveside service. The cemetery was right behind the church. Remember, my grandfather gave the land they built the church on, and he gave a lot of money to help build the church, and he got a plot to be buried in. So did my daddy, who gave the church additional land for the cemetery before he died. I've got a plot, too, in that cemetery. And John Tarver preached the graveside service for my daddy, a white man he had known all of his life and who he helped raise when south Georgia was as segregated as segregated could be. I will never forget that day.

My daddy, and a man like John Tarver, taught me a long time ago that you don't judge any man by the color of his skin. I've always believed that. I've tried to live my life by that belief. I guess that's one reason it hurt me as much as it did to be accused of running a racist program by one of our own players a lot of years later at Auburn—even though it was an untruth, by a weak and vulnerable young man. You can ask the other hundreds of young men, black and white, who have paid the price of blood and sweat to carry on the football tradition at Auburn. They will tell you we are all part of the same family. We win together and we lose together.

There wasn't one of 'em who sometimes didn't quit the team, or think about quitting, the same as I did all those years ago at Georgia. Football is tough; football is sacrifice; football ain't for everybody; but if you love the game, and play it with heart and soul, you will have an inner strength that others don't have and will never understand. We ain't perfect in the Auburn family. But I hope we grow up to take responsibility for our own lives together. It hurt me to hear a false charge of racism. But I come from the man John Tarver put in the ground that day. And he taught me a long time ago to treat all men with respect, and to stand tall and to stand tough, and I mean to be standing here at Auburn as long as I have something to give back to the game and the kids who play it.

Let the earth shake when it will.

11

CLOSING OUT AT ALABAMA

The man in the street will tell you Sam "Bam" Cunningham and Southern Cal integrated the Alabama football team at Legion Field, in 1970, by the score of 42-21. Actually, it's not true. I had already recruited the first black high school player to Alabama, Wilbur Jackson, of Ozark, Alabama.

In 1970, we did sign defensive end John Mitchell from a California junior college. He was originally from Mobile. I believe Southern Cal Coach John McKay actually told Coach Bryant about him. Hayden Riley and I flew back from the Bluebonnet Bowl in 1970 and met with John and his family. We had lunch at a restaurant somewhere in Mobile. Hayden ended up signing John.

But I had already recruited Wilbur Jackson in the winter of 1969. Of course, freshmen weren't eligible then, and he didn't play until 1970. When did Coach Bryant tell me we could recruit a black player? He didn't. I told him. I said, "There's a black kid at Ozark that I'm gonna recruit." What did Coach Bryant say? Nothing. By that time, it was no big deal to him. He didn't ask me what kind of kid he was. He knew I wasn't going to recruit a sorry person. I mean sometimes you do but only by accident. You must remember the local high schools hadn't been integrated, and we had been recruiting only the white high schools. Later I also signed Woodrow Lowe and Gus White, both of them early blacks in our program.

I talked candidly with Wilbur about being the first black player at Alabama. I said, "Wilbur, there's no way for me to tell you what it's going to be like, because I don't know. I don't know how the other students on the campus will treat you. I do know our football players will respect you as a man. I know what you can expect from them. The other problems you will have to deal with, and probably they won't be any different from what you deal with here in Ozark. Or anywhere else."

Who else was recruiting Jackson? Tuskegee. Notre Dame never heard of him. But he was an outstanding young man. Had a fine mama and daddy. He was a lot of fun to recruit. It was an exciting time for me. I knew what kind of talent he had. He could run the 40-yard dash in 4.4 seconds. I don't guess Alabama had ever had anybody who could run a 4.4.

The kids liked him, accepted him. You couldn't help but accept Wilbur. He was just a class person. He became an all-conference football player. He had a good pro career with the 49ers and the Redskins. And the last I heard he had his own business back in Ozark.

I mentioned Gus White. I have to chuckle at how I recruited him. He came from Dothan in the high school class of 1973. I promised Gus a scholarship his junior year. I guess that helped spoil him. He played awful, ballooned up to about 280 pounds, a big, old, roly-poly doughboy. Tore his knee up, to boot. Nobody else offered him a scholarship. I probably wouldn't have either if I hadn't already obligated myself. I went down to see him. I told him, "I promised you a scholarship, Gus. I'm here to see if you still want it. I'm gonna tell you right now, we ain't gonna put up with your playing like you played this year. You are gonna play for Coach Donahue, and he's the toughest, meanest, orneriest guy in the world. He's gonna run you back to Dothan. We've got a scholarship for you, if you want to come under those conditions." He came on. Got in shape. His knee was a mess. But he was tough, mentally and physically. We got about 10 plays a ball game out of him as a freshman. After I'd gone to East Carolina, Gus became a first-rate player.

The nature of our football business was about to change at Alabama in the fall of 1971. And it was to affect my coaching life for a lot of years to come.

We'd had two disappointing seasons. Coach Bryant called a summer meeting. I never will forget it. He walked into the room and went to the blackboard. He started off kinda rambling about running formations. He picked up the chalk and put up the wing T. He put up the full house T. He put up the I formation. Every time he put up a formation, he told why it was a great running formation. And when he used it. And how he used it. Oh, yes, he was sound. Then he stopped. Then he said, "You know we've got the best running back in America in Johnny Musso. And the best running formation in football today is this right here."

And he drew up the wishbone. You can say we were all surprised.

Looking back on it, Coach Bryant was very close friends with Texas Coach Darrell Royal, and I expect he had a lot to do with talking Coach Bryant into the wishbone. Another thing, beating Tennessee was an obsession with Coach Bryant. And Texas had killed Tennessee, a good Tennessee football team, in the Cotton Bowl, running the wishbone.

What did we assistant coaches think about the change, after we had already taken spring training? Well, the way Coach Bryant presented it, it was the thing to do. We had Musso at one halfback. And quarterback Terry Davis to run the offense. He was terrific on the option. We would have had trouble with him as a dropback passer.

We opened the 1971 season with Southern Cal. I believe they were ranked No. 1. From what I saw out on the field, they should have been. We caught them unprepared for the wishbone. We scored the first three times we got the ball, led them 17-0. They scored just before the half to cut it to 17-7. We just hung on the second half and won, 17-10, the way my old high school team hung on against Lanier. We didn't lose a game all year, until Nebraska in the Orange Bowl. It was the best coaching job we'd done since 1965.

Coach Jordan had done a heckuva job getting Auburn through the season unbeaten. Pat Sullivan won the Heisman Trophy and deserved it. They were a little predictable by the time they got to us. We put two men on Terry Beasley on every play. And we won the game, 31-7. Nebraska manhandled us in the bowl game, 38-6. That Nebraska team wouldn't win the National Championship today. But it was the best team in America that year, with Oklahoma close behind. Remember, there are no miracles out there. We began to recruit bigger, stronger, faster people.

I don't think the Auburn people will ever forget 1972. At Alabama, we were undefeated and ranked No. 2. Coach Jordan did one of his best coaching jobs, winning 10 games without Sullivan and Beasley. To be honest, we dominated the Auburn game. Statistically. I think they had a total offense of only about 85 yards. But we didn't score enough points. They also did a helluva job on defense. And they dominated the kicking game. The two identical blocked punts for touchdowns were remarkable. But they weren't flukes. And I don't think it was a pure lapse on our part. I think Coach Paul Davis, who designed their kicking game, spotted a weakness in our alignment and took advantage of it. If memory serves me correctly, they also blocked an extra point and came close on a couple of other kicks.

How did Coach Bryant take the loss? Hell, I can't remember. I'm sure he was sick. I remember how I took it. The way I've always taken a defeat. I wanted to do something positive. I couldn't wait to get on the road and recruit. That one was gone, and I couldn't do anything about it.

Of course, we didn't lose a game in the regular season in 1973. No team even came close to beating us until we played Notre Dame in the Sugar Bowl. It was a truly great college football game.

But before we played it, I had accepted the job as head coach at East Carolina.

MY OLD ALABAMA PLAYERS

I think my close friends, my former players at Alabama, whom I loved and who loved me, we still have strong feelings for each other.

I think they respect me and the job that I'm doing. I'm not saying that they would ever pull for Auburn to win a football game. But I don't think they would pull against me personally.

EAST CAROLINA

At the end of the 1973 season, I got a telephone call from Dr. Sonny Lowry. Remember we shared a house for six months after my senior season at Georgia. Until Dean Tate put me back in a dormitory. Sonny's a terrific fellow. Cut out of the same mold as my south Georgia hunting buddies Cleve Wester, Jimmy Sealy, and Talmadge Watson. Sonny had gotten his degree at Georgia in veterinary medicine. He'd met a girl from Greenville, North Carolina, and moved up there and started a practice. He called me and said the East Carolina coach, Sonny Randle, had resigned to take the job at Virginia. He wanted to know if I was interested in the job. I said, hell, yes, I was interested.

In my years at Alabama, I'd been offered jobs as an assistant coach at Georgia Tech and Georgia and Tennessee. Well, if I was going to be an assistant coach, the place to be was Alabama. The name of the game is winning. I knew we were going to win at Alabama.

I also knew I wasn't going to be the next head coach at Alabama. They would pick one of Coach Bryant's old boys to follow him, as they did when they picked Ray Perkins. And I knew Coach Bryant wasn't ready to retire, but I didn't know he would coach *nine more years*. I also knew no major university was going to name me head coach from the job I had coaching linebackers at Alabama no matter how many games we won. Many coaches have made it to major college football through the smaller schools. My soon-to-be rival, Bobby Ross, went from The Citadel to Maryland to Georgia

Tech; Lou Holtz went from William and Mary to N. C. State to Arkansas to Notre Dame; Dick Sheridan moved from Furman to N. C. State. It was time for me to find out if I could be a head coach.

I tried to catch up with Coach Bryant and tell him I was going up to interview. But he was travelling, and I never caught up with him. I was recruiting a kid, a linebacker, up above Chattanooga; he finally went to Tennessee. Sonny Lowry joined me in Chattanooga, and we flew to Greenville for the interview. I met with Dr. Leo Jenkins, Chancellor of East Carolina, and with the rest of the selection committee. I told 'em I had never interviewed for a job before, except to be an assistant coach at Alabama. I told 'em I didn't know if I could be a head football coach or not. But if they had enough guts to hire me, I had guts enough to come find out.

Who else did they interview? I don't even know. What did they ask me? Not much. They asked if I were going to run the wishbone? Yes, I was. They wanted to know who I would hire. I told 'em I'd bring in young people that I knew who had coached at Alabama. Did they ask me anything about running an honest program? I don't think it ever came up. I certainly didn't intend to run any other kind, and there wasn't no money to cheat with at East Carolina, anyhow. What did they know about me? Not much more than Sonny Lowry had told them. But they more or less offered me the job that day.

They didn't offer me much money. The athletic director, Coach Clarence Stasovich, told me what the job would pay. It was $21,000, or something like that. I was making more than that at Alabama, maybe $22,000. Dr. Jenkins, the Chancellor, called me after I got back home. He was an outstanding Chancellor and an outstanding man. I told him I wanted the job, but I didn't feel I ought to take a cut in pay. They ended up paying me $24,000, and $2,500 for my TV show. A total of $26,500.

I finally got up with Coach Bryant. He'd been to the National Football Foundation Hall of Fame dinner in New York. I caught him on the elevator. I told him I had talked to the folks at East Carolina.

He said, "You ain't going to East Carolina."

I said, "Well, I'm thinking pretty seriously about it, Coach."

He said, "Hell. You done made up your mind."

I said, "As a matter of fact, I have." His quick intuition, realizing I had already made up my mind, I'd say it was typical of him. But Coach Bryant didn't advise me not to take the job.

He said, "You'll be trying to schedule us and come down here

Coach Bryant came to my coaching clinic at East Carolina in 1978.

and make some of this gravy."

Yeah, he was hustling me already. He probably would have played me that first year. It was hard for us to get a game like that at East Carolina. We played North Carolina four times, and played N. C. State every year, played Duke a couple of times, played Wake Forest once. Always at *their stadiums*. Every one of those schools ought to be playing East Carolina right now. They won't play 'em. I do know East Carolina made asses of themselves a couple of years ago. It was a game with N. C. State; I don't know who won, but they had a big free-for-all. I don't say the problem was all East Carolina, but if they'd had their asses in the stands where they belonged, it wouldn't have happened. I'm getting ahead of myself.

I told Coach Bryant we had worked mighty hard to get in a National Championship game with Notre Dame, and I wanted to stay and coach in it. He said, fine. We were ranked No. 1 in the nation in both polls. And Notre Dame, No. 2. It was for the National Championship, and I wanted to be there. Remember, too, I'd recruited 27 of the kids who would make the trip, kids like Woodrow Lowe, Leroy Cook, Skip Kubelius, Greg Montgomery, Randy Lambert.

They ran the wing T. Lot of deception, faking of the backs, hiding of the ball. We had great respect for Coach Ara Parseghian. Everything started off that hard dive by the fullback; he was a good blocker, tough runner. Two tremendous tight ends, one was Dave Casper, played a long time in the pros. Of course, Parseghian made the call that won the game. We had 'em backed up to their two-yard line in the last minutes. Their quarterback, Tom Clements, on a play action fake, threw to tight end Robin Weber out past the 35-yard line for a first down. They had the lead, 24-23, and that was the final score. Before the pass, we had the momentum. Parseghian knew if they punted they'd lose. The pass was a helluva call.

A play that really hurt us in the game was a 93-yard kickoff return for a touchdown by a freshman, Al Hunter. I'd never heard of him until I went up to Greenville to interview. They told me that Greenville that year sent a great back to Notre Dame, who had run the 100 in 9.3. Name was Al Hunter. I was standing right beside Coach Bryant on the kickoff return. Paul Spivey, I believe, was our deep safety and the fastest we had, but he couldn't run a 9.3. When Hunter hit that crease, I said, "Coach, we ain't got nobody who can catch him."

It was one of the all-time great football games and a gut-wrenching game to lose.

I saw Coach Bryant the next morning. I'd never seen him like that before. I mean he looked like he was dead. He was still just gritting his teeth, probably been up all night drinking. Replaying it. And in all his damn frustration, and all his anger, he had the insight to know that we might want to get together for the last time down there in New Orleans as a coaching staff. I was leaving the next day for North Carolina. He gave me the keys to his suite; he and Mary Harmon were leaving for somewhere. So we assistant coaches got together one last time. It meant a lot to me. As it had at the end of the season when they had a going-away party for us up at the lake in Tuscaloosa. A lot of guys had left in my nine years without a get-together. Coach Bryant even came, which he never did any more. I was lucky in my career to be around truly good assistant coaches and came to understand what a good assistant coach is all about. And I hope I got to be one before I became a head coach. The bottom line for a winning assistant coach: he can teach a player what he needs to know, and get him to carry it to the field on Saturday, and get him to play at the top of his game. It was my luck to be among such coaches at Alabama. I look back, as I look back at my days at Georgia, and I know I loved those years, and I gave all I had to give.

East Carolina had enjoyed back-to-back 9-2 records under Sonny Randle. But they graduated over 20 seniors, including the quarterback and a talented tailback. The four previous seasons had been losing seasons. Stasovich had had some outstanding teams in the late sixties, before he gave up the head coaching job to be athletic director.

There're a lot more good coaches around the country than there are coaching jobs. And I've been fortunate. I was lucky to get the job at East Carolina. It was a great coaching job because it was important to Dr. Jenkins and the people there to have a good football program. I couldn't know that four years later, when Dr. Jenkins left, football wouldn't be important to the guy who took his place. But I'm getting ahead of myself again.

What did I find when I got to East Carolina? It's an outstanding school academically. And like Florida State, it began as a girls' school. Good people, hungry and appreciative of what we were trying to do. Oh, the football facilities were about as meager as you could imagine. Coaches' offices, dressing rooms, all just the bare necessities. No weight room. A stadium that seated about 18,000. We later expanded it to 35,000. It was an opportunity to grow and to find out about yourself. To coach hungry kids who just wanted to play. They weren't spoiled. And we brought in a coaching staff that was young and eager and hungry.

I was 34. I hired Jim Fuller from Jacksonville State to coach the offensive line. He was a kid and already a good one. My old college roommate, Frank Orgel, coached the linebackers. He'd been a graduate assistant at Florence State. Lanny Norris played at Alabama and had been freshman coach at Arkansas; he coached the defensive backs; he would've been a great college coach, but he later went into business. Wright Anderson of Wake Forest coached the running backs. Watson Brown came from Vanderbilt to coach the quarterbacks. Henry Trevathan was the only coach off the old staff to stay; he coached the wide receivers. In 1978, I hired Wayne Hall to coach my defensive line and he's been with me ever since. He'd been coaching the linebackers at VPI. Wayne is just a smart guy, a great coach, who knows how to work kids and get 'em to play their best; he just doesn't accept anything else. How much was I able to pay the assistants? Not much. I remember I had to take one salary and split it between Lanny Norris and Watson Brown, paid them $4,800 apiece. We were all young and eager. Like any young staff we made mistakes. But you couldn't accuse us of not working or trying hard.

I don't want to go any further without mentioning Cliff Moore. He's dead now. But to me he was the heart and soul of East Carolina, both as the financial guy in the administration and in his support of football. He helped us every way he could. We improved the practice fields and the locker rooms. We got a little old place to build a weight room. We started a training table while I was there. All the kids lived on a couple of floors in regular student housing. We eventually doubled the size of the stadium.

When we got there they were recruiting a lot of players from Virginia, some from the Washington, D.C., area. We started recruiting North Carolina kids. That's when we got better athletes. We worked with them, and developed some great players.

We had some of those, you know, long, tough practices, trying to separate the men from the boys. We had some quit. If you haven't got a few quitting, or some of 'em thinking about quitting, you aren't working them hard enough. Because football ain't for everybody. What kind of coach was I then? Early on, I was a lot more involved in the detailed planning of practice. I had so many kids coaching for me. Some of 'em I had to teach how to coach. I guess I'd describe myself as a young, impatient coach, impatient for us to improve. When things weren't going right, all I knew was to work harder. I'd say it's still a part of my coaching philosophy. When you get in a crisis, and your back is against the wall, as a coaching staff and a football team, if you work hard enough the weak ones are gonna fall by the wayside, and the strong ones are gonna step forward, and that's who's gonna win for you anyway. A certain group will follow the strong ones, and there's gonna be some that'll go with the weak ones. And I still believe when you get in trouble, go back to basics. I made the mistake of trying to do too much, trying to be too fancy. If you are going to get the most out of your players, they have got to play hard; they've got to be fundamentally sound, and they've got to know what to do. You can't perfect everything, just a few things.

Did the kids take to us? You'd have to ask them. I don't know what they thought. But I'm still close to a lot of 'em. I still hear from a lot of 'em. And they were winners.

That first year, 1974, we were 7-4. Then we went 8-3. And 9-2. And 8-3 again. And in 1977, we were 9-3 and beat Louisiana Tech, 35-13, in the Independence Bowl. Our last year, we were 7-3-1 and tied our greatest rival, North Carolina; actually, they tied us in the last seconds, 24-24.

We were fortunate that first year. We didn't inherit a good football team. Most of the talent had graduated. But we found some pretty tough kids at East Carolina. And some of the toughest stepped forward. You could start with inside linebacker Billy Hibbs, and a big old tackle named Ken Moore. That first year Cary Godette got hurt, but he was a big ol' defensive end, the rock we built future teams around. Later, we had another tough defensive end come in, Zack Valentine. A little free safety, Jimmy Bolding, led the nation in interceptions one year. We had two outstanding cornerbacks, Reggie Pinkney and Ernest Madison. Had a little old nose guard, weighed about 215, Oliver Felton. Our offensive line averaged about 185. Had a good fullback, Don Schink. And running backs Kenny Strayhorn and Bobby Myrick. The sophomore quarterback, Mike Weaver, stepped forward to be a leader. I wish I had room to call every name for every year. But they know who laid their guts on the line.

We won our first three games. Then we were *at* N. C. State. All our big games were *at*. They wouldn't come to our place. We led N. C. State, 14-0, after the first quarter. They scored just before the half. That's when I asked our players at the half who among them had a scholarship offer to N. C. State or North Carolina, I asked 'em to hold up their hands; nobody did. But we lost the game, 20-24. The year before, N. C. State had beaten East Carolina, 57-8. I'm reminded a bit of our 10-7 loss to Tennessee my first year at Auburn;

Tennessee had won the game the year before, 42-0. Lou Holtz was the State coach in 1974. I think he's a great offensive coach. I still don't think he's a very good defensive coach. He's at his best when he has a top defensive coordinator and leaves him alone. It was the third year before we beat N. C. State, 23-14. We opened the season with 'em the year after that and beat 'em again, 28-23. I remember our quarterback Leander Green went 60-something yards for a touchdown. By then we had some real speed at halfbacks with Sam Harrell, who could run a 4.5 40, and Anthony Collins, who could run 4.4. Both became NFL players. I hate it Collins had all that trouble with drugs up in Boston. Fullback Theodore Sutton could also run a 4.4. And Green could fly. We signed Eddie Hix in 1975. He weighed 215 and could run 4.3. By 1979, our halfbacks were averaging over seven yards per carry; our fullback was averaging 6.8 yards, and our quarterback was averaging over six. We never had that much speed at Alabama.

We slipped by Furman in 1974 and won four of our first five games. If a coach is going to last in college football, he has to be able to absorb the shock of a defeat. Probably the worst I ever handled a loss in my life was our next game that first year with Appalachian State. We were down, 20-0, at the half. We came back and went ahead, 21-20. They kicked a field goal to win, 23-21. I was so upset, mad, that for a year, starting the week after the game, we ran a lap around our whole practice field—coaches and players both—after every practice. Just to remember that game. Called it the "Appy Lap." Well, I thought it was the right thing to do. The next year we went up there and they beat us, 45-27. They had a terrific little quarterback named Robbie Price. He was like Houdini. We couldn't hem him up. I got in front of the team, players and coaches, after the game and apologized. We never ran the "Appy Lap" again. We whipped 'em the next year, 45-14, and then 38-21 our last year.

We lost our first two games the second year. I thought we'd turned it around, beating William & Mary and Southern Illinois. But we jumped ahead of Richmond, 14-0, and they beat us, 17-14. I challenged every player and every coach. I got through talking to them, I think on a Monday. A second string split end walked in my office. He said, "I know I'm not a very good player. But I love this team, and if there is anything I can do to help us win, I want to do it." I said, "How many people feel like you feel?" He was a white kid. He started naming off some of his buddies. And they were all white.

And I began to name some of the black players. I said, "What about this one?" He said, "I don't know about him." I said, "What about this one, and this one?" And he didn't know. I said, "Hell, they are playing just as good as these other kids are playing. The team means just as much to them." I said, "That's the damn problem with the football team. We ain't playing together." I said, "We are going to have a meeting this afternoon. I'm gonna leave you players in the room, and when you come out of the damn meeting room, you better be together. If you ain't together, we got no chance to win." That's what I did.

We were going to play The Citadel. East Carolina and The Citadel is like Georgia and Georgia Tech, and Auburn and Alabama. It's like Southern Cal going to South Bend to play Notre Dame. The guys play as hard as they can play. The fans pull as hard as they can pull. It's a game you play for keeps. Bobby Ross, who coached Georgia Tech to a share of the National Championship in 1990, was The Citadel coach. And I was about to find out how good a coach he was, and that's plenty good. We were struggling. We weren't playing 60 minutes. We weren't playing with heart and soul and everything we had is what it amounted to. And we were leaving our No. 1 quarterback at home with a virus. We got on the bus and went to Charleston.

Our second-string quarterback, Pete Conaty, broke his collarbone, but not before he kicked our only field goal. We had a little kid, Jimmy Southerland, who was a walk-on, had never taken a damn snap in a ball game. We ended up playing with him.

I believe it was the hardest fought football game of any football game I ever coached in. We won it, 3-0. The Citadel had a punt return for a touchdown called back. The game turned my whole coaching career around. We got on the bus to make that long ride back to Greenville, and they were bloody, and beat up, but you could see in their faces, there was no doubt they were together. And let me say The Citadel boys played their guts out. We probably had more speed, more talent than they did. But they had that pride, and they were well coached. We came back home and won the rest of our football games in 1975, which included beating North Carolina at Chapel Hill, 38-17, and Virginia at Charlottesville, 61-10.

We were playing at North Carolina, and had 'em beat, and were on their five yard line, going in; I had the quarterback lay on the ball and not even try to score. Bill Dooley was the North Carolina coach, and he had some terrific teams.

Early in the season, when we had won three and then lost two straight, the people, you know how people are, were getting on me pretty severely. Of course, we didn't have any special boxes for coaches' wives to sit in. Sue had to sit out there and hear all that stuff. Then I heard it when she got home. It was a great lesson every head coach has to learn. Because the same ones who had been cussing me, and abusing me...when the clock ticked down at Chapel Hill, they were crowding around, ready to run out on the field and celebrate. One of 'em in particular—I won't call his name—was standing right beside me. I looked over at him, and I said, "When the ship's sinking," I said, "the rats are the first ones that leave the ship. But you know, when the ship's sailing where it ought to sail, and everything's going good, the same rats will crawl out of trash cans and out from under rocks and old houses and climb right back on, won't they?" And he was just a-grinning, and he said, "They sho' will." Hell, he didn't have enough sense to know I was talking about him. But that's football. And if you don't understand people and can't live with the way they are, you aren't going to be very happy as a football coach. You have to realize the best friend you have in the world will sit up in the stands on Saturday and say, "This is the sorriest coached football team in America." And maybe that day he'll be right. And on Monday, he'll be your best friend again, and probably out helping you raise money. You can't expect people to be perfect. And believe me, coaches aren't perfect either.

We lost to North Carolina twice. In four games. But they never truly beat us. They just outscored us. We won once, and once it was a tie, 24-24. When you are always playing at their place, with their officials, you are just not gonna get the close calls. It doesn't take but one or two to make the difference. I don't mean any ACC official was ever out to get us. It's just human nature, in the heat of combat, for the home team to have the advantage. I would be a lot more critical of ACC officials of the game we lost at home to Wake Forest my first year at Auburn, in 1981. We get three 15-yard penalties in their last, 80-yard drive for the winning touchdown. Two of the penalties—all three were called by the umpire—were on our *nose guard for holding the center.* And they were passing on every down. Why the hell would we be holding the center? And show it to me on the film. And here I am replaying a game 10 years old. I made plenty of mistakes that day, too. And I made my mind up that year, after the

Mississippi State game, that I wasn't going to build a program that was built on excuses. But I'm getting ahead of myself again.

Let's go back to that 24-24 tie our last year at North Carolina. I can't tell you how big the North Carolina game was to us at East Carolina. It was a fierce rivalry. At the same time, we had lots of North Carolina friends, and Duke friends, and friends from N. C. State and Wake Forest. If they were football fans and lived in eastern Carolina, they tended to also pull for us when we weren't playing their own school. But the North Carolina rivalry was big for us. They had the name and the tradition. Well, our visitors dressing room at Chapel Hill was right under the Carolina Rams Club, and we were all heart-broken because we hadn't won. They'd kicked a field goal in the last seconds to tie us. Our wives and girl friends were all standing around outside the dressing room door. Well, over their heads, out on the deck, the Rams Club members were pouring drinks, and spittin', and ridiculin', and my wife was standing right below 'em. And Sue is FEISTY. She looked up and said, "All my life I've heard about Carolina Class, but it's a shame I don't see any." And about that time, I came out the door, and somebody told me what had happened. I looked up and there was nobody, not one soul, standing up there on the deck. They'd all gone. But fans can be fans when you don't win. Carolina people are good people, no matter what school they pull for.

We won 12 straight games at East Carolina, including the first six of the 1976 season. Then we lost at North Carolina, 10-12. Like I say, they outscored us; they never whipped us. We also lost at Furman, 10-17. That was the first year Art Baker was the head coach at Furman, and they had our offensive signals. They had an open date before the game and just did a heck of a coaching job, including picking up our signals. They also whipped us physically. But we won the Southern Conference championship in 1976.

In 1977, we opened the season, as I said, beating N.C. State, and also Duke, 17-16. We won our first four until we lost *at* South Carolina, 16-19. We never got to play a big team at home. Maybe that's why I love playing our big games, especially the Alabama game, in Auburn.

Coach Bryant, the next year, came up to speak at our clinic, and he drew a big crowd.

Unhappily, things changed at East Carolina after 1977. Dr. Jenkins retired as chancellor. Dr. Thomas Brewer came from

Texas Christian. The first thing that scared me about Dr. Brewer...he told our Pirates Club director not to contact any more East Carolina graduates in raising money for athletics. I mean, who the hell were we supposed to contact if we couldn't talk to East Carolina graduates? I'd speak to 35 Pirate Club meetings a year, in every little ol' town in eastern Carolina. And fund raising was the big thing. We had gone from raising about $60,000 a year to raising close to a half-million dollars. As I said, we doubled the size of the stadium, and for the first time in history, football was paying for itself at East Carolina. Then came Dr. Brewer and football was not important anymore.

It's been my experience, before and since Dr. Brewer, that some people give money to college academics, some people give money to college athletics, many people give money to both. The people, and the money, and the giving are compatible. One helps the other. It's true, at that time, we were raising more money for athletics at East Carolina than we were for academics. Now whose fault was that?

Already, I was being asked to interview for coaching jobs, but I wasn't out looking to leave East Carolina. I interviewed at North Carolina, after Bill Dooley left, and they hired Dick Crum. I interviewed at Missouri. And Florida State called me before they hired Bobby Bowden from West Virginia. I told 'em at FSU not to call me back unless they were ready to offer me the job. That I didn't want to come down there, right in the middle of recruiting, just for a token interview. That was on a Friday afternoon. They called me the next morning and said they wanted me to come down the next day for an interview. I talked to Sue about it. I had talked to the FSU president, and to Athletic Director John Bridges.

They were trying to hire Bowden, and that's who they wanted, I'm sure. They just wanted to use me as leverage to get him to make up his mind. That's my opinion. I called 'em back and told 'em I wouldn't take the job. That I really hadn't finished what I'd come to East Carolina to do. Of course, they hired Bobby, and I'm sure they are glad; he's been a brilliant coach.

Later on I was offered the Mississippi State job. When Emory Bellard went there. I turned it down. I just didn't feel it was right for me. So I stayed at East Carolina. That was after the 1978 season. But I quit after the 1979 season.

I knew then we were headed down a no-win road. The straw that broke the camel's back was a decision by Chancellor Brewer. We had a little ol' quarterback who went through spring practice with us that year, 1979. You know, I can't remember his name. He was a walk-on. I had promised him a scholarship for the coming season, and I was going to sign him. He went through spring training as our backup quarterback.

Well, there was a coach at Duke who had recruited him in high school. After our spring training, Duke offered him a scholarship. Now it *just happens* we were going to play Duke in the third game of the 1979 season. They couldn't give him a scholarship unless we released him. He would have to walk on and pay his way for a year, which was more money than he could afford. If it had been a different set of circumstances, if he had quit the year before, or if we weren't playing Duke in the third game, I would have certainly given him his release. But I'd groomed him through the spring to be our backup quarterback. I wasn't going to release him. I told Dr. Brewer the reason I wouldn't release him. Bill Cain, our athletic director, called me, and I told him the same thing. Nobody said anything more to me, but the kid ends up that fall at Duke.

It's tough for a team that doesn't run the wishbone to prepare for a team that does run it. One main reason is the difficulty a scout team quarterback has in giving you a true picture of how the offense operates. The speed with which plays develop. Suddenly, Duke has a scout team quarterback who not only can run the wishbone, but who has been executing *our version* of the wishbone all spring.

Duke beat us, 28-14. I don't say they beat us because they were able to practice against our quarterback running our plays. Let's say it wasn't a handicap.

But I didn't ask the athletic director or the chancellor if they had given the kid his release. I didn't want to know. I didn't want to go through the season upset about it. I put it out of my mind. When the season was over, I walked in Bill Cain's office. And asked him, "Did y'all give that kid his release to Duke?"

He said, "Yeah."

I said, "Why?"

He said, "Well, Dr. Brewer thought that was the best thing for the relationship between the two schools."

I said, "You mean to tell me you released him without talking further with me about it, or even bothering to tell me."

He said, "Yeah."

I said, "I'm resigning, effective right now."

Either that day, or the next day, I called the football team together and told them.

I had resigned, and I didn't have a job. But the N.C. State job was open, West Virginia was open, Tulane was open, Wyoming was open. There were all kinds of jobs out there. And I knew I could always get work as an assistant coach if I had to.

I was not going to coach in a situation in which I didn't trust the man who was running the show. I wasn't making much money. Money at that point in time wasn't that important to me. The opportunity to build a program at East Carolina was all the motivation I needed. By the time I left, I was probably making $50,000 a year, with TV bringing in $18,000 or $20,000 of that. I still believe that you could build a major football program at East Carolina to rival what has been done at Florida State. There are two million people living in the eastern part of North Carolina. Maybe three million. It's a great area to live in. It's got it all: wonderful coastline; you're two hours from Virginia Beach, where there are another two million people, and three hours from Washington, D.C. The football team is competitive right now. They could have beaten Georgia in 1990, probably should have. They upset Syracuse and Pittsburgh in 1992. Every year they've had a couple of good kids drafted in the NFL. Earnest Byner comes to mind, the big running back with the Redskins; he came to East Carolina the year after I left.

We've still got close friends in Greenville we hear from two or three times a year. Two of the closest friends I had in Greenville both died a year ago. Cliff Moore, I mentioned, was the heart and soul of the school and the athletic program. Pat Draughon was the East Carolina alumnus I was closest to. He was a former high school coach who had gone into the international catering business in a big way. He fed the people who built the Alaska pipeline. He'd go all over the world, setting up military mess halls. Roddy Jones was another good friend of mine. Roddy, I think, is now the chairman of the Board of Governors for the State of North Carolina. And I still hear from my old players all the time. I would say it was just a great six years in our lives. For our whole family. We loved Greenville.

A few years ago we played East Carolina, twice, at Auburn. Of course, all the kids I had recruited were gone. But they played us tough. They hit us. One year, it was 7-0 at the half. We won, 35-10, but they gave a good account of themselves.

East Carolina had been a great job when Dr. Jenkins was chancellor. Dr. Brewer just didn't understand what it took to win, as far as total support, everybody being on the same team. Of course, since I've been at Auburn, we've had that total support. We've had our controversies, our ups and downs, but through it all we've been on the same team. Academics and football are both important to the folks here. I guess we've also raised more money in those years for academics and athletics than any time in the school's history.

But even today I remember East Carolina with affection. I would say that throughout my coaching career, each stop along the way has had a special significance for our family, and none of them to me was more special than East Carolina.

I interviewed with Chancellor Joab Thomas of N.C. State after I resigned at East Carolina. It was ironic that Dr. Thomas wound up as president of the University of Alabama, with me at Auburn. It was a short interview. Dr. Thomas wasn't on the N.C. State selection committee. And I'm sure the committee didn't recommend me for the job to Dr. Thomas. The old N.C. State athletic director was in the hospital when I went through the interview. He knew me and knew my background. I don't remember who was on the selection committee. Evidently I didn't say what they wanted to hear. I didn't wait around to find out. Of course, I didn't get the job.

A YEAR AT WYOMING

That left Wyoming. Well, the people from Laramie flew down and offered me the job, and I took it. I told my assistant coaches, "We're fixing to find out if we can coach." Wyoming hadn't had a winning season in eight years.

I didn't go to Wyoming to stay just a year and leave. But I didn't go out there to spend the rest of my life either. I knew that. And they probably knew that, too. I knew that Bob Devaney had been there and won, and it led to a great opportunity for him at Nebraska. Bowden Wyatt had been at Wyoming before Devaney; he won, and it was a stepping stone to the job at Tennessee. Fred Akers won at Wyoming and got the job at Texas. I knew if we went to Wyoming and won, somebody would be looking.

I loved Wyoming. It's a place I'd like to go back and see again. I could spend a summer there and love it. And the fall would be better. Now I wouldn't want to spend another winter. And the spring in Wyoming you don't know about; it can be any temperature. It's the most gorgeous country that the Lord ever created. When people say the Rocky Mountain region is the backbone of the United States, I believe it.

The people are just as enduring as the landscape. They've got to have each other to survive. If everybody lived their lives, depending on one another, the way the people in Wyoming do, it would be a better world. When the ranchers gather their cows up, they all go together and brand 'em together. If you get stranded on one of those lonesome highways in a blizzard, and you are praying that somebody will come by and help, if somebody does come by, they will stop and help you. It might be them stranded the next time. When you live in Wyoming, you've got to respect the elements. They are a tough people. Most of them will take a drink. Cuss a bit. But they are good, honest, God-fearing Americans. And I don't know how you could not love the countryside. Looking at the Rocky Mountains, up the eastern slope, coming down the western slope, the rivers and streams and snow-capped mountain tops, you can see for fifty miles. The air is clear. No pollution. I just marvel at the beauty of it.

Wyoming is a great school. Academically, it's one of the best in the country. When I was out there, they had an abundance of money because of a tax on coal.

We got there in December. I mean it was December. Cold. That wind blowing from Canada. But our family enjoyed Wyoming. We got into snow skiing. In the summer, we spent a week up at Jackson Hole. It's unbelievably gorgeous. The rest of the time I was working so hard I didn't really have time to get close to anybody in Laramie, to develop friendships.

What kind of kids did they have playing football? Let me say again, I find that kids are the same everywhere—they're all good kids. But there are only 400,000 people in the state of Wyoming. Lot of little towns might play six-man football, and high school football just wasn't that big. Kids had to travel a long way to go to school and didn't have a lot of time to practice, and to be honest, rodeoing and that sort of thing was bigger than football. I mean it was a tough, Western way of life. Now the people who did follow football loved it. We could expect two or three college prospects each year from Wyoming. We'd get a few kids from Nebraska. Occasionally, one from Montana or somewhere up there in the high country, and one or two from Denver. But when you left Colorado, you had to go to California, or in the other direction to Chicago or New Jersey or down to Texas to find a prospect. We'd take a few from junior college, and they might have grown up anywhere. We had a broad variety of kids from different backgrounds. But I'll tell you this, when it came to football, they got after it pretty good.

Did we have as much talent as we had at East Carolina? Not really. Not overall. We didn't have the speed we had at East Carolina. We did have an outstanding quarterback. A kid named Phil Davis from Cerritos, California. He was a good one. And we had a dominating defensive end, Guy Frazier, from Detroit. We had a punter, Gil Wiel, who led the nation, averaged about 48 yards a punt, and he was from Pinedale, Wyoming. And we had a kick returner, Darnell Clash, from Cambridge, Maryland, who was as good as I ever saw. He had over 1,000 yards in kickoff returns and over 500 yards in punt returns. You can see our players came from all over. That fall, we won six games. And we lost five. We played hard. We won some we might should have lost. We lost a couple we should have won. We should have beaten Colorado State and Air Force, but we didn't. We lost big only once, to Brigham Young, 52-17. I love Lavell Edwards to death, the coach at Brigham Young. He and his wife, Patty, are close friends of Sue and myself. But one thing about our game in 1980 stands out in my mind. Jim McMahon was the Brigham Young quarterback. He later led the Chicago Bears to the Super Bowl title. I can remember distinctly being behind, 52-17, and McMahon is still out there throwing to try and get another touchdown. Last year, I was watching the Texas A&M–Brigham Young bowl game on television. And the announcers were getting on A&M Coach R.C. Slocum mighty hard for running up the score on Brigham Young. He got about 60 points. But I wasn't quite so sympathetic for Lavell and Brigham Young as those announcers were. I wasn't necessarily pulling for Texas A&M, but that's one game I can't say the big score bothered me that much. I never believed in embarrassing any coach or any team.

We had a few big wins, including the first three games with Oregon State and Richmond and Hawaii. Hawaii came in with a pretty good football team, and we beat them, 45-20. We just lost to New Mexico, 24-21. Then Brigham Young buried us. We came back and won against Utah and had a big win over San Diego State, 34-9. We lost close games to Colorado State and Nevada-Las Vegas, and Air Force beat us when they shouldn't have. And we finished the season against big rival, Texas-El Paso, and we whipped them good, 52-7. I can promise you we weren't trying to score on the last play.

If we had stayed at Wyoming, I don't doubt we could have built teams to compete for the championship of the WAC conference.

We had some memorable times. We started working on a world class indoor facility that they use now. At that time, we practiced in a big arena. After they'd have a rodeo, we'd scrape off the playing surface and put down tree bark and practice on that. It was a little rough to fall on, but it was better than falling on hard dirt.

In the winter, they'd put down a hardwood floor and play basketball in there. Now they have a state-of-the-art indoor facility.

I would say that one year at Wyoming confirmed all the things I believe about football and what makes a winning team: heart and soul, character, conditioning, the intangibles. And defense, always add defense. And don't ever underestimate character when you recruit a kid. You can sense it and you can feel it, in him, in his high school program, in his home life, but you really can't be sure he has it until you put him to the test. A kid may have strong character in a weak high school program, where he's never really been tested. You don't know where his breaking point is. I've seen kids in a weak program, who didn't display the kind of character you thought they should have, but when we put them in our program, they responded with outstanding strength of character. We can put 'em to the test after they put on that blue jersey. And we do. But a football team can't live under the fist all the time. Sooner or later, each guy has got to take up his own fist, be his own man. Take responsibility for his own actions. And then he's a grown man, and that is what we try to accomplish with our program at Auburn.

One Sunday night, in 1980 a good friend of mine from my Georgia playing days, an old teammate, Don Leebern, called me. Just recently, Don was elected to the Board of Regents at Georgia. He owns Georgia Crown, and that's who my brother Nat works for. I guess Don called me the Sunday night after the Auburn-Alabama game. He called and asked if I wanted the head coaching job at Georgia. If I was interested in it. I certainly was. Don said, "I think Vince Dooley is going to Auburn."

I talked to Don. And I talked to some of the people I knew on the Georgia selection committee. Then, I guess, it was Tuesday I talked with them again. And they said, "Well, it looks like Vince is going to stay at Georgia." What if he had gone to Auburn? I don't think I would have gotten the job. I would have probably come in second. I think Erk Russell would have gotten it, and he would have deserved it. I think Vince made the wise decision staying at Georgia. He'd earned a great deal of success, had just won the National Championship. He wasn't at a hungry time in his life. And a few years later, he got a warning signal from his heart. He also had Herschel Walker for, it turned out, two more years. And he had an outstanding freshman class that won 10 games after Herschel went pro. I guess Vince used the Auburn opportunity as leverage to be appointed athletic director. Speaking as a Georgia alumnus, Vince deserved to be athletic director; in fact, he deserves all the success he's enjoyed. Vince has been good for college football. In the first place, he was a dang good coach. His teams played hard, and they played a full 60 minutes. They pulled a lot of games out in the last few seconds. They played good defense, had a good kicking game, good offensive line; they were conservative on offense. And they won, for 25 years. Vince was good for college football, the things he believed in. We've come down on opposite sides of some issues. But he was standing up for Georgia's best interest, and I was standing up for Auburn's. I guess our teams won five out of eight games with Vince's teams. But football can be a game of high times and low times. After Herschel's class, with the Jan Kemp problems, Georgia experienced something of a sinking spell, though Vince's teams were all contenders. And he was a gentleman, win or lose. Don't expect Georgia to stay down long; they have too many fine athletes in my old home state. Vince Dooley is headed for the Hall of Fame. It's just a formality, voting him in. I respect the job Vince did as a great coach at Georgia. And I will always be grateful to him for not taking the Auburn job.

Well, Wednesday night, I called Fob James, the Alabama governor and old Auburn halfback. He said, "You don't need to talk to me. As a matter of fact, the committee is meeting right now in Auburn." And he gave me Auburn President Dr. Hanly Funderburk's telephone number. With Vince bailing out on them, the committee was desperate for a coach. I called Dr. Funderburk, and his secretary got him out of the selection committee meeting. I made an appointment to talk with them on the following Friday, I think, the 12th of December. I met them in Atlanta.

I mentioned earlier how, when I was a kid growing up and getting ready to go on a big quail hunt, or dove shoot, I could never sleep the night before. That's the way I was that night. Hell, I woke up at 12, two, and three o'clock. Finally, I looked over, and it was 3:59. I got up and walked outside the hotel. It was December. It was a cool morning. The kind you can wake up to in a thousand little towns over the South. There was a different smell in the air, a different dampness, not like the dry cold of Wyoming. That old, damp, cool air hit me in the face, and at that moment I missed the South more than I'd missed it in the year I'd been gone.

You come to those moments in life, of opportunity, and there are not so many of them.

One of the things I found interesting in Bo Schembechler's book—he was the third or fourth choice to be the head coach at Michigan. I don't know how far down the line I was at Auburn, but I damn sure wasn't the first choice. They tried hard to get Vince. They tried to hire Bobby Bowden. I don't know who all they talked to. I do know Ray Perkins called and asked about the job. He was still coaching the New York Giants. They talked to a lot of 'em.

Let's see, who was on the Selection Committee? Dr. Funderburk, Mike McCartney, Dr. Wilford Bailey, Morris Savage, John Denson. Bobby Lowder wasn't on the committee, but he sat in on the meetings. He was there because he was putting together a radio and TV package for the coach they hired. Bobby was the only one who didn't say a word. I asked him about it later, why he didn't ask me anything. He said he made his living hiring people, that he had checked me out long before I walked in the room. He didn't have to ask me anything.

Something funny happened after we finished eating lunch. We were sitting around talking—Sue was talking with the wives—and I was talking to the committee. I said, "Why don't y'all go ahead and make a decision, go ahead and do something?" And one of them, well, it was John Denson, said, "We want it to be unanimous." I said, "If it's gonna be unanimous, I'm gonna get the job." He looked at me just as funny. He said, "How do you figure that?" I said, "Well, because there are some people on this committee who want me to be the head football coach at Auburn." I said, "If I'm not, then it ain't gonna be unanimous."

One of the things I told the selection committee was that if Auburn was to be successful in football, it had to be able to beat its two biggest rivals, Alabama and Georgia. I don't mean beat 'em every year. But I mean compete with them on even terms. And I told them that I had played at Georgia and coached for nine seasons at Alabama. They weren't going to find a coach who knew more about those programs and what made them work than I did.

I guess the most famous question they asked me was, "How long will it take you to beat Alabama?" And I answered, "Sixty minutes." I wasn't trying to be smart. I didn't mean we were going to beat Alabama the first time we played them. What I meant was it would take a complete game, all 60 minutes. Auburn had played Alabama close several times in the last eight years, but had been unable to put them away.

I couldn't help but feel I had been preparing for the job at Auburn all my life. As I said, I had played at Georgia, and I coached at Alabama. My family had been close to Shug Jordan all the 25 years he was head coach at Auburn and for years before that. And I had known him from the time I was a small boy, and had been recruited by him, and played against him, and coached against him, and had all the respect in the world for him; I always thought he was a perfect gentleman, and he was plenty tough. I often wish he were still alive. He was Mr. Auburn. It would be a pleasure to have him come to practice and to see our teams play heart and soul football, the way he coached it. And I could durn sure learn from him.

I went back to Wyoming, and Auburn called and asked me to come back and bring Sue with me. They called the following Monday week. And we flew down on Sunday. All the students were gone. The campus was empty. I met with the committee. We had dinner. Visited. We spent the night in Dr. Funderburk's house. Everything was friendly and went fine, but they didn't offer me the job. I knew they were still looking at a lot of candidates.

The next morning we got up and flew back to Laramie.

When we got off the plane, our athletic director, Bob Hitch, was waiting for me. We were good friends.

He asked, "What are you gonna do?"

I said, "I don't know. I haven't been offered the job. But if they offer it to me, I'm gonna take it."

He said, "Well, you've got to make a decision."

I said, "What do you mean?"

He said, "You've got to either sign a contract with us, and we are going to hold you to it. Or you can resign. Or we're gonna have to fire you."

I had never signed a contract at Wyoming. Just came on a handshake. We lived only two blocks from the president's house. So I went to see Dr. Jennings.

Dr. Jennings said virtually the same thing Bob said. Their board had given them an ultimatum. They weren't going to let me stay at Wyoming while trying to get a job at Auburn. I told them I didn't know if I was going to get the Auburn job or not. I said, "Let me go and talk with Sue."

I went to the house and told Sue what the situation was. I also called Dr. Funderburk. Jackie Sherrill was at his house when I called, interviewing for the job. Jackie and his wife were there. His Pittsburgh team was in Jacksonville, getting ready to play in the Gator Bowl. I think Jackie made a lot of demands, a lot of financial demands, more than Auburn was interested in. I told Dr. Funderburk what my situation was. How the people at Wyoming had to know something. I said I had to know something. I asked him, "Am I going to get the job? What's the deal?"

Well, the search committee was in Auburn meeting. Dr. Funderburk got three or four of the committee members together. But they weren't ready to make a decision.

I told Dr. Funderburk, "You know, I have to make a decision. I don't have any doubt I'm the best man for the job. I'm going to resign at Wyoming."

He said, "I can't promise you you are going to get the Auburn job. The only thing I can tell you...you know you are one of the top contenders." He didn't say he was supporting me, but I felt like he was. But Dr. Funderburk couldn't give me a firm answer. I said, "I'm going to resign from Wyoming. I've never been without a job in my life, since I started working when I was 10 or 11 years old. I can always find a job. I can go back and be an assistant coach if I have to. But I know I'm the best man to coach the football team at Auburn."

I think Sue understood. If she didn't she pretended she did. In fact, she wrote out a short resignation note for me. And I signed it. We took it up to Dr. Jennings's house. Bob Hitch was still there. We talked, hugged and kissed, and cried, and left.

I went over where the assistant coaches were gathered up and told them that we were unemployed. I never will forget what Bobby Wallace said. He said, "Coach, we'll get a job somewhere, and it doesn't make any difference where it is, we can win."

That was the kind of spirit we all had. But I also had to smile. I said, "Bobby, we ain't got a job anywhere; I may be trying to get the same assistant coaching job you'll be trying to get." I had no idea what would happen to us. But I knew there wasn't a loser in the room.

Anyway, that was all in the middle of December. And we stayed in Laramie through Christmas. Just sat around and looked at each other. You can imagine, after I resigned, I wasn't a very popular person on the streets of Laramie. They began looking for a new coach. They didn't promote my offensive coordinator, Al Kincaid, until after we were gone. Later he was fired. He lost the job as head coach at Arkansas State in 1991. But he's a good coach.

We were sitting around the house waiting on the word from Auburn, and I told Sue and the kids we might as well go to the slopes. So we went snow skiing for three or four days. We got back around the first of the year. And I watched all the ball games on television. Seems like I talked to Dr. Funderburk one time while he was in New Orleans. My old school, Georgia, was playing for the National Championship in the Sugar Bowl. And Georgia won the game with Notre Dame and the championship.

Well, Dr. Funderburk called. He said he was going to offer me the job, but they didn't want anyone to know about it yet. He said I needed to meet a private plane in Atlanta. They'd pick me up on the second of January. Or maybe I flew to Atlanta on the second, and they picked me up the next day. I can't remember.

Anyway, Bobby Lowder's plane picked me up in Atlanta and flew me to Montgomery. The selection committee's work was supposed to be over.

When I got off the plane, I asked Bobby Lowder, "How are things going?" I could see in his face...I think it was the most scared I've ever seen Bobby.

He said, "Not too good." He said, "You've got to meet with the whole board. They won't vote on it without meeting you."

I said, "Well, good." I said, "If I can't convince them I need to be the head football coach at Auburn, then I may not need to be." I think it was the best thing that could have happened. I had a chance to get them on my side.

What kind of questions did they ask? Oh, just some general questions. No real football questions. I think somebody asked me something about my University of Alabama ties. As I remember, I said your loyalty is to where ever you get your paycheck. Something like that. It was no big deal. And you know my loyalty to Auburn now goes a lot deeper than my paycheck. I stayed in there 10 or 15 minutes, with the whole board and the search committee. They asked general questions. They didn't ask me anything to try to provoke me. It was friendly conversation. I think they just wanted to get a sense of the kind of guy I was.

Anyway, I stayed in there a few minutes, and Dr. Funderburk said, "Pat, how about stepping outside and let us take a vote." I guess he felt the mood in the room was right.

They took the vote. I think everybody voted yes, but one. And that one wouldn't—he was the kind of guy who would vote against anything.

I went back to Bobby Lowder's and spent the night, getting ready to go over to Auburn the next day and publicly accept the job. That night was the first time that we ever talked about, or even mentioned, salary, or anything about money.

Well, I got a contract for $50,000 salary and a $50,000 personal services contract with Bobby Lowder. It was a four-year, revolving contract; every year it would renew itself for four more years. I think I still have the same four-year revolving deal.

When I came to Auburn, I really wasn't concerned so much about the money. I just wanted the opportunity. I knew if I did the job, then I'd be compensated for it. The money wasn't that important to me.

The truth was they really had no guarantee of radio or television revenues. That was part of my contract. I would have to handle my own radio and TV arrangements. Now I have built them into a profitable thing. But in the beginning, in my opinion, Bobby Lowder took $50,000 out of his pocket and paid me. Because I don't think he was making anything to speak of on the television show, or on the radio show, or on anything I was doing.

The next four or five years, I built up our radio and TV revenues into a pretty nice thing. We have had some outstanding and loyal advertisers. In no real order, Coca-Cola, and Great Southern Woods, and Colonial Bank, and Alfa Insurance, John Deere tractors, and Blue Cross and Blue Shield and Golden Flake have been steady advertisers. And some good ones have come in and out, such as Zeigler's. We've built one of the top coach's shows in the country. I think the photography, by Channel 12 in Montgomery, is outstanding. And I've enjoyed working with my co-host, Phil Snow.

I have made personal endorsements with some of our advertisers, and with others I haven't. But our relationships have been positive both ways. Where I have given personal endorsements, I think people do identify Pat Dye with Great Southern Woods, and Colonial Bank, and John Deere tractors, and Coca Cola, and Golden Flake potato chips. I haven't suffered any backlash response from viewers. I don't think the companies have, either.

My son, Pat, Jr., is a lawyer and an agent, and has helped me a great deal in negotiating contracts, but not with the university, as far as my pay is concerned. Because I believe that a coach's contract should be between him and the university. I feel strongly about that. But my private endorsements or other business ventures are a different matter.

And I would say the university has always been fair to me and very good to me when it comes to my salary. And they have given me the opportunity to be involved in endorsements and other commercial areas available to me because of my job as head football coach. I don't think I have done anything with my name that other football coaches around the country haven't also done.

In many cases now, universities themselves are controlling the radio and TV commitments. Which is fine. I don't have a problem with that. But when I came to Auburn, radio and TV were a burden. They were not a source of income. Now, of course, they are. I would assume that whoever comes after me will probably have his radio and TV contracts handled through the university. And he'll inherit a nice radio and TV package. But I had to develop those relationships myself. The same with our car loan program. When I got here, the athletic department was loaned twelve cars. Now we have almost five times that many. It's a matter of giving business people the chance to affiliate with a solid program, and of treating them with professional respect. And, I believe, they get those things at Auburn.

The Auburn Alumni Association has also been generous to me. When I first came, there really was not a place to entertain. I knew that I had to build more house than I needed. And more house than I could afford. To give us a class place for me to entertain the alumni, the press, the people we have got to have interested in our program in order for us to succeed.

So I built a large house. And then, over the next few years, the Alumni Association bought my house. And they still own it. The original contract called for them to own the house as long as I was head football coach at Auburn, and I would live in it and at the end of 14 years, the house would come back to me. Since then, they have told me I can take possession of the house anytime. The Alumni Association also gave me a $200,000 annuity after the 1987 season. It's supposed to be mine after five years.

Auburn and Auburn people have been good to me and my family. We appreciate it, and we love Auburn, and I love coaching. I didn't get into this business to make money. I've already talked about that and how when I became an assistant coach, there was no money to be made. I got into coaching to work with kids and to help influence them to live better lives. I still feel that way, even though today I am well paid.

And when I came to Auburn, I meant to stay. My original thought was, if we were successful, I was going to make Auburn my home. I'm not a mover. I coached at Alabama nine seasons, and I had a job offer for more money every year I was there. I took the first head coaching job I was ever offered, at East Carolina. I stayed there seven years, and left for Wyoming. And I left Wyoming after one year and came to Auburn. I guess that's four moves. Many coaches make five times that many in their careers. I made my last move in 1981. I'm an Auburn man now so long as I live. I love what I do. I'll be carried out of here in a box.

TO THE PLAINS

You could say I was pretty excited to get the job. At my first press conference, I called it "the University of Auburn." From the first day, I felt I was home. From the first day, I worked to be here for the rest of my coaching career.

I knew we were going to win when I came to Auburn. How did I know? Because it is a people game, and I believed in our people. I already knew our coaches. And I knew something about Auburn people from having played against them in the days, as I said, when those blue jerseys put the fear of God in a lot of people. And from having coached against them. But even with my experience competing against Auburn, I quickly learned I had underestimated the strength of Auburn. When you are an opponent, you can respect a school, but you don't really have a true insight into the heart and soul of what makes a school what it is. And you find the heart and soul of Auburn in the Auburn people.

When I came I didn't worry about Alabama and Georgia getting all the best high school players. And I don't worry about that today. I'm not a coach who believes that you have to have an All-America at every position to win. You do have to get your share of the top prospects. And Auburn proved to be a lot easier school to recruit to than I had imagined. A lot easier! And I mean to get the top guys to visit and to come here. And we only want those kids who *want* to come here.

As far as Alabama dominating Auburn in football, they had won the last eight games in a row by 1981. Well, I don't think winning is a matter of institutions. I think winning is a matter of *people*.

You must remember I have been at both Auburn and Alabama. I think to understand the rivalry, you have to understand the history behind both schools. A lot of people, in my opinion, are misinformed. They believe that Alabama has always been the dominant football school. But that's not true. Some people might not want to read this, but as a matter of fact, before Coach Bryant came back to Alabama, Auburn had won more of the games between the two schools than Alabama had. And since Coach Bryant has been gone, Auburn has won more of those games than Alabama has.

I realize the game wasn't played for many years. And during those years Alabama won more championships than any team in the South. What I'm saying...it's the *people* involved who make the difference in winning and losing.

Auburn's football tradition was generated by John Heisman and Mike Donahue and Ralph Jordan. Auburn was a dominant force in Southern football for more than a quarter of a century. And the Auburn-Alabama series was suspended in many of those years or Auburn would have won more of those early games. Anyway, I respected Alabama's great football tradition. But I knew Auburn had one of its own. I knew I was the man for the Auburn job. This part of the country is my home. I've been up and down every corn field in Georgia and Alabama, walked every practice field; I knew all the high school coaches, I'd been in their offices, I knew all the back roads, the pig paths, talked to all manner of families and high school athletes. And I knew my own coaching staff. There was one thing I underestimated: how popular Auburn was to recruit to as a school. It is a very popular school with certain types of kids.

Another thing I found, I already knew: we live in an age, and it will probably last forever, where the black kids in this region make the difference in football. If there are 10 college prospects in Alabama, seven are gonna be black.

Some people said, at the time, you couldn't recruit the top black athletes to Auburn. That proved to be the biggest bunch of baloney of all time. We've had great black athletes in our program, and they are loyal to it. Now every athlete, white or black, isn't happy all the time. Football is a demanding sport. But our black athletes have loved Auburn, and Auburn has loved them. Their mothers and fathers, when they come on the campus, see the ease and peace of the atmosphere here, and they feel comfortable. We're a long ways from being downtown Atlanta or downtown Birmingham. We don't have a lot of outside distractions. It's a quiet, easygoing Southern community. Social life here is among the students. It's a young peoples' town. They are not out competing in public with adults. Conservative mamas and daddies like to send their children to Auburn, which is a conservative school. I mean by that, it stands for the old values of family and work. And so does our football program.

That January 1981 recruiting was almost over. That first year was grab as grab can. Pat Sullivan, who had his own business at the time, had helped organize recruiting when Auburn didn't have a coach. One thing we did, we started a tradition of signing kids who were not much sought after who became terrific football players. I think specifically of defensive lineman Ben Thomas from little Ashburn, Georgia, in Turner County. We were the only school after Ben. He went on to an all-Southeastern Conference career, and a career in the NFL. The little defensive back, David King, from Fairhope, also started for us and eventually made all-SEC.

I believe we've signed more kids nobody wanted who turned out to be football players than anybody in this part of the country. I mean kids who turned out to be GOOD football players. I think of defensive end Aundray Bruce, who was a late signee and became the NFL's No. 1 draft choice. I think of fullback Tommie Agee, now starting with the Cowboys, and safety Tommy Powell, who would be in the NFL if he hadn't gotten hurt. I think of receiver Trey Gainous, who made two of the biggest plays that have been made at Auburn, the punt return against Tennessee up in Knoxville, and the fourth-and-six catch against Alabama. Nobody wanted Gainous.

Anybody can pick out the great high school prospects. I don't mean they will always be great college players, but they should make it. It takes a keen eye to pick out the marginal player who can play the college game, and our staff has been able to do that. I think of our 1983 team, one that could have played any team in the nation by the end of the season. The 12 or 15 seniors who played were hardly recruited by anybody. Tackle Pat Arrington was probably recruited. And guard David Jordan. Tight end Ed West, who's still in the pros, wasn't recruited. Split end Chris Woods wasn't recruited. Tackle Donnie Humphrey was about half-recruited. Nobody wanted center Bob Hix. We've been lucky. But we've been *smart lucky.* A lot of credit goes to Coach Frank Young who coordinated our recruiting and had a knack for picking out a kid with potential, in person and on film. Rodney Garner from Leeds, who played here for us, now coordinates our recruiting, and he's doing a terrific job.

So, what did we find when we got to Auburn?

A lot needed to be done. But nothing is more important than the players and where they live. First thing we did was spend a million-and-a-half dollars renovating the athletic dorm. We needed practice fields. The stadium needed a good deal of attention.

I didn't go to Auburn with any intention of also being the athletic director. Vince Dooley was being asked to come as head coach and athletic director, but Vince decided to stay at Georgia, and Auburn's athletic director, Lee Hayley, joined him in Athens, leaving the Auburn AD job open. When the search committee asked me if I wanted to be AD, I told them, no. But when I got to Auburn and saw the state of morale in the athletic department, I was concerned.

Dr. Funderburk was under a lot of pressure at the time and was later forced to resign. I knew that I had to have support from the athletic director and the president to build a program. If I became AD, that would solve one problem. I couldn't do anything about the president's situation, except support him, which I did until the very end. It hurt to see Dr. Funderburk lose his job. I still have great respect for him, and I realize he is the reason I am at Auburn. He put his reputation on the line for a guy who was not famous in big-time football.

A lot of people, Auburn supporters, asked me to apply for the athletic director's job. And there I was, sitting between Coach Bryant, who was also athletic director at Alabama, and Coach Dooley, who was suddenly athletic director at Georgia. I didn't have the same kind of strength my two biggest competitors had. So I talked to Dr. Funderburk and the board of trustees.

They were for my taking the job. Now that I've had the job these last 11 years, and the football program and the athletic department are a solid, profitable enterprise, a lot of people don't remember the state of things in 1981. But as I've said, I was called to be a football coach. I wasn't called to be an athletic director.

In 1981, the big question was, who would be the associate athletic director. My first recommendation was Oval James, who was already on the staff. He knew athletics. He knew people. He has also gone on to do a tremendous job as AD at Colorado State, and recently took the AD job at Pittsburgh. But the board wanted an Auburn man.

So, we settled on Dr. John Cochran. I think John did a great job, considering he had no experience in athletic administration. He is a scientist, an aerospace engineer. A couple of years later, he went back to the engineering department, where his talents are put to greatest use. And Oval took over and did an outstanding job, allowing me to coach the football team. Then Hindman Wall had it for several years until he left for Tampa. Hindman took a good job in a stable situation in that league, and he doesn't have to worry about the football coach beating Alabama every year, or the basketball coach trying to get to the Final Four.

We've hired a brilliant young man, with a powerful financial background, Terry Windle, as associate athletic director. To tell you the truth, I don't know how we got along without him. He managed a $100 million budget as controller of the international construction division of Harbert International. He has helped put the Auburn Athletic Department on an even financial keel.

It's an interesting question, the value of having an Auburn man coaching the team here or running the athletic department. Or of having a Georgia man at Georgia. I think being an Auburn person coaching at Auburn could offer certain advantages. But I think there would be more handicaps than assets to coaching at your own school. You've got too many strings attached to you. Too many people can get to you. If I was in Athens, every person I ever knew growing up and going to school would feel they could pick up the phone and get me involved in a long-winded conversation when I ought to be coaching. Hard to say no to your old friends and teammates and classmates. Here at Auburn, we have friends, and I try to be open with all Auburn people, and available, within reason, but it's easier for me to come in here quietly to my office and go down on those practice fields and do my job. Easier than it would be for me at Georgia. I'm sure of it.

There were two great coaches in the SEC whose careers denied the idea that it's tougher to coach at your own school. One was right here, Coach Jordan, who won 176 games at Auburn where he played. The other was Coach Bryant, who won all those games at Alabama. I think it helped that both had been gone for more than

20 years before they came back. I don't know how Coach Jordan handled it. But I can tell you how Coach Bryant handled it. He came back in 1958, and they had a bunch of townspeople who felt they had to be on the inside of everything going on in the athletic department. Some of them were powerful people. They'd come over there and walk up and down the halls, and in and out of coaches' offices, and on the practice field. Coach Bryant just ran 'em all off. Period. He just decided he would sink or swim on his won-loss record, and he mostly swam. He didn't care what was being talked up around the town. A lot of coaches aren't strong enough, don't win enough games to do that.

Most coaches who have succeeded did not coach at their alma maters: Dodd at Tech, Butts and Dooley at Georgia, Schembechler at Michigan, Devaney at Nebraska, Royal at Texas, Neyland at Tennessee, Vaught at Ole Miss, Switzer at Oklahoma, Broyles at Arkansas, Paterno at Penn State, and a lot of others. Of course, there are exceptions: Johnny Majors has done a fine job at Tennessee, where he was a great player; I guess he had his biggest success, a National Championship, coaching at Pittsburgh. I believe good people are good people. And good coaches are good coaches. It doesn't matter where they come from. Our job at Auburn is to turn out good people, where ever they wind up, and it will be fine with me if many of them wind up here, or one of them winds up in this chair I'm sitting in. Just so they are good people and good coaches.

Laying the Foundation

Recruiting was about over in the winter of 1981, and we hadn't started spring training, and a funny thing happened. Alf Van Hoose, sports editor of the *Birmingham News*, got up the idea of a rabbit hunt, to get Coach Bryant and myself together for the first time since I'd taken the Auburn job. I said, yes. Nobody loves a rabbit hunt better than I do anyway.

I went over to Tuscaloosa and spent the night with my old friend Rufus Deal, which is always a treat. Then the next morning drove to Moundville for the rabbit hunt. We were hunting on the late Judge "Tigger" Burke's place.

Coach Bryant sent word that he was tied up in some meeting and couldn't get there until noon. Van Hoose tells this story better than I do. But somewhere between what he tells, and what I remember, is the truth. Or some of it.

We had a good hunt that morning. Killed 28 rabbits. Coach Bryant finally got out of his meeting. And by the time he'd been driven to Moundville, he'd caught up on his double vodkas. He was feeling pretty good.

Coach Bryant didn't know a whole lot about shotguns in the first place. And he had borrowed one for the afternoon hunt. Between his feeling no pain and the strange shotgun, we had a little trouble getting volunteers to go out in the woods with him. Finally, they got him out there. And they kept putting him ahead of the dogs where he was sure to get a shot. But something kept happening, the rabbit would turn, or somebody would shoot it first. After about an hour, and no shot, Coach Bryant got bored. And sleepy. It had rained the night before, no standing water, but it was damp. And Coach Bryant walked over and leaned against a clay bank, just an old, damp, country clay bank, and he went to sleep.

The hunt was about over, when the dogs jumped a rabbit opposite where he was leaning up there—sleeping it off was what he was doing. The dogs were making a commotion, and a rabbit was flying about a hundred miles an hour. Pig House took aim, but he thought the rabbit was too far away to hit. Coach Bryant woke up, raised his shotgun, and KA-BLOOM! That rabbit went head over heels. Pig House stepped it off. Some people say it was fifty yards. Some people say it was sixty. I can tell you it was way out of range to be killing a rabbit on the dead run. I still think that rabbit died of a heart attack.

Pig said, "I started to shoot, but I thought he was out of range."

Coach Bryant said, "I started to let him run on some more so I wouldn't tear him up." Then he said, "That rabbit knew who was shootin' at him."

Now you can believe almost all of that because it's mostly true.

What did we talk about? We reminisced about old times. What did I say? To tell you the truth, not much. I'm not too smart, but whenever I was with Coach Bryant, I was smart enough not to talk much. I did a lot of listening. I know one thing happened that day. Mal Moore called Coach Bryant at Moundville and told him he had just signed the big tackle from Sylacauga, Jon Hand. Jon hadn't signed on signing day. It was a big catch for Alabama. Coach Bryant loved it, signing Jon Hand and having me out there with him in the woods. Did he kid me? It was more like sticking a knife in you and turning the blade slowly.

We had a good visit. None of us could have guessed Coach Bryant would be dead before two years had passed.

I remember my first meeting with the Auburn football team. The kids were sitting around the room…I know they were wondering what they were in for. I could sense their frustration. They hadn't experienced a lot of success, hadn't won a conference game the year before. And here they had another coach on their hands.

I said to them: "My name is Pat Dye. But you don't know me. And the truth is, I don't know you. It would be asking too much to ask you to win football games for a man who didn't recruit you, for a man who hasn't coached you, for a man you don't even know.

"Well. You all made the decision a while back to come to Auburn. It was the school you chose to go to and play football for. And I also made the decision to come to Auburn. And to coach the football team. We both made commitments to Auburn.

"If you'll play for Auburn, and I'll coach for Auburn, and if we all live up to our commitments to Auburn, then we'll be all right on the football field."

And that's what we did. And, finally, we got to know each other, too. And that is the true glory of coaching, knowing the kids and seeing them grow into men.

Well, I took on the job as Auburn AD after my first spring training in 1981. And that was some spring training. It was just an old-fashioned, hard-coaching, hard-playing, blood and guts, wolf-sign-everywhere kind of spring practice. "Wolf sign," that's damn blood and hair and tore up ground all around.

We had a scrimmage for the high school coaches at our clinic, and when they left, we locked the gates, and had that kind of practice where you pick 'em up and throw 'em back in the huddle and keep on going. Not too many quit. Some did. A few good ones. Sam Dejarnette could have been a great player for us, but he quit, transferred to Southern Miss. He and Lionel James and George Peoples could have been a pretty decent backfield.

Adjusting to the wishbone was not easy. It was not easy for James. It was pretty rough on all that first crowd. But there's a tradition of toughness at Auburn that's handed down through the generations. I can tell you this, when we came out of that spring, they weren't afraid. Of anybody. I think they had a different feeling about themselves. They knew there weren't any faint-hearted people playing for us.

That fall, we went out to Nebraska in the rain, and all they had was Roger Craig and Mike Rozier and Turner Gill and one of the best teams in the nation, and I can tell you we hit 'em, and if we don't leave the ball on the ground seven times, it's gonna be a mighty close football game. It was a case of an 80 percent team playing 100 percent, and a 100 percent team playing 80 percent. That's how you get big upsets in college football, and we had a chance. The next year I thought Nebraska was the best team in America. They whipped us at Auburn and just kept on whipping us.

That first spring we had some kids rise up and meet the

challenge. On defense, the kids hadn't been tied together, from the standpoint of playing hard, and playing hard on every snap. I remember our first scrimmage that spring of 1981. We had 32 missed tackles. The next day we practiced tackling for an hour-and-a-half. We used every tackling drill any one of us coaches had ever heard of. The next scrimmage we had fourteen missed tackles.

Gradually, the kids grew into football players. Edmund Nelson started our long tradition of outstanding defensive linemen. For years every starter on our defensive line eventually made all-SEC. Mark Dorminey, Bob Harris, Dowe Aughtman, Jeff Jackson were solid. Linebacker Danny Skutack was a leader and a tough kid. Gregg Carr, an outstanding student, became an outstanding player. He made it in the pros, and also became a doctor. I believe Donnie Humphrey got hurt. Quency Williams ended up being a good player for us.

In the secondary, Nat Ceasar ended up playing and Dennis Collier and Tim Drinkard and Dorminey. Al Del Greco was our field goal kicker and kicked for years in the NFL. We had some people to build on on defense. I mean guys you could go around the world with. Some juniors, some seniors. Of course, the juniors came back the next year and helped us beat Alabama and win nine games and go to a bowl.

I don't want to take anything away from the kids I coached at East Carolina and Wyoming. They were all good kids. But I think boys growing up in Alabama, and in this particular part of the country...to them, football is very, very important; it's a way of life, and they'll work a little harder; you can demand a little more of them, and they are willing to give a little more.

Football has changed in the Deep South in the last 10 or 15 years. And I'm speaking of the emergence of the black athlete. It's been a big and good transition, ain't no doubt. The black athlete has speed and size and hunger. And all the intangibles. And the kids are good kids. My experience, down through the years, has been: if you are sorry, you are sorry. It doesn't make any difference if you are white or black. If you are a good person, you are a good person. It makes no difference if you are black or white. Color has nothing to do with it.

I think background has something to do with it. I'd say that kids who come from solid families, whether it be a single parent, mother and father living together, or being raised by a grandmother—it doesn't make any difference, as long as there is a stabilizing force in that youngster's life. Then he's got a better chance to make it. Yet, I see great kids come from unbelievably tough circumstances, and I've seen some of the sorriest kids I have ever coached come from the best circumstances possible. There is no ultimate pattern. There is certainly no black and white pattern. A good person is a good person.

One or two great teachers can influence a young man's entire education. A Sunday School teacher or somebody in the community can influence his entire life. One great high school coach can be the difference in a young athlete's future.

Looking at the film of Auburn's 1980 season, you could see they had a pretty good offensive football team; they moved the ball extremely well. I knew we didn't have a James Brooks coming back at halfback. Defensively, they gave up a lot of points. I felt we could have a big impact on defense immediately. And I think we did.

It was pretty obvious we were struggling at quarterback. And we would keep struggling in the fall. We didn't have a lot of talent on offense. Little Lionel James did a man-sized job running and blocking in the wishbone. We were searching for another halfback. Mike Edwards, a split end, was the best, most courageous guy we had, so we moved him back there. They were a sight, 5-foot-6-inch James and 6-foot-4-inch Edwards. We moved Ed West from fullback to tight end, and he became a full-grown man and is still playing in the pros. We had three or four on the offensive line who had pretty good ability: Pat Arrington, David Jordan, Keith Uecker. Chris Woods grew into a football player, and he learned a lesson against Alabama we're still teaching.

We kicked the ball off that fall against Texas Christian. There were 48,000 fans in the seats. That wouldn't seem like much of a crowd today at Auburn. As I remember, it was as much a surprise to me as it was to the fans to see a pure freshman from Atlanta, Ron O'Neal, run 32 yards for a touchdown and put us in position to score twice more. We won the game, 24-16.

I didn't have any illusions as to how good a team we were, because I knew TCU wasn't very good. I did know our players were going to play hard. And that they would have a chance in most of our games. I still say if we had done a better coaching job, we'd have beaten Tennessee, Wake Forest, and Mississippi State, though State had a fine team.

Also, we didn't do a very good job of handling Ron O'Neal. He wound up quitting the team and quitting school. Neither academics nor football was important enough to him. If a guy cares enough about either one, he will do what he has to in class to play football, or in football to stay in school. Ron would be the first to tell you, if he could do it over, he would do it differently. But sometimes it's hard to get their attention when they are 17 or 18 years old. And it's sad. Ron could have been something special in football. I think he's back in Atlanta working, and I hope he's taking responsibility for his own life.

Wake Forest was one of the few games I feel we have lost at Auburn, that we absolutely should have won. You might add a couple in 1990 and 1991 to that list. Good coaches don't lose the games they should win, and they win some they shouldn't.

We flew up to play Tennessee. It's an exciting place to go play. I like playing up there. I don't like *losing* up there. We've lost there four times, in '81, '85, '89, and '91. We got thrashed in '85, and I'd say '89 was a pretty good whipping, but I guess we could have won it at the end. We've won once and tied once in Knoxville. Some people say we are jinxed in Knoxville. Well, hell, the jinx is *where* you play, and *who* you play. We got a *jinx* in Gainesville, Florida, too. And I'd say a lot of people have had a *jinx* in Auburn, Alabama. You damn right they have. Tennessee hasn't beaten us in Auburn, yet. We tied in 1990. That makes the series, 5-4-2, in our favor.

I like going up to Knoxville. Everywhere you step there's tradition. General Robert Neyland. The stadium's named after him. He was one of the coaching greats. He helped plant the seeds the game grows from. Those letters, VOLS, sitting up on top of the stadium, must be fifty feet high. The stadium is in a bend in the river, but we don't see the river when we go play, that's for the spectators, the river is. We hear "Rocky Top." I like "Rocky Top." I just like to hear it early in the game, rather than at the end. In Knoxville, you can hardly hear anything. It's loud; 95,000 fans make a lot of noise. First time we went, they had that old sorry Tartan turf. Now they've gone to something new. Three years ago, it rained on us. But we wouldn't have won that year indoors on a dry field.

By the time we played Tennessee that first year, we were a pretty good defensive football team, not great, but pretty good. If we had done a better job of taking care of the ball, we could have won on defense; our punting wasn't bad, and we were pretty good on field goals.

We also created a state of confusion that day on the sidelines. We were trying to compensate for a lack of ability, here and there, running substitutes in and out, trying to give the kids a chance to win. We got caught for delay of game two or three times coming down the stretch, and that really hurt us.

But we had a chance to win. We were down on the goal line, one play left in the game, the score was 10-7. We could have kicked a field goal and tied. I've never played for but one tie in my coaching career, and that was in the last seconds against Syracuse in the Sugar Bowl. I'll talk about that later. Often, tying a game is the best way to win it, but obviously not on the last play. We drove the length of the field, 80 yards in 15 gutsy plays, and fumbled the ball on the goal line.

A true freshman, Ken Hobby, was our quarterback. He also gave up football and school. In my years of coaching, I've seen many kids throw away great opportunities. I've seen an awful lot of talent wasted. If they don't want the opportunity, you can't force it on them. Hobby was a good athlete, but I never saw him throw the ball well enough to classify him as a great quarterback prospect. Let me make one thing clear: football is not for everybody. It requires a special kind of sacrifice, of effort and time. I see absolutely nothing wrong with a young man's decision to give it up for other interests. I do hate to see young men, or women, not complete their formal education. That, I think, is a great waste. We do everything we can at Auburn to encourage our kids to get their degrees. But they have to want it, too. You can't force it on them.

Speaking of Tennessee, I like Johnny Majors. Sue and I both like Johnny and Mary Lynn. Johnny and I are from the Old School. Only thing about Johnny is, he never played with both hands on the ground. I kid him about that. I was an old guard at Georgia. He was a tailback in the single wing, letting those guards do all the work up front. To tell the truth, he was a great player, a senior on an unbeaten team when I was being recruited by Tennessee. And I liked Tennessee. I've followed his career ever since. One thing with Johnny, to me, he's always been the same. What you see is what you get. Some people don't like him. Some people love him. I like him. We trust each other, although his people did send Texas some scouting stuff on us before our 1991 game; I got mad, but I can't stay mad at Johnny.

We've played some raging games, and have shaken hands afterward, and gotten together under the stands when the press had all gone home, and talked about what happened, like we did after the 26-26 tie in Auburn in 1990. I got him that year before the game. I called him up, and we talked around, and I asked him straight out, if he was gonna play for a tie, if it came down to it. Caught him by surprise. He sputtered around. Durn if his kicker didn't miss a short field goal, and it did end in a tie. Football has always been a way of life to Johnny. Like it has to me. He grew up in a football family. He and I have been coaching in the league longer now than anybody else. I've got special respect for people we have played who have beaten us, and I try to learn from them, and Johnny has beaten us about as much as anybody. We're still friends. His job's winning at Tennessee. Mine's winning at Auburn. I feel the same way about Bobby Bowden at FSU, and Billy Brewer at Ole Miss, and Gene Stallings at Alabama, and Tom Osborne at Nebraska, and Ray Goff at Georgia, and all the other coaches. I'm not envious when they win, I'm not jealous. I try to keep our programs in perspective, and leave the wins and the losses on the field. I have a lot of friends in the business. I hope I don't have many enemies. Life is too short for that. The game is tough enough without that.

Did any team ever win a game in the Southeastern Conference playing four quarterbacks, one play at a time? We did, against LSU. It was the first time Auburn had beaten LSU in 40 years. Between injuries and indecision, we couldn't settle on one quarterback, so we played 'em all. When you turn the ball over seven times, as we did against Nebraska, you are looking for help at quarterback. We started with a little walk-on from Birmingham, John Murphy. Then, Joe Sullivan...Randy Campbell...Clayton Beauford. Each one of 'em could do at least one thing. All four had a hand in winning it. The score was 19-7. Our defense held 'em to 38 yards rushing. We've played LSU three times since I've been here, won twice and lost once.

I remember a fun thing about that 1981 game. We were warming up in the rain and mud. And LSU came on the field with no pads, just jerseys. Coach Stovall told 'em, don't get on the ground. Don't get muddy. Don't soil your clothes.

And we were fixin' to go out there and play in that stuff. When I saw that, I told our coaches, "Get 'em good and muddy before we take 'em in." Bud Casey had the backs doing the three-man roll. The offensive and defensive linemen were going one-on-one in the end zone. Oh, we were a mess. And we were ready to play, mud or no mud.

Coach Stovall lost his job after that season. It's a reality all coaches live with. One coach wins, and one coach loses, every Saturday. It's not like Coca-Cola and Pepsi Cola. One can outsell the other, but they can both make millions. One coach wins, and one coach loses. That's why I never try to embarrass anybody in a football game. I've been on the other side. Stovall played at LSU after I played at Georgia. I followed his career. He was a great player, in college and in the pros. But that day against LSU, I wasn't thinking about Jerry Stovall being in trouble. I was only worried about Auburn, getting our program started, turning us in the right direction. There have been a lot of coaches lose their jobs in my 11 years in the league. It's an occupational hazard.

Georgia Tech. When I played at Georgia, Tech was a household word. And after Bobby Ross took over as coach, Tech was back; they even won a share of the 1990 National Championship. I also think getting into the Atlantic Coast Conference has helped their identity. But the years I coached against Tech at Auburn, they were independents; they had dropped out of the SEC, and, to me, it never was the same. Our players didn't feel that old passion to play Georgia Tech that we did as players. And the game came in the middle of our SEC season. Sometimes we struggled to beat them. But I guess we never lost to them.

That first year, we were leading them, 10-7, in the last quarter. But they were about to kick a field goal, and Chris Martin swears he told David King, if you block it, I'll run it for a touchdown. David blocked it, and Chris ran it 77 yards for a touchdown.

We might as well bring it up. The snap that wasn't supposed to happen against Mississippi State. The game we lost, 21-17. With the play we called, you don't really have room for error. We were leading, 17-14, in the last two minutes in our own stadium. Had the ball on fourth down at mid-field. We called, "Long count, no play." If they don't jump offsides and give us a first down, we'll take a five-yard penalty and punt. Somehow, between the sidelines and the center, we didn't get it communicated. Though the State kid did jump in the neutral zone when the ball was snapped, we didn't get the call. They drove it 50 yards for a touchdown. Their fine quarterback, John Bond, completed a 32-yard pass on fourth down.

I complained after the game to the press about the no-call. At the time the play happened, our little ol' football team had risen above its limits to have a chance to beat a very talented Mississippi State football team. We're not gonna beat Nebraska or Georgia or Alabama. But we can have a winning season, instead of a 5-6 season. I let my emotions get the best of me second-guessing the call. The next day on my television show I tried to make it plain that I wasn't blaming the loss on the officials, or on that one play. I didn't want to run a program looking for excuses. I still don't. If there is ever a wrong call, it isn't made against me, or us, it's just a human mistake. I've made more than anybody. If you are in the game long enough, they will even out.

Well, it didn't take long for the missed calls to even out. The next week, Florida kicks four field goals, but misses one in the last seconds, and we win, 14-12. Florida had a touchdown called back; they caught a fumble of ours in the air and scored, and the official missed it. Butch Lambert, *Sr.* was the official. The very next year, in Gainesville, two things happen to us: We have a touchdown called back on a holding penalty, and, on their last-ditch onsides kick, Lionel James comes up with the ball, and the official gives it to Florida. The same official made both calls: Butch Lambert, *Jr.* We lost, 17-19, on a last-minute field goal.

Charlie Pell, of course, was the Florida coach. I knew Charlie, but not well. Did I know they were headed for trouble with the NCAA? I knew they were doing some things they didn't have to do. There were plenty of athletes in Florida. And Charlie was a sound football coach. I talked to Charlie, and he told me to run my program like I wanted to, and he'd run his like he wanted to. So that's what I did.

After we beat them in 1983, in one of the most competitive games I ever coached in, they beat us three years in a row, 1984-85-86. And I'll tell you this, their 1984 team was as great as any team we have played since I have been coaching at Auburn. They were as great as the Nebraska team of 1982. As great as the Texas team of 1983. As great as any of the Alabama teams. They might even have been better than the Florida team that whipped us so badly in 1990. In 1984, they had three running backs as No. 1 draft choices. The Redskins paid linebacker Wilbur Marshall $6 million. Alonzo Johnson, Jarvis Williams, Lomas Brown, the Newton boys. They all looked like blocks of granite. But they only really whipped us in 1984. We had our chances to win the other two.

I thought the 1985 Florida game was a great football game. I mean it was hard fought, jaw-to-jaw, and we couldn't move it much, and they couldn't either. I think it was one of the hardest hitting Florida games we have played. The Bell kid, Kerwin Bell, took a lot of punishment and hung in there for them at quarterback. They beat us, 14-10. And that was about the difference in the game. The next year in Gainesville, we jump out ahead, 17-0. Should have won the football game. Fumbled it going in. And Bell came off the bench, injured, and beat us, 18-17. They go for two in the last minutes, and Bell runs it in on one leg. Tough kid. Tough loss.

All the times we've played Florida, they've had an open date before our game, with an easy team to play before the open date. So they've been ready. But then they've had to play Georgia the week *after* they played us, and they've had a helluva time getting ready to play Georgia. And Georgia, having to play them the week before our game, has had a tough time getting ready to play us. All of that will change with the new SEC schedule. We've finally gotten our own Auburn schedule arranged the way I want it now, with an off week in mid-season. It should help.

Georgia. Vince had a helluva team in 1981 and 1982. And it wasn't all Herschel. As I said, that Georgia class won 10 games their senior year after Herschel left school to turn pro, and they upset No. 1 Texas in the Cotton Bowl. We were the only team to beat Georgia in 1983. Don't think they weren't tough *with* Herschel in 1981-82. We just didn't match up with them. But we hung in there and made football games both years. I guess we actually led the game in 1981 in the second quarter. But they were too strong for us. No doubt Herschel Walker was a great, great football player. He was different. All the great backs are different in their own way. I never saw two of them who ran alike. Herschel was speed and strength. He could run over 'em, and he could outrun 'em. It didn't surprise me that he carried it 44 times against Florida once and hammered it the length of the field to win the game at the end. Against Notre Dame in the Sugar Bowl, he dislocated his shoulder in the opening minutes, had it pulled back into place, and carried it over 30 times to help them win the National Championship. He was amazing.

I've been asked when I first knew that we had the Auburn

program headed in a championship direction. Was it after playing Tennessee as close as we did in 1981? Was it beating Tennessee the next year in Auburn? No. Actually, I knew we were going to get it done after the fourth quarter against Georgia in 1982, a game we lost to a tremendous team. Lionel James ran 87 yards for a touchdown to put us ahead in the fourth quarter, 14-13. I understand it was the second longest run in Auburn history.

Georgia came back Georgia style: Herschel four yards here, and Herschel five yards there. Fourteen plays for 80 yards. They went for two and missed it. We came right back at 'em. Jaw-to-jaw. Length of the field. Took it to the 14-yard line. But we couldn't get it in. Randy Campbell's fourth-down pass was incomplete. Georgia ran the clock out. But the way we took it to them on that drive, as great a team as they had, I knew we were made of the right stuff. And if it hadn't been for that effort on that drive against Georgia, a drive that failed, I don't believe we could have had the confidence to make the last winning drive two weeks later against Alabama in Birmingham.

But, first, let's talk about 1981 and Alabama and Birmingham. You couldn't turn on the television without seeing that Coach Bryant was going for his record 315th victory. Against *us*. Was it a distraction for us? I have to chuckle at that. It was probably more of a distraction for them. They must have felt a lot of pressure to win it. I was never concerned about it. I was concerned about Auburn. If Alabama had done what it was supposed to have done that year—they lost to Georgia Tech and were tied by Southern Miss—they would already have won his 315th. I have to laugh at that statement; I guess most of us coaches would be content with winning 314 games.

Anyway, our football team learned some lessons in that 1981 game. Our fullback George Peoples ran 63 yards for a touchdown and the game was tied at the half, 7-7. I wish we'd had George in the wishbone another year. He could have been a good one. Well, the game rocked on. I believe Joe Sullivan was our quarterback at the time. He hit Ed West with an option pass. Their free safety missed the tackle, and Ed is gonna score a touchdown. But Chris Woods didn't come off the line full speed on the backside to make his block. His man, Benny Perrin, makes the tackle about the 18-yard line. We end up having to kick a field goal. A touchdown puts us ahead, 21-14, instead of 17-14, and might have made the difference in the ball game.

When Alabama scored in the fourth quarter, the game would have been tied, 21-21, instead of putting us behind. They were a lot looser, more confident team after they got ahead. Well, they beat us, 28-17.

I made a big issue out of Chis Woods not coming off the ball full speed and making his block, not only to him, but to the entire football team. There are five or six plays that decide any big ball game, and if every man isn't ready when the opportunity is there, you lose. Two years later, up in Birmingham, it's Chris Woods who throws the final blocks to spring Bo Jackson on both his long touchdown runs against Alabama in a game we win, 23-20. And the world keeps turning, and the same old truths stay with us. In 1990, Herbert Casey didn't block his man on the long run by Alex Smith, and Casey's man made the tackle 40 yards down field. It would have been a touchdown to put us ahead in a game we ultimately lost. So, we are still learning, all 11 players have to play on every down.

In 1981, when we went ahead, 17-14, in the fourth quarter against Alabama, there was a lot of jubilation on our bench, a lot of screaming and hollering and celebrating on the sidelines. I knew there was plenty of football still to be played. When Alabama scored to go back ahead, it was like letting the air out of a balloon. Auburn had been close before in the last nine years. We knew what it was like to be close. But when Alabama went back ahead, we didn't know what it was like to win, and it was over.

Myself? I wasn't intimidated playing in Birmingham. I'd coached at Alabama for nine seasons, and we'd won a lot of big games there. I hadn't had the same experience the Auburn people had had: losing eight, then it was nine years in a row, playing before a mostly partisan Alabama crowd despite the ticket split, with all the ushers, concessionaires, whatever, pulling for Alabama. I've said Coach Bryant was an intimidating man. He loved to walk out on the field before a big game, in front of a loud, partisan crowd that was watching every step he took, and intimidate the opposing coach. I met him at mid-field. I said, "Coach, before you say a word; you ain't gonna intimidate me; we're fixin' to get after your ass." What did he say? He just looked at me. And laughed. But I wasn't intimidated. Oh, I knew what Coach Bryant was telling his players at practice before our game. No question he wanted his football team to feel superior to Auburn. Well, my job is not to be intimidated by

ANYBODY, whether it be Coach Bryant, or Darrell Royal, or Bo Schembechler, or anybody else. I wasn't. I ain't. And I never will be. I guess it's partly the way I was raised. My daddy was never afraid of any man alive. Part of it has been my own experience. And part of it is because I just ain't afraid. Somebody said, maybe I'm not smart enough to be scared. That probably hit the nail on the head.

I said it would take a full 60 minutes to beat Alabama. And they proved it to us in 1981. But we were learning. We'd be more sure of ourselves in 1982. And who could have known we would have one of the greatest athletes ever to step on a playing field. To be honest about it, I knew. I had known since the weekend we lost to Wake Forest to open the season. We'll get to that.

Up ahead, there was also a bigger game within a game. Moving our half of the "Iron Bowl" to Auburn. We'll see how that came about, a little later. It's still the biggest single happening in my 11 years at Auburn.

So the 1981 season ended. We won five, lost six, the first losing record one of my teams ever had. But it is important to remember what those kids did. They put a foundation in our program that stands to this day. A tradition of effort and guts and belief in the Auburn family. I want to be sure they are remembered for that. The Auburn people weren't fooled by the 5-6 record. Auburn has good football fans. They know when the kids are playing hard, and when they are not. They can tell when they quit, and when they don't. These kids never quit. I think every Auburn person knew there were better days ahead. What kind of grade would I give myself for that first year? I'd say a B minus. We put a bottom in 'em. That'd earn the B. We should have won three more games. I believe that. But the foundation was built, with a lot of blood and sweat.

ALL THE RIGHT THINGS

Vincent Jackson. Bo. Now you can get on a plane and fly up to Canada and go fishing, way out on one of those lakes, and get you an old guide who has been working up there about 40 years, and you are gonna have a hard time finding one who doesn't know who Bo is. A lot of people consider him the greatest athlete of this century. I do. I mean, here was a high school kid, with very little training in track and field, who could run the hurdles, could high jump *6-10*, broad jump 20-something feet. Nobody was gonna outrun him for 100 yards. He goes on to win the Heisman Trophy in college football. He makes the Pro Bowl in the National Football League, playing part time, as a "hobby." He gets voted to the All-Star game in major league baseball, and they vote him the Most Valuable Player of that game, and he has played very few baseball games in his whole life.

I know there was Jim Thorpe early in this century. A great football player and track and field man, but he was just a journeyman player in baseball. And now Bo's career is maybe lost to a hip injury forever. But don't bet the house on it.

I think back to the first time I ever saw him; actually, that first time I saw him was not in person, it was on film. It was the spring of 1981, my first year at Auburn. Bobby Wallace was recruiting the Birmingham area for us, and he did a heckuva job. Of course, we had all been up in Wyoming the year before, and none of us had ever heard of Vincent Jackson. I guess Bobby had the high school send us a film of him. I know the first time Bobby and several of our coaches saw Bo in person was when he entered the State decathlon at Shades Valley High School in Birmingham. Of course, he won it. Bobby and the other coaches came back to Auburn saying this kid Jackson was a world-class athlete. He must have weighed about 190 pounds then. He went to McCalla High School near Bessemer, Alabama, which is near Birmingham.

The film his high school sent us was of the Dental Clinic game. It was played at the end of Bo's junior season in 1980. McCalla was playing Leeds High School, which is also near Birmingham. I have to stop a minute and realize Charles Barkley, the basketball player, was playing at Leeds about the same time, and both he and Bo came on to Auburn and became two of the most famous athletes of all time. Anyway, I was looking at the film of this game between McCalla and Leeds. This kid Jackson is out in front, leading a play—McCalla ran the wishbone, just like we did—and this kid blocks three people at one time; he just runs through 'em, stacks 'em up like cord wood; I'm not sure he ever hits the ground, just runs through the three of 'em. Oh, goodness! He was the type athlete we loved to coach in the wishbone. He was a halfback with a linebacker's mentality. In Bo's career at Auburn, if my memory is correct, every time that we threw an interception when Bo was on the field, *Bo* made the tackle. Every time. He would have been a world-class linebacker. In high school, Bo played defensive end and kicked and blocked and did about everything you could imagine on that team. He also ran for about 250 yards in that Dental Clinic game. I didn't realize it, but Bo also pitched and hit 19 home runs in just 24 games on the baseball team his senior year. I didn't know it, but it doesn't surprise me.

So, was Bo the most famous high school athlete in America, another Herschel Walker? No way. He was hardly known at all. How could that be? That's a good question. Herschel Walker's senior year, the University of Georgia put an assistant coach in an apartment in his home town the whole season; I guess they wanted to let Herschel know they wanted him, and Southern Cal and everybody that had a major team recruited him. I understand Bo didn't get listed among the 100 best high school players in America. That will show you how the crowd that gets up that list can screw things up. I don't guess in 11 years at Auburn we've had a handful of players on that list, but we've put more players in the NFL than almost anybody in college football. The biggest newspapers in Bo's own state, just 40 miles away, didn't rank him very high, about the fourth best prospect in Alabama.

How could that be? A decathlon champion, a sprinter, a world-class athlete, a complete football player, a baseball phenomenon; the Yankees offered him hundreds of thousands of dollars to sign a contract, and George Steinbrenner got furious when Bo wouldn't take it. How could the "experts" have overlooked Bo? Because all the "experts" only look at statistics. Herschel Walker gained more yards than any high school back in the history of Georgia, starting in the ninth grade.

Bo played on a wishbone team. He started on defense his junior year, but he didn't also start on offense until the season was two or three games under way. A little kid at the other halfback was actually the team's leading ground gainer. Of course, he had Bo blocking for him. And Bo's senior year, they had a good season, but they just missed the playoffs. Bo played defense and offense and blocked and didn't run up a spectacular number of yards. The recruiting "experts" were looking the other way.

Did I hold my breath, that the University of Alabama would realize what a phenomenal athlete he was, just 40 miles from their campus? I think, probably late, they did realize it. But it was too late. Coach Bryant never visited in his house. Bo did take one unofficial visit to Alabama, but he made only one official visit and that was to Auburn. Bo didn't visit a single out-of-state school. I think he made up his mind early he was going to stay in the state, and if he stayed in the state, he was coming to Auburn. Why waste the money of Notre Dame and Nebraska and Tennessee if he knew what he was going to do. I'm not sure any of those schools ever heard of Bo, maybe Tennessee. Bo is such a private person, visiting a lot of schools just wasn't his way of doing things. He wasn't seeking publicity. He didn't want to be bothered. When time came around for recruiting, he wanted to run track, then he wanted to play baseball.

I'm not sure how hard Alabama was working in recruiting, how seriously they took Auburn. They'd beaten us nine years in a row. Maybe Alabama was just gonna throw their hat on the table at the end of recruiting and get who they wanted. One of their coaches told Bo, maybe he could start for them his *junior year*. Another more highly-recruited player from Gardendale, tight end Jeff Parks, would also normally have gone to Alabama. But he didn't. He came

At the Heisman Memorial Trophy ceremony, with Bo's mother, Florence Bond, Sue, and Bo.

to Auburn. Bobby Wallace recruited him, too. We signed a lot of fine players in the winter of 1982. Of course, so did Alabama. I wouldn't say we signed more outstanding players than they did.

Back then, you could take a summer visit to a player's house. I visited with Bo and his mama, Florence Bond. I liked them both; I liked their sincerity.

A few pages back, I told you I knew Bo was coming to Auburn before our opening loss to Wake Forest. I did. Bo doesn't remember it, but he actually told me in a roundabout way that he was coming to Auburn. Bo and his mother, Florence, and his sister, Janice, came by our apartment before the Wake Forest game. The game we lost. Sue and I and the family were living in Sewell Hall at the time while we built a house. I'm not 100 percent sure exactly what I said to Bo. But it was something to this effect: "We need you in our program. You can be our Herschel Walker." And then I asked him, "How would you like to come here?" And Bo said, "I'd like that." He told me, "Coach, I want to play football, I want to run track, and I want to play baseball." I told him, "Fine." Those might not have been my exact words or his exact words, but they are close. After they were gone, I also told Sue, "Bo can be our Herschel Walker." I didn't doubt it. I wasn't looking at his high school statistics. I was looking at Bo, the athlete.

I think I asked Bo one other time if he was coming to Auburn, and then I never asked him again. He just showed up on signing date.

There had been a rash of discipline problems at Alabama Bo's senior year. That bothered his mother. But that wasn't the reason Bo came to Auburn. Bo saw we needed him. He could come to Auburn and play immediately. And he felt comfortable, he felt at home at Auburn. He made up his mind that's where he was coming, and that's what he did. He wasn't a wishy-washy kind of person. He never has been. He'll keep the public guessing; he always wants to challenge the odds, but what Bo says he will do, that's what he does.

I remember Bo's senior year at Auburn. There was a lot of speculation he was going to turn pro, in football or baseball. Agents might have been after him; I don't know; at that time, I was naive and ignorant about agents. I've learned more about 'em in later years; there are capable, honest agents, like my son, Pat, Jr., and there are the other kind. Bo came to me and said, "Coach, I've got a lot of people bothering me about whether I'm going to turn pro. I'm not going to say anything to anybody but you. But I'm coming back my senior year to play football. When the season's over, I'll see if I get drafted, and then I'll make a decision as to what I'll do." I didn't tell anybody what he told me, not even my coaches. Sure enough, about a month later, Bo said publicly he was coming back to Auburn. If you become a superstar, people—the media—have a tendency to put words in your mouth, to sometimes make you out to be something you are not. Bo was always just what he was, and did just what he said he would do. I could never have guessed that he would later turn down millions from the NFL to sign for hundreds of thousands with baseball. I couldn't have guessed, but it didn't surprise me either. And it turned out to be a brilliant business decision, playing both sports. But I expect Bo did it for the challenge, not the money.

I also remember the first day Bo stepped on the practice field at Auburn. The freshmen had reported. They were in shorts. Bo must have weighed 200 or 205 pounds his senior year in high school. By the time he got to Auburn, he weighed 222. He was a full grown man. And he was such a magnificent athlete. You're talking about a perfect specimen, for a football player or a baseball player or for anything you wanted to play. And I still think the one thing that nobody has ever given him credit for is how smart he is, how quickly he picks up techniques and adapts to anything new. I know this is true in football. It just came so easy for him. Wishbone, I formation, split backs, it didn't make any difference to him. He could do it all.

While he was at Auburn, and in the years since, Bo has become a skilled outdoorsman, a hunter and a fisherman. He didn't start out that way. I ran into Bo's roommate, Tommie Agee, one day, and he said, "Coach, last night I caught a record bass."

I love to fish; I was excited; I said, "How much did he weigh?"

Tommie said, "Two hundred and twenty-two pounds. I caught Bo."

They had been out fishing, and Tommie hung his lure in Bo's head. They had to take him to the hospital to get the hook cut out. Bo and Tommie were roommates and great competitors and great friends. Tommie now starts for the Dallas Cowboys.

Some of Bo's teammates had a bow and arrow at Auburn, and they were shooting it off the balcony at a target way down in the woods behind the athletic dorm. They swear Bo came by and picked up the bow and put an arrow in and hit the target on his first try. Bo's not only a skilled outdoorsman, he's an enthusiastic one. And sometimes his enthusiasm runs away with him like it does all the rest of us hunters. He was out at my farm a couple of years ago turkey hunting. We'd been out all day and hadn't seen a turkey. We went back to the cabin, and I was doing something, and Bo left in his truck. About 45 minutes later he came running in, all excited. He'd been driving across the dam on our lake, and there was a big tom turkey right at the end of the dam. Bo had been out trying to get close enough to shoot him. He said that turkey was "high as a horse." Now I'm still looking for that monster turkey.

I remember, as if it happened this morning, that first day on the practice field, the first time someone pitched Bo the ball, the first time he put his hands on it, he put it away and carried it *perfectly*. That's usually the first thing you have to teach a young running back, how to carry the ball, and you have to work a long time on it.

Somebody in high school had done a good job with Bo. And he is a quick learner who only has to do something once to get the hang of it. You just watched him work; you could see he wasn't afraid. There was nothing wrong with his techniques, of running, blocking, catching; you could see he was going to be a great football player.

The day the varsity reported, we put Bo at the starting right halfback. Two reasons: we didn't have anybody else, and we weren't scraping the bottom of the barrel with Bo. He belonged from the first day. I've been asked why I'm not afraid to play talented but untried young players. I'm not afraid if *they're* not afraid. Bo doesn't know fear. Which is why I'll never quite get over the article *Sports Illustrated* wrote about him in 1985. But we'll talk about that later.

We had Lionel James returning at left half. So we put Bo at right half. I don't know why some people made such a big deal of his playing right halfback instead of left halfback. One thing that all the people critical of playing Bo at the right half position didn't realize is that when you run to the left, 98 percent of the time you are running at the weakest defenders. And it didn't matter to Bo. He made long runs that first year against Georgia Tech, Florida, and Alabama. He would have won the Heisman Trophy at either halfback. In fact, he won it at tailback.

Anyway, from the first day, Bo Jackson and Lionel James struck up a very special and very close relationship which lasts, I guess, to this day. Little Lionel would knock their feet out from under them for Bo, and Bo would knock 'em on their backs for Lionel. I was looking at the film the other night of our 1982 game with Alabama, and there was Bo, blocking two Alabama players on Lionel's 14-yard touchdown run. Bo also became close friends with defensive backs Mark Dorminey and Bob Harris. Mark and Bob were leaders on our football team, and they knew early on that Bo would be a big part of it. And let me say that Lionel was also a great leader. Two running backs, Tim Jessie and, of course, his roommate, Tommie Agee, were also close to Bo.

Bo was not a boastful person. He was very confident, fun-loving, most of the time he was in a good mood. He had his good days and his bad days like everyone else. The kids liked him. In fact, Bo, when he became an upperclassman, got every vote for captain.

You never had to question if Bo was fooling around with drugs or whatever. He was always a clean-cut young man who stood for the right things. He still does. I understand in his own book, Bo says that he had a lady friend during those first two-a-days at Auburn. That they set some kind of "NCAA record." Bo certainly may have had his lady friends. But I have to smile a bit; he may have exaggerated in that book. People have been known to do that about that subject; but then it's dangerous to bet against Bo.

Bo Jackson was never, ever a discipline problem. He had that little episode his first season, before the Alabama game, when he sat up all night in the bus station, wrestling with the angels, trying to decide what he was going to do, stay in school and keep playing high-pressure, big-time football, or go home. He was depressed. Bo had a tendency toward depression. He had his tough times. Every college football player goes through them. I'll say again, every player quits some time, or thinks about it. Football is a demanding sport. It's not for everybody. Well, Bo stayed. We would never have beaten Alabama that year without him. I believe we would have built a winning football program at Auburn without Bo Jackson. Even with Alabama long established across the state. And with Georgia the National Champions in the next state. But it would have been tougher. And taken longer. And look at the career Bo has gone on to make for himself. And what he has meant to Auburn.

The only other sinking spell Bo had at Auburn in his four years came in 1984, after he was hurt in the Texas game. He hurt his shoulder and missed six games and got real depressed. He was in treatment, and he wasn't able to practice. And then he began to come to practice, but he couldn't take any contact. He came on the field late one day, and it just seemed to me he was a little less involved with the team than he should have been. I called him over, and I said to him, "Bo, I'll help you do anything you want to do. If you want to play pro football or pro baseball or whatever, I'll back you and support you 100 percent. But if you are going to play football at Auburn, you are going to have to do what the rest of the players do and do it on time." He took it like a man, and there was never another cross word between us.

Bo wasn't the kind of guy who was going to go out every day at practice and kill himself. He'd turn it up and turn it down. When he had his motor running in practice and felt like he needed some extra work to get in shape to be sure he was ready, he could turn it on out there and do things you couldn't believe you were seeing. His hand-eye coordination, his just pure speed. And then when it was game time, he was a great, great competitor. There's never

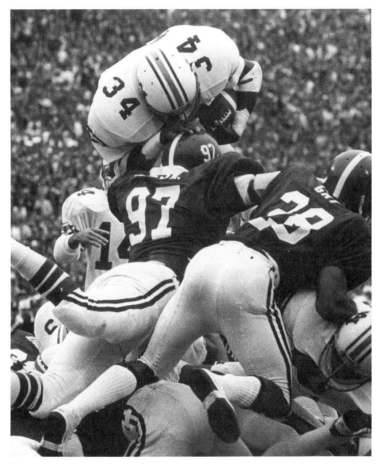

Bo over the top: I know there's never been a greater competitor.

been a better one. Most of the time, after we went to the I formation, Bo was going to get hit 30 or 40 times a game, because that's how many times he was going to get the ball.

Before a big game, how did Bo respond? Most often he went to sleep in the dressing room. Maybe that was a sign he was nervous, I don't know, but I know he'd get sleepy. All the great ones—Bo Jackson, O.J. Simpson, Jim Brown—they had their own way of building to the moment. Bo got sleepy.

I remember Bo's first year we were struggling against Mississippi State. Bo had hurt his leg, had bruised a thigh. We held him out of the first half. They hit a long touchdown pass to pull within three points, 17-14. And we put Bo in. He made a helluva block on Lionel's 32-yard touchdown run. Just Bo's presence on the field picked up the football team. We won the game, 35-17. Bo played the whole game against Alabama in 1985 with broken ribs. He was almost unstoppable. They beat us with the kid's 53-yard field goal in the last seconds. But I still think it was the greatest game that's been played between Auburn and Alabama since I've been here.

Of course, after Bo's senior year, he was drafted by the Tampa Bay Bucs football team. Tampa Bay thought Bo was the best football player in America—and they were right about that—and they drafted him No. 1. I doubt they would have wanted him to play baseball. My guess is they didn't talk to him about baseball or about what he planned to do after he got out of school. They might not have talked to him at all before they drafted him. I know they never called me. They made a mistake, in my opinion, not getting to know Bo better.

If they had called me, I could have told them exactly what Bo was going to do. Remember, he came back and played his senior year when everybody speculated he would go professional. And he told me he was going to play football his senior year, play baseball in the spring, see where he was drafted in both sports, and then make a decision what he would do. And that's exactly what he did.

What Tampa Bay didn't know was: you don't push Bo. You just don't push him. That's not the way you deal with him. You sit down and reason with him. He's a smart person. And he's got all the good qualities: he's smart, loyal, and he has a tremendous amount of self-pride and self-discipline. He wants to be in control of his life. He won't tolerate someone else being in control of his life.

In dealing with Bo over four years, I couldn't help but learn a lot about him, the way he thinks, how he reacts, what turns him on and what turns him off.

Of course, he shocked Tampa Bay and the NFL by turning down millions to sign with the Kansas City baseball team for several hundred thousand dollars. He even agreed to go to the minor leagues. But he didn't stay down there long. And then, of course, after he made it to the major leagues, he also signed a football contract with the Oakland Raiders, who had been smart enough to draft him in a middle round. I expect Al Davis was smart enough to talk with Bo. I don't know that. But I know how shrewd Al is.

Even playing part time, Bo had some tremendous games for

the Raiders. He helped turn their team around. A lot of people have questioned Bo's decision to play football, too. But why not play both sports if he was capable of doing it? Why not do something that nobody else could ever do? He's one guy who could do it. And that sets him apart from all the rest of the great athletes. That's Bo.

Not that he would ever boast about it. I have never, ever heard Bo boast in my life. He's got that old, country smarts about him. He doesn't have to brag on himself. Because other people are glad to do his bragging for him. That's something I learned coming up. An old timer told me once, he said, "If you ain't good enough for other folks to brag on you, you ain't good enough to say anything about yourself." Bo let his greatness speak for itself.

I've said more than once that I've found the kids I've coached everywhere to be great kids. And it's true. Bo Jackson is a great talent, and he is an outstanding young man. Auburn has had two Heisman Trophy winners, Bo Jackson and Pat Sullivan. Pat last year was elected to the College Football Hall of Fame. Both Pat and Bo stand for all the right things. Our rivals at Alabama, with their great football tradition, have never had a Heisman Trophy winner and never had a Bo Jackson. But it's not Bo's athletic success that makes him a hero of mine. It's the kind of person he is. You can see it when you are with him, one on one, and when you see him with his children and his wife and his mother. His mother died recently. I went to see her for the last time in a Birmingham hospital. Nobody knows how it hurt Bo to see her sick. And I'll say again, he stands for all the right things. Bo Jackson has a strong personality; everything about that personality is not perfect, but his heart has always been in the right place.

THE TIDE TURNS

Our spring practice in 1982 was probably not as tough as the year before. But we weren't running any baby-sitting service. We had one coaching change. Jack Crowe came from Wyoming to coach the offense. He replaced Alex Gibbs who had taken a job at Georgia. Jack had coached at North Alabama and Livingston. He was a good teacher, a smart coach. The time had come to settle on a quarterback. We settled on Randy Campbell. He'd been a third string wide receiver most of the last season. Randy wasn't very big. He wasn't very fast. Didn't have the strongest arm. But he was a winner. He wanted the ball in his own hands when the game was on the line. He did enough things well enough to win. Randy was from Hartselle. He didn't make the "100 Best Athletes in America" list in high school. But he led us to 20 wins in two seasons, and to two bowl victories, and to the Southeastern Conference championship. Randy won the job during all of spring training. But we had a big, tough scrimmage after the spring game, and his performance that day confirmed our decision that he would be the quarterback.

Spring training also showed us we needed plenty of help at positions other than quarterback. And a good bit of that help would have to come from the incoming freshman class.

The world didn't know it, but we had some instant help on the way from one member of the class we've talked about, Vincent Jackson. I mentioned Jeff Parks, a tight end. He came from sort of an Auburn family, but Gardendale boys had been headed for

Alabama for a long time. Getting Jeff was a big sign that Auburn was a school to be reckoned with in recruiting in Alabama. The biggest name we signed that winter of 1982 was a halfback from Enterprise, Alan Evans. He was the top-ranked back in the state. Alan didn't make it as a football player at Auburn. Or at Texas A&M. Football isn't for everybody. But Alan's back at Auburn, back going to school, trying to graduate. I guess I've helped Alan a whole lot more since he left the team here than I ever did when he was playing football. I'm still pulling for him to get his degree. We didn't sign so many famous kids that year, just kids who would prove they could play the game: running backs Tommie Agee from Maplesville and Tim Jessie from Opp and safety Tommy Powell from Greenville. Jeff Lott, a lineman from over in Gainesville, Georgia, and Steve Wallace, a tackle from Atlanta who starts for the San Francisco 49ers, became good players for us, and so did Ron Middleton, a tight end from Atmore, who's still playing for the Redskins. Running back Collis Campbell from Florence helped us win six straight games when Bo got hurt in 1984, and had a terrific night in the wild game at Florida State. Gerald Williams from Valley, another little-sought-after lineman, had a good career at Auburn. I doubt anybody much had heard of Gerald Robinson of Notasulga, who became a heckuva player and a top draft choice. I don't have room to call all their names. But I can tell you this, 17 true freshmen got in the game with Alabama that year, and we couldn't have won it without them. Five of 'em were in the game on the winning touchdown drive.

There weren't any miracles out there for Wake Forest in the '82 opener. I guess we gained 500 yards. Lionel James ran 67 yards for a touchdown. Ticket Manager Bill Beckwith says there were 59,350 fans there. I expect twice that many "remember seeing" Bo run 43 yards for a touchdown in his first college game.

We beat a good Southern Mississippi team. Barely. The score was 21-19, and they had first down on our 27-yard line when the clock ran out. Five more seconds and we lose. Not many realized at the time how good Southern was. They had the great quarterback, Reggie Collier. They went on to beat Alabama in Tuscaloosa. First time they'd lost at home in 57 games. I'm sure that loss had Coach Bryant thinking about retirement, even before they lost to us.

Tennessee. We had the first sellout in our first two years at Auburn. 73,600. That would be a disappointing crowd now for Tennessee. Johnny Majors always has a bunch of fast receivers.

Where does he get these guys? He got Willie Gault in Griffin, Georgia. Willie caught one touchdown pass for 38 yards and another one for 78. If we'd have had a longer field, he'd have run further. I said Majors is from the Old School. I believe the truth is, he would rather run the ball than throw it. But what he got into, in my opinion, is an automatic system on offense that allows the quarterback a lot of freedom on the field to change plays. Whenever you do that, you are going to get a lot more passing.

Does everybody remember that Lionel James threw a 43-yard halfback pass that day to Bo? Gregg Carr played a great football game against Tennessee. Made 16 tackles. We took it away from 'em four times. At Auburn, we've got to get back to making things happen on defense.

We held Nebraska, 7-7, until they scored just before the half on a long pass from Turner Gill. The second half they whipped us and kept on whippin' us. Mike Rozier is still running up in the pros for the Atlanta Falcons. And we still had a ways to go to be able to beat Nebraska. But by the end of the next year, we could have played Nebraska or anybody else.

Little Al Del Greco kicked six field goals to beat Kentucky. It's still a Southeastern Conference record. We shut out Georgia Tech, which always warms the heart of an old Georgia guard. Bo missed the game with a thigh bruise. But Lionel had 200 yards running, catching, running back punts. Carr and Chris Martin made 19 tackles. I enjoy seeing Chris still up there playing for Kansas City. I like to think Chris *became* a football player at Auburn, like a lot of other dedicated kids have done. We already talked about the Mississippi State win and the loss to Florida. Nobody in the league has had better football players than Florida in my 11 years here. And let me say this about Florida Field, I think it is the toughest place to play in the Southeastern Conference. Tougher than Knoxville, with its 95,000 seats. And Florida has recently expanded its own field to over 80,000. The fans are right on top of you. It's hard to hear. Sometimes it's impossible. And they always have good players. Noise doesn't help much without the athletes. They have replaced the artificial turf with grass. It's not quite as hot. But that didn't help us much down there in 1990.

Let me get ahead of myself again and say, I think the toughest of all places we have played since I've been at Auburn is Tallahassee. You must remember the home team is Florida State. But let's wait and talk about that in the middle of the wildest game I've ever been involved in as coach or player.

We didn't beat Georgia. We got as close as the 14-yard line. But I knew our day was coming the way we played them. I guess we've won four of the last five games with Georgia. They caught us last year in Athens in a game we had a chance to win. And we've had success recruiting in Georgia. Auburn fans and Georgia fans have both misunderstood our success recruiting in Georgia. I've said that several times. They both think we have outrecruited Georgia in their own state. It's not true. When we've gone head-to-head with Georgia for a kid who is interested in both schools, we have rarely won. We've mostly gotten kids who, for one reason or another, wanted to go out of state. Or, Georgia didn't want them. Tracy Rocker wanted to go out of state. We had to beat Notre Dame for Tracy, not Georgia. So he came to Auburn. We've gotten a few, like noseguard Benji Roland, who was interested in Georgia, and Georgia wanted him. Stacy Searels, a fine tackle, Georgia wanted him. But we've gotten a number of players Georgia didn't want, such as Trey Gainous. I think I mentioned earlier that Trey made two of the great plays in Auburn football. We'll remember those plays as we get to those years.

Auburn is only 35 miles from Georgia. It's a lot closer from south Georgia to Auburn than it is to Athens. Auburn has always gotten its share of good players from Georgia, and it always will. Some of my Georgia friends have said they are gonna lock the gate and keep us out of the state. But that won't happen. Everybody doesn't want to go to Georgia, fine school that it is with a great football tradition.

What about my own family, and the personal friends I grew up with, and played ball with? How has it been between us, with my being at Auburn? I didn't come to Auburn expecting all my Georgia friends to follow me. My closest friends, and family, have become Auburn fans, including my brothers who were captains at Georgia. I think that's natural. Some of my best hunting buddies have become Auburn fans. And then there are other old teammates and friends who are still very much Georgia fans, and we are still very much friends. I think of my old roommate, Tommy Ash. He's been in the real estate business since he got out of Georgia. He lives outside of Augusta. I see him and my Richmond Academy classmates from time to time. Sue and I go back for class reunions, that sort of thing. We went back a couple of years ago for our 50th birthdays. We turned 50, and all of our old friends turned 50, and we had a party. And we had a terrific time. That's the way it ought to be. I still love my home state and my alma mater. I even read Lewis Grizzard. Now I don't read everything he writes, and everything he writes ain't funny, but a lot of it is. Even when he writes how many days it is before Georgia has to play Auburn again. It'll get here soon enough for both of us, Lewis.

In truth, in my personality, my interests, my way of life, I'm more Auburn than I am either Georgia or Alabama. Auburn University's got agriculture, the veterinary school, business, engineering, the liberal arts, Auburn's got it all. And unless our own people are lying to me, a bigger percentage of Auburn applicants get accepted into law school and medical school than graduates of any school in the South except Vanderbilt. My oldest son is a lawyer, and he graduated from Auburn. I said earlier, a man's loyal to his paycheck. And he is. But Auburn has also become my home. I love it. And I don't mean ever to leave.

Where were we? Alabama. Oh, yes. That game at the end of the season. You remember that one. All of our six wins over Alabama have been big ones. But the biggest one was 1982. Because it was the first one.

There was the great crowd up in Birmingham. Cheerleaders urging 'em on. The two teams on the field, warming up. Bands playing. Flags waving. National television on the sidelines. And there was Coach Bryant coming across the field before the game. His old houndstooth hat on his head. I got a tape of his interview before the game. On national TV. I play it now and then. In fact, I'll put it on right now. They're asking him, "Coach, if Auburn beats you, are you going to retire?" Coach is saying, "I'm not going to retire. Period. If Auburn beats us tomorrow, I've already invited the University to look into the situation. I want Alabama to go UP. We have enough players to have a great team next year..." And the next afternoon, down on the field, amongst all that pre-game commotion, we talked. Coach Bryant and I were as close as we could be, with him coaching Alabama, and me coaching Auburn. If you were sitting here in my house, you could see this picture on the wall. It's of Coach Bryant and myself talking before the game. He told me, "Pat, I'm thinkin' about gettin' out." I said, "Well, if you're gonna get

Looking up to Coach Bryant before the 1982 Iron Bowl.

out, if you *promise* to get your ass out, I'll let you beat me one more year." He laughed at that. He was 72 years old. I was about to find out he could still coach a football team.

To tell the truth, I thought we'd win, going into the game. I'd already told our sports information director, David Housel—and he's the best one in the business, by the way—I'd already told David, if we won the game I was going to bring the team out of the locker room back on the field. It had been a long time since Auburn had won a big game, one of that magnitude. I knew our kids had paid the price to be winners. I wanted them to experience the moment. I also knew what a frenzy our fans would be in. I wanted to show them our appreciation for their support. I did not want to rub Alabama's nose in it. How did Alabama fans take it, our players coming back on the field after the game? I don't know. I didn't care.

I also didn't know Alabama was going to play its best game of the season.

We were ready to win the game. We were ready to win a game like that. And Alabama had been kinda struggling. I really thought they did a masterful job of getting their kids ready to play us. And they had a great game plan. They kept us off balance all day. At one time in the fourth quarter, they had thrown for 219 yards and rushed for 219 yards. That's a balanced offense. But we got two touchdowns off of turnovers and that was the difference.

Their quarterback, Walter Lewis, always gave us problems. He was quick, hard to hem up. And Coach Bryant always got more out of the passing game from the wishbone than anybody. They worked at throwing the football. They wound up with 507 total yards to our 257. But we had the most points. We took the ball away three times, twice on interceptions by Bob Harris and once on a fumble. The fumble came when Mark Dorminey nailed their pass receiver, Joe Carter, and Tim Drinkard caught the ball in mid-air and ran it back half the length of the field. Dorminey and Drinkard were two kids who weren't big enough or fast enough, but nobody said they weren't tough enough.

Lewis threw a 22-yard touchdown pass to Joey Jones in the first quarter. Lionel James came back with his touchdown run when Bo blocked two men. We held 'em to a couple of field goals in the second quarter. And Randy Campbell scrambled in for a touchdown. We had half as many yards, but we led at the half, 14-13.

Coach Bryant made a couple of questionable decisions in the game. They had it down close for an easy field goal early, and he went for it on fourth down and didn't make it. Big Doug Smith got in the way. Then, late in the game, when a touchdown puts us out of it, they had it on our goal line with a yard to go and kicked a field goal. That kept us in it.

After the half, they came back and scored on an eight-yard run by the kid from Mississippi, Paul Carruth. They went for two, but they didn't make it. That put the score, 14-19, against us. They got it back down and kicked a field goal and made it an eight-point game, 22-14. It would take two scores for us to win.

Now it's the fourth quarter. Bo breaks one for 53 yards. Del Greco cuts the lead to five, 22-17.

We hadn't stopped 'em much all day. But we stopped 'em this time. We took the ball on our 34-yard line. We had four minutes and 40 seconds left. We took it 66 yards in 14 plays. Randy Campbell hit Mike Edwards for 16 yards on third down and 14. I say again, if we hadn't made the drive that died against a great Georgia team, we wouldn't have had the confidence to take this one in.

I mentioned that five true freshmen were in the game on the last drive against Alabama. I know for sure Bo was there, and Jeff

Parks, and Steve Wallace, and Randy Stokes, and maybe Jeff Lott; he was in the game plenty that day.

We were deep in their territory when a critical call was made. Jeremiah Castille ran through the back of Chris Woods to make an interception that would have beaten us. Ain't no question it was a foul. It was a sound call. And it took more guts to make that call than any since I've been at Auburn. There are not many officials who would have had guts enough to make it. Billy Teas made it. Billy was a great running back at Georgia Tech. There were some out there on the same field with him who didn't make the call, who didn't have guts enough to make it.

Well, Bo goes over the top. And we lead, 23-22. But the game isn't over. They still have 2:26 to win it. They had come back and won many times in the past 10 years against Auburn. But this time the emotion, the determination along our sidelines was different. This time our players KNEW they could stop them. And they did. We played a 60-Minute Game, and we won it. If you were there that day, you remember the sound and the feel of what those kids accomplished. Nobody hates to lose more than I do. But I know this: winning isn't the most important thing, to me. It's *having paid the price* to win that matters. That can change a kid's life.

I do not remember what Coach Bryant said to me at mid-field. I was too excited. I do remember what I said in my interview after the game. I remember because I can put the video tape of it in the VCR. Like this: "...I'm mighty proud of our coaching staff and our people...it's been an unbelievable year for us. Our fans, against Georgia, and all year long, they have been encouraging us...hungry...They kind of pulled us out of it at the end." About that time the interview trailer lurched; it fell off one of its supports or something. I said, "...I don't think somebody is trying to blow us up..." But I didn't call for the FBI.

If you are laughing, you know what I mean, but we'll get to the 1989 Alabama game in a little while. I went on to say: "Alabama did a tremendous job. Coach Bryant and his staff, there is no question about it...I thought...based on what I've seen of Alabama's games...I thought they played as well today, or better, than they played all year. I was mighty proud of one thing...we *won the fourth quarter.* That didn't happen a year ago. There is no question Coach Bryant is still the greatest coach in the business. There is nobody that is even close to him. To be honest with you, I didn't think our effort

The win over Alabama in 1982 was our biggest because it was our first.

was that good...at times, they just outmuscled us..."

I guess I was still coaching at the end. But what if we hadn't won that game? How much tougher would it have been to build the program at Auburn? It would have been tougher.

A very short time after the game, Coach Bryant retired. I guess we were at the Tangerine Bowl, getting ready to play Boston College, when I heard about it. Was I surprised? He'd told me he was thinking about getting out. So I guess I wasn't surprised. When you are 72 years old, it's amazing that you are still coaching college football. It's an age when you have to prepare yourself.

I said Coach Bryant and I were as close as we could expect to be, coaching at the state's two biggest rivals. I think back to just that past summer of 1982. We were both playing in a charity golf thing in Memphis, to fight cystic fibrosis. I got ready to come back. We were flying right over Tuscaloosa. I asked Coach Bryant if he wanted a ride home. He said, "Yes, if you won't tell anybody I got in that damn Auburn plane." Of course, he was just needling me. From time to time, Coach Bryant would go on the wagon. But he wasn't on it that day. He drank a fifth of vodka from Memphis to Tuscaloosa. He could sober up with an act of will when he had to. I can tell you this, he was a sober sight for an opposing coach across a football field.

I was recruiting in Georgia. In fact, I was in the home of quarterback Jeff Burger in Cedartown. Somebody phoned me. Coach Bryant was dead.

Did I weep? I don't guess I did. But the memories that rolled through me. I went to his funeral, just as he had once gone to the funeral of his great rival, General Bob Neyland. In the church was a common bond of players who had played for him and coaches who had coached for him, and many who had coached against him. It occurred to me I was born lucky. I came along as a player in the last age of the men who bore the seeds of the game I love. I got to play for Coach Wally Butts. I got to know and love, growing up, Coach Shug Jordan and play against his greatest teams. I got to meet and respect and play against Coach Bobby Dodd. Men who knew the game and learned it from the men who knew Rockne and Heisman and Donahue and Wade and Alexander and the great coaches of the East. Men who knew what the game could mean in the life of a young boy about to become a man. Coach Bryant gave me my own chance to be a college coach. I often wonder what would have happened in my life if I had not played against his teams and seen, jaw-to-jaw, how well prepared they were, if I hadn't met him at the banquet in Washington, if I hadn't played service ball with three of his old players? Would he have hired me? Where would I be if I hadn't coached for him for nine seasons and learned from him and from all his assistant coaches and from all the coaches we played against? Just as I learned from my high school coaches and my college coaches and all the kids I played with and against. I'm grateful for the life I've had. And I try to carry the seeds of the game as best I can for the next generation.

FORGING A CHAMPIONSHIP

We had a terrific time in Orlando at the Tangerine Bowl. Now they call it the Citrus Bowl. It was Auburn's first bowl in eight years. We beat Boston College, 33-26.

Every time he stepped on a playing field, Bo Jackson seemed to do at least one thing you never saw before. Randy Campbell was a little late and behind Bo with a pitchout about their five-yard line. Bo reached back and caught it with one hand, tight-roped down the sidelines, with his feet in bounds and his head out of bounds, and just got the ball in the corner of the end zone for a touchdown. No other back alive could have made the play.

Randy had his best game passing the ball. Completed 10 of 16 for 177 yards and a touchdown. Was voted the offensive MVP. Lionel James had a 100-yard day. Mark Dorminey was his usual tough self and intercepted a pass. He was voted the Defensive MVP. We gained nearly 500 yards against 'em.

We won. But we all came away Doug Flutie fans. You couldn't help but like him. A terrific little player. You could hardly hem him up. And he had a big-time arm. And he was a competitor. I don't think people realized how good a team we beat in Boston College. Until they went on to upset Miami on national TV, on a Hail Mary pass from Flutie. They beat Alabama the next two years in a row, in Boston and Birmingham. And they beat an outstanding Houston team in the 1985 Cotton Bowl. By then there were a lot of Flutie fans. He won the Heisman Trophy in 1984, the year before Bo won it.

I enjoy great performances by players on the other team. I

don't enjoy their whippin' us. But to me, if you can't appreciate courage and performance in the other team, you are losing...you are missing the boat in college football. There are times I point out to our own players how hard somebody on the other team played against us. As I said, we were all Flutie fans. We knew how good he was, early on. I think of little Joey Jones of Alabama, and how hard he played. And Terry Hoage of Georgia, what a competitor he was. They had a linebacker at Georgia, Knox Culpepper, back in the middle eighties. I liked to watch him play. Of course, it was awesome to see Herschel Walker run the ball. Florida's had all those fine linebackers. The big, great ones, and the small kid, Jerry Odom, who gave us fits for two years. Tennessee's had so many fast receivers you can't remember them all.

I guess I have always had an affinity for the underdog, the little people. There weren't a lot of rich people around where I grew up. And the bigness in the community wasn't who had the most money. It was that person who showed up first in time of need, when there was a problem, a sickness, a death. Growing up in a rural environment, I came to appreciate the struggles and tribulations that the less fortunate go through. I don't mean to sound too high-flown. I still want to kick the other side when the whistle blows. Nobody, nobody, hates to lose more than I do. And I don't believe good coaches lose many games they ought not to lose. Luckily, it hasn't happened to us too many times. But as much as I despise losing, especially a game we ought to win, I can understand how the kids on the other side feel. I've been there myself too many times, especially when we were always playing the big schools on their own fields at East Carolina, and sometimes we whipped them. I think I said on the radio, after Southern Mississippi beat us two years ago, that "it ought to be a great experience for those boys to come in here and beat Auburn in front of 85,000 people." I meant it. Not that Southern was a poor team. Heck, they beat Alabama and should have beaten Georgia. And they beat us again in Auburn in 1991. But I've been there before, winning a game you had no business winning. I can understand what the feeling can do for a kid, can make him reach higher than he ever thought he could. I believe that's why you plant the seeds of the game.

Where were we? The winter of 1983. All the winter talk now is recruiting. What high school football player is going where. It dominates all the radio talk shows, the newspapers. I hate it. I think it's terrible. This time of year we ought to be excited about Tommy Joe Eagles's basketball program at Auburn and the basketball program at Alabama. I mean we have quality basketball programs. It's not that I don't love coaching in a state for which football is an obsession. But all the talk of recruiting is just that...talk.

I mentioned earlier how few members of this 1983 senior class were recruited by anybody but Auburn. And it's true. There are plenty of good football players in the South, and especially in our area of the South. Georgia is going to get good players; Florida, Alabama, Tennessee, LSU, the Mississippi schools, all of us in the Southeastern Conference are going to get good players. You better worry about teaching them the fundamentals, and the intangibles, and getting them to play together with one heartbeat, and getting them to play as hard as they can...every down. That's what you better worry about if you are going to win in this league.

But the subject of recruiting doesn't go away. It didn't in the winter of 1983. It was even said that the loss of one player to Auburn had something to do with Coach Bryant deciding to retire, even before he lost to Southern Miss and to us. That player was lineman Ben Tamburello. But it really wasn't so much a case of Alabama losing him. Here's what happened:

Tamburello grew up in Birmingham in an Auburn family. He really hadn't finished growing when he finished high school. So he went for a year to TMI prep school, up in Tennessee. To be truthful, we lost track of him at Auburn. Somehow Alabama connected with him, and I'm sure Ben went there and had a good visit. Coach Bryant was a very intimidating person. And Coach Bryant said, "How's your visit?" and Ben said, "It was good." And Coach Bryant said, "How would you like to come to Alabama?" And Ben probably said, "Yes, I'd like to come to Alabama." And Bryant said, "Good. We'll count on it." Those might not have been the exact words, but it was that kind of commitment.

But Ben had never visited Auburn, or LSU, two schools he was interested in. As I said, we got onto Ben late. He made a visit to Auburn. Thanksgiving weekend, I guess it was, after he visited Alabama. Then he went down to LSU. We got back with him the next Monday. He was in a mess, because now Alabama was *third* on his list. Auburn was No. 1 and LSU No. 2. As a matter of fact, my whole conversation with Ben and his family in the last day or so before he committed again was to try to persuade him to stay in the state. Because I knew Alabama wasn't any longer in the picture. Ben did commit to us. I know it was hard for him to call Alabama and tell them he was coming to Auburn. But he did. Possibly Ben's decision influenced Coach Bryant's decision to retire. I have no idea. Tamburello became a tremendous offensive lineman. And the days were gone, as I said, when Alabama just threw its hat on the table at the end of recruiting and got who it wanted.

Recruiting. The subject doesn't go away, so we might as well explore it a bit more. As you know, at Auburn, *only* our coaching staff recruits. Period. We love our alumni. But the NCAA rules are complicated. We don't want alumni talking to high school players about Auburn, much less recruiting them. And how do our coaches recruit? We sell our program. We sell Auburn. We sell the Auburn family. We work hard. But we want kids who want to come to Auburn. Each of our assistant coaches uses his own personality recruiting. If I have got to sit down and tell somebody how to recruit, then I've hired the wrong guy.

Just as we got Tamburello in 1983, we've gotten our share of players at Auburn. But we've never dominated Alabama recruiting in the state. In my opinion, Alabama is gonna sign good players every year. We depend on our out-of-state recruiting a little bit more than maybe Alabama does. But we are only 30 miles from Georgia. We feel we can sign three or four kids out of Georgia every year, and two or three out of Florida, maybe one from Tennessee or wherever. That's basically the way we operate. We signed a top kid from Louisiana in 1991, a halfback, Roymon Malcolm, a good prospect, who did not pass his ACT test but came on to Auburn. In fact, he was Most Valuable Player in the Louisiana All-Star Game. But we don't try to go to Texas. Why go to Houston when we've got a prospect in Montgomery?

We took a chance on a young man, Otis Mounds, a promising halfback from Ft. Lauderdale in 1990. Steve Dennis recruited him. He'd fallen in with the wrong crowd as a kid, got into trouble with the law. But he's taken responsibility for his own life. And he's been a fine young man in our program. Otis worked his way into our playing rotation in 1991 and has since moved to defense and has a chance to be an outstanding football player. Last year, four of his former Dillard High teammates decided, independently of Otis, and of each other, for that matter, to come to Auburn. I'm sure the fact

Otis was comfortable at Auburn influenced them. These four kids are mentally tough, and all have a chance to be outstanding players for Auburn. That was a rare happening, signing four quality kids from one high school team. I'm not sure I know of a similar case.

I mentioned Auburn has signed more unsought-after high school players who became GOOD college players than any school I know of. I also mentioned Aundray Bruce of Montgomery. He was not recruited by anybody but Chattanooga. He was not a good high school football player. But he was a good athlete. He was voted MVP of the state basketball tournament. He became an All-America player at Auburn.

I don't mean to say we have all the answers. We don't. I do think what you see now are youngsters coming out of high school, who've seen Auburn on television seven or eight times a year— we've played on TV 67 times in the last 11 years. They've seen Auburn win championships and go to bowl games. They are just as excited about Auburn football in this state as they are Alabama football. I think of John Hudson. He grew up in Tennessee. Alabama recruited him hard in 1986. They told John, you go to Auburn, you'll never beat Alabama. John came to Auburn and never lost to Alabama.

The schools are different, Auburn and Alabama. The kids who choose between the two schools are a little different. Now the children of some Alabama graduates choose to go to Auburn. And the children of some Auburn graduates, much to their parents' dismay, choose to go to Alabama. I've been at both schools. They are both quality institutions. I think that kids who come to Auburn—I'm not only talking about football players, I'm talking about average students—in my opinion, they choose to come to Auburn for most of the right reasons. It's not the social life. We certainly have our share of that and social life is important to you at that age. But fraternities, sororities, the social scene are not the main reason kids come to Auburn. Kids who grow up in conservative families— I don't mean politically conservative; I mean families of old fashioned values—kids who feel comfortable in a small town environment, who are seriously looking for an education to make something of themselves, these kids tend to like Auburn. And grow to love it.

But Auburn football is not for everybody. We are careful to see that any recruit, when he visits us, spends time with our players. It's hard for a kid to come in and spend a weekend with us—with our players, our assistant coaches, with me—and leave without his having a pretty sound opinion of what our program is all about. A lot of times these kids will eliminate themselves, and do us a favor in the process. They will find an easier route, find a program that does not have quite as much discipline as this one, where they don't have to work quite as hard. And does that frighten me? No, no, and no. Because we realize that some of the good athletes, some of the good prospects are going to come to Auburn *for* those reasons, *for* that discipline. You can ask our players. We don't water down the demands of our program to young athletes we recruit.

Let's get back to 1983. Of course, Bo played baseball in the spring. I don't know if that hurt him some in football. But I promised him he could do it. I think now we can all see he was wise to play both sports.

That fall, no college team in America had a stiffer challenge than we did. Our schedule was voted the toughest in the NCAA. We only had to play *eight* bowl teams from the season before. We played Maryland with Boomer Esiason; we played our first game with Florida State and it was everything all the others would be; we caught Texas, which would go undefeated, untied, and ranked No. 1 until the Cotton Bowl; and we played a great Florida team and a terrific Alabama team and a Georgia team in Athens that *beat* Texas in the Cotton Bowl and cost them the National Championship. Don't forget Tennessee in Knoxville, Georgia Tech in Atlanta, Kentucky in Lexington, and we opened with Southern Mississippi, which went to a bowl after beating Alabama the year before. The first five teams we played had open dates the week before our game. And that has gotten to be a tradition, scheduling an open date the week before you play Auburn. Finally, as I mentioned, we've scheduled an open date in the middle of our own season.

An amazing thing...we played that tough '83 schedule and only *three* of our starters missed a total of only three games. We've had our share of injuries at Auburn. But I think we stay as healthy as we do because of the way we work in the off season. And how hard we go at it in practice. A young man learns to protect himself out there on our practice fields. He better, if he's gonna survive. It also helps that we practice and play on grass fields. But football is a collision sport. You have injuries.

And in the pre-season of 1983, we had more than an injury. We had a death. Senior Greg Pratt suffered heat stroke and died. Greg's death affected me more than any one incident that has happened in my life. In some ways, it was more difficult that my daddy's death. My daddy had lived his life and had been sick a long time.

We were testing the physical condition of our players. They were down on the baseball field running four 440-yard dashes, against time. We are awfully careful about the effect of heat on our players now. And we were awfully careful then. Greg was struggling on his fourth 440. With two teammates helping him along, he made it. But he was struggling. Our trainers immediately packed him in ice. They got him up to the coliseum and called for an ambulance. That's when I got word that Greg was in serious trouble. The medics came, but Greg never regained consciousness. It was heart breaking.

I think you can ask any kid who played on the 1983 team, and he will tell you that the pain of Greg's death helped bond that team together. But I don't think that's unusual. I think it's typically American. The way the love and courage and ultimate death of Chuckie Mullins affected all his teammates at Ole Miss.

Greg had come to Auburn as a transfer. His home was Albany, Georgia. He was a wonderful young man, studying math education. He played in 1982. He was a good player. He wasn't a great player. He was scheduled to be our starting fullback.

We took the whole team to Albany for the funeral. Greg had a brother and other kin. But his mother was the strong force in the family. I can't tell you how terrible, how helpless we all felt for her.

I don't think there is any way to rationalize, to justify the death of a young athlete. But I know this: I know that Greg Pratt loved his family, and he loved his teammates, and he loved his coaches, and he loved Auburn, and he loved football. And all of those people, and Auburn, loved him.

Well, the 1983 season finally started. And the "Little Train," Lionel James, ran over Southern Miss in our opener. He gained 172 yards, including an 84-yard run. Gregg Carr got off to a great season. He made about 15 tackles. Gregg was one of the smartest linebackers, smartest players we've ever had. We beat a good team, 24-3.

I wish we could have played Texas later in the season. We could have played anybody later in the season. I wish I would have known the Texas team was going to be throwing up its guts in the heat in the fourth quarter. I might have been more patient when we got behind. All those are wishes. What happened was, they beat us, 20-7. It was a great Texas team, with about 18 or 20 future NFL players on it. We got behind, 20-0, at the half. They returned a punt over 50 yards and kicked a field goal. Our defensive back fell down, and they completed an 80-yard touchdown pass. We were struggling. We held them to only 20 yards total offense the second half. But it was too late.

How do you get a team over the shock of a big loss early in the season? You've got to immediately set new goals, and turn your attention to reaching them. We lost to Texas. We could as easily have lost to FSU, Maryland, Florida, Alabama, Georgia, any one of six or seven teams.

Next up was Tennessee. In Knoxville. It didn't look good. We could run the ball. But Randy had completed only three passes in our first two games. He hit 10 of 16 up in Knoxville. That's what winners do, when you got to have it. But it was close at the half. We led, 10-7. Bo scored for us, and they threw a 30-yard pass to one of those burners, Tim McGee. You can change their names, but Johnny always has one, or three, or five of them who can run and catch the football.

They get ready to punt in the third quarter, and we send out a little fellow to return it, about 5-10, 170 pounds: Trey Gainous. How did he come to be out there in all that noise, him a true freshman?

Frank Orgel and I went down to Americus, Georgia, two years before to look at a quarterback who later went to Tennessee. I think his name was Sims. We watched his team play Cairo, Georgia. Trey Gainous was a junior on that Cairo team. And he had two long punt returns that night for touchdowns. He wasn't big. He wasn't that fast. He had a knack. I told Frank that night, "You go ahead and recruit this kid Gainous. I don't care how big he is or whatever."

So, Trey's first year we put him out in front of 95,000 fans at Neyland Stadium to return a punt in a close, tough game. He breaks it up the middle 81 yards for a touchdown. It was Auburn's first punt return for a touchdown in *nine* years. It was the fourth longest punt return in Auburn history. And it turned that Tennessee game upside down. We've got a young freshman around here now, Thomas Bailey, from Enterprise, who might break the punt return record. But he'll have to do it on the field. He can't do it in this book.

Trey Gainous made two of the biggest plays ever at Auburn.

(A funny thing. I was talking about Trey Gainous for this book a couple of weeks ago. And the two sentences about Thomas Bailey were typed last Thursday. On Saturday, Bailey caught a punt against Ole Miss and, with some solid blocking, took it back 83 yards for a touchdown. It broke the game open on the field and in time to get in this book, too.) As I said, I'm not afraid to play a freshman, so long as *he's* not afraid. There was no fear in Trey Gainous or Thomas Bailey. In 1991, Trey came back to Auburn as a graduate assistant.

We ran for nearly 300 yards against a tough Tennessee defense. Gerald Robinson had a big game, made four tackles for losses. There wasn't any "jinx" up there in Knoxville for Auburn that day. We won, 37-14.

The next week, we didn't get much relief. We played the first of our seven games with Florida State. All seven of those FSU teams were outstanding. Our kids did a heckuva job winning four of those games. We could have won almost every one of 'em. We could have lost almost every one of 'em, too. FSU coach Bobby Bowden, I think, is as good an offensive coach as there is in the country. His teams have always done a great job with the kicking game. They block punts and run 'em back, too. Since Mickey Andrews has been down there, they've been a good defensive team. I'm smiling. They had some great defensive teams when my coach Reggie Herring played linebacker down there in the late seventies and early eighties. Bobby and I have always gotten along. I know he respects Auburn and our football team. And we have the same kind of respect for Florida State. I'm proud to have his son, Tommy, on our staff today. It takes time to establish a new offense, but our fans will learn there's a lot of his daddy in Tommy.

Playing FSU is not for the faint of heart. Randy threw touchdown passes to Jeff Parks and Tommy Agee. Del Greco kicked two field goals. But Florida State scored again with less than seven minutes to play, and we were behind, 24-20.

A trivia question: who returned the kickoff? Bo Jackson, the best we had. We didn't ask him to return many. He had to carry it too many times from scrimmage. Bo got to the 26. We had 73 yards to go. Twice we converted fourth down and long. Once, Randy hit Ed West to the 32. And then, on the second fourth down, Randy swung it out to James for 15 yards and a touchdown. We led, 27-24. Against FSU, no lead is safe until you're in the showers. They always have a great quarterback. Kelley Lowrey passed them quickly to our 26-yard line. Donnie Humphrey was hurt, playing on a bad knee. But the winners play when they hurt. Donnie pressured Kelley who hurried the ball directly to Gregg Carr who intercepted it and fell on it. We had won three out of a tough four games, and now we were in the national rankings.

We played a night game in Kentucky. Little David King picked off a pass and ran it 40 yards for a touchdown. It put us ahead, 14-7. They never got that close again. I said every time Bo stepped on the field he did something you couldn't believe. He took the ball that night on the 19-yard line and ran over half the players Kentucky had for a touchdown. It was just astounding. It was like one of those Kentucky thoroughbreds coming down the home stretch. He couldn't be stopped. We had a damn good team. They couldn't just watch Bo with 11 guys. Jerry Claiborne did a good job at Kentucky. He didn't win a championship, but he got them competitive again.

We'd played so many tough games in a row. Facing other teams all rested up with open dates. We were tired. And like I said, playing Georgia Tech was not the same anymore since they got out of the conference. Our kids had a let down. I had to jump 'em at the half. Their little ol' quarterback, John Dewberry, hit the tight end on a play action pass for a touchdown. They went in the locker room ahead, 10-7. We had a little session. About pride. About the Auburn way of football. I guess I got their attention. Tech only got 107 yards and three points the second half. We won, 31-13. Collis Campbell and Bo scored and Randy hit Chris Woods with a long touchdown pass. It will always mean something to me, an old Georgia guard, to beat Georgia Tech, especially in Atlanta. I have tremendous respect for their football tradition.

You forget how many long plays Lionel James made in 1983. The second play of our game the next week with Mississippi State, he ran 74 yards for a touchdown. Tommy Powell intercepted a pass to set up another touchdown. We pounded out a win the rest of the way. A name to remember scored one of our touchdowns: Fullwood, Brent Fullwood, from St. Cloud, Florida. We were gonna hear from him in years to come.

Auburn-Florida. It was one of the great football games ever played in Jordan-Hare Stadium, or in any stadium. Pro scouts say there were more future outstanding professionals on the field that day than have ever played in a college football game. More than 50 players off those two teams signed pro contracts.

Bo was sick all week with a stomach virus. But he played one of the greatest games of his career against a tremendous team, which only lost to us and Georgia. First time we had the ball, Bo ran 55 yards for a touchdown. Florida had three No. 1 draft choices in their backfield: fullback John L. Williams, and running backs Lorenzo Hampton and Neal Anderson, a great star with the Chicago Bears. They had a durn good quarterback in Wayne Peace, who threw a touchdown pass to Rick Nattiel, who is still catching 'em up in the pros. Randy scrambled in for a touchdown, and James ran in from the 17-yard line and we led, 21-7. Neal Anderson appeared to score,

Lionel James, number 6, "the Little Train": You forget how many long runs he made in 1983.

but he was hit at the goal line and lost the ball in the end zone. The official ruled it was a fumble. I think it was Billy Schroer who made the call. Coach Charlie Pell was upset. But films of the game clearly showed it was a fumble. Bo didn't take any chances. The next play he ran 80 yards for a touchdown. He gained 196 yards that day. We won, 28-21. You might live a long time and not see that much talent on the same field again.

How is it that Miami, Florida State, and now Florida all have such powerful football teams when they once were ordinary football teams? Simple. The growing population of the state, the high caliber of high school football being played. It used to be said that Florida boys weren't tough enough. Nobody has said that who has played those three teams lately. They get a little different kind of kid today. Of course, many of them are black kids. I think they are playing with hungrier athletes. And now with Steve Spurrier at Florida, and Dennis Erickson at Miami, and Bowden at FSU, all three schools have outstanding coaches.

Now all we had to do was beat a terrific Maryland team. Boomer Esiason hadn't been sacked all year. We sacked him on the first play of the game and on the last play of the game. Donnie Humphrey recovered the ball in their end zone on the last fumble. We needed all the pressure we could get to win, 35-23. I enjoyed visiting with my old rival, Coach Bobby Ross, before the game. I'm glad I didn't know how good Boomer Esiason was or I wouldn't have enjoyed it at all. I think you know by now I believe Bobby is one of the best coaches in the country. He did a great job at Georgia Tech, and I'm sure he'll do a fine job in the pros. Tommy Agee, Lionel James, and Bo Jackson each ran for more than 100 yards. Sometimes I miss the old wishbone offense. But I don't miss it when we need to throw a pass. We pressured him, but Boomer passed for 355 yards. I didn't think the game would ever end. We even went for a first down deep in our own territory to keep Boomer from getting his hands on the ball.

Now we had to go to Athens and play unbeaten Georgia. How was it for me, returning again between the hedges where I had played? Well, I never do carry sentimental feelings into a ball game. You can't afford to let yourself do that. You can't let anything distract your concentration, your ability to give your football team the best chance to win that you can.

It was a tough game. Close. Hard-fought. Georgia was trying to win its fourth straight Southeastern Conference title. We were in contention. To be truthful, we dominated the game. We rushed for 261 yards to their 51. But their defense wouldn't let us put 'em away. Coach Dooley's teams have won a lot of games by hanging around and pulling them out in the last seconds. They went on to do just that to No. 1-ranked Texas in the Cotton Bowl.

Quency Williams jumped on a Georgia fumble inside their 25. Lionel scored our only touchdown in the first quarter from about the four. Al Del Greco kicked two field goals in the second, and we never scored again. Georgia took the ball deep in our territory after the half. But on fourth and one, Doug Smith stopped 'em behind the line, just as he had done at Alabama the year before. Georgia finally scored with about two minutes to play. Then they did a heckuva job recovering an onsides kick. If they could score, they could win. We threw them for four yards of losses in four plays. Jimmie Warren, who broke up a pass for a touchdown against Tennessee, broke up a fourth down pass in Athens. And we won, 13-7.

It was pretty simple up in Birmingham. We win, and we're the undisputed conference champions, and we play in the Sugar Bowl.

Of course, Alabama had something to say about that.

They had a new coach, Ray Perkins. I can't say I was entirely surprised he left the job as coach of the New York Giants. He had called Auburn about the job here. And I'm sure he liked the idea of going back to his old school as head coach. I think he even owned property in Tuscaloosa. In New York, the coach of the Giants can never get away from the press. And if you know Ray, you know he has something of a thin skin. He certainly went back to Alabama with the idea of following Coach Bryant in his own way. I've said before how tough I think it is to go back and coach at your old school.

I like Ray. He was a great football player. He wasn't a natural receiver; he made himself a receiver. And he was a fierce competitor. He was late getting to college. When I coached at Alabama, Ray and I were about the same age. He might have been older than me. He was married. He was the kind of guy who always had something going. He would fix up old cars and sell 'em. He once sold me a pickup truck.

When Ray took the job, I visited with him and said the same thing I said to Coach Bryant, and later, to Bill Curry: "Look, your job is tough enough at Alabama; I don't need to make it any tougher." I said, "My job is hard enough at Auburn; you don't need to make it any harder. If there is a problem with Auburn, call me. If there is a problem with Alabama, I'll call you." We did that. Ray and I always got along. He was doing it the best way he knew how. And I was doing it the best way I knew how. We had a conflict once in a while. It didn't keep us from being able to communicate, to talk to each other. After Ray went back to the pros, we visited; he came here to Auburn to scout players for his Tampa Bay team. There weren't any real "public" problems between Coach Bryant and myself, or between Ray and myself. Now, I didn't agree with everything Ray said. And I'm sure he didn't agree with everything I said. But we didn't have any public flare-ups. I can't say I was shocked when Ray suddenly resigned at Alabama after the 1986 season and went back to the NFL. I think he got several million dollars for going down to Tampa. And I suspect the press and the fans and a lot of things about college football annoyed him. I was sorry to see him lose his job in Tampa in 1990. I wish him the best at Arkansas State.

Speaking of coaches getting along...there used to be a tradition in the SEC of coaches settling their differences among themselves. I remember my first Southeastern Conference meeting. I think it was in Destin, Florida. Coach Bryant went to that one. Coach Dooley told me they used to end the meetings by running everybody out but the head coaches, and they'd get across from one another and say, "You SOB, you know you did this or that..." They'd talk about whatever was bothering them and try to settle it in the room.

I have to tell a golf story on Ray. I'm not much of a golfer. I enjoy playing *at* it. And I think Ray is a typical golfing coach, kind of erratic, but he's a pretty good player. Most football coaches don't have time to be very consistent on the golf course. One day we were both playing in Birmingham in a charity event. I forget the course, maybe Inverness. I know Bubber Majors and Mailon Kent and Earl Morgan were on my team. Perkins was playing with some of those hot shot Alabama golfers. We were playing right behind their team in a scramble; everybody plays the best drive, the best second shot, everybody hits the same putt, that kind of thing. Well, we were gonna get up a little bet, the money would go to the charity. And Perkins says, "Let's make it a thousand dollars." So we did. His team finished something like 18 under par. And they were sitting in their carts around the 18th hole. We were tied with 'em. And we had about a 20-foot putt. And I lucked that thing in the hole, and hot damn, you should have seen Ray's team wheeling those carts out of there. I don't know if they've paid the $1,000 to charity yet.

Ray is a good football coach. I think for a while he ran the offense and was head coach, too, at Alabama. I got to tell you, I remember his teams more for their defense than their offense. I'm smiling while I say that. But, Lord, they had some great defensive football players: Jon Hand, Cornelius Bennett, Curt Jarvis, Willie Wyatt, Derrick Thomas, maybe Derrick was a freshman under Ray. Now they weren't unarmed on offense, with Walter Lewis, and backs like Ricky Moore and Paul Carruth, and Bobby Humphrey, and Gene Jelks, and receiver Joey Jones, and the great field goal kicker, Van Tiffin.

When the 1983 game started, the sky looked awful. We were supposed to have bad weather for the kickoff, but it didn't come...yet. But the wind was blowing. As it turned out, we got the wind in the first quarter, and then it turned completely around when the front came through, with rain and lightning and tornado warnings—but I don't think two people left their seats—and we had the wind in the fourth quarter, too. It was that kind of night.

Alabama had a good football team. But Bo Jackson had one of the greatest nights of his career. And we played strong defense, especially in the second half, when they didn't complete a pass, and in the fourth quarter, when we shut 'em out. Vic Beasley intercepted two of their passes.

Bo ripped off runs of 69 and 71 yards for touchdowns. He started to his left on the first one, and reversed his field, and used all his great speed to get outside. You remember Chris Woods made the last block on both runs. The first play after Moore ran 57 yards for a touchdown to put Alabama ahead 20-16, Bo broke the 71-yard touchdown. It was in the third quarter and it was the last score of the game. That night, Bo averaged over 12 yards a carry. He gained 256 yards. Al Del Greco kicked two field goals. Randy Campbell only threw 14 passes. Completed five. Best of all, he didn't have any intercepted.

I remember in the dressing room, after the game, Greg Pratt's old roommate, Terry Walker, stood up and said, "We've got one more to win for you, Greg: the Sugar Bowl." Fifty years after that 1983 season, any kid who played on the team will remember Greg Pratt.

I said Ray Perkins and I had no big public disputes. We didn't. I also confessed I didn't agree with everything he said. Ray can say some strange things. One year he said that I couldn't understand the magnitude of the Auburn-Alabama game "because I hadn't played in it." What did I think of that statement? I thought it was bull—baloney. I only coached in nine of those games at Alabama, and I've coached now in 11 of them at Auburn. Besides, it doesn't make any difference if it is Auburn-Alabama, or Georgia-Georgia Tech, or East Carolina-The Citadel, or it could be Parker and Carver High Schools. It's the same life and death feeling. Perkins tried to build the game up as high as he could, as big in the life of the people in the state as he could. He said it was bigger than the Super Bowl. I know it was big enough to give me the hives. I could have made an even bigger something out of it, a monstrosity. What it boils down to is blocking and tackling, just a football game played by two good teams on a 100-yard field, each fighting its ass off to win. That's what it is. The newspapers and the television, the media, try to build it up to be more than it is, but that's what it truly is, a football game. After our loss in 1985, I decided to take the opposite approach to Ray. To prepare for it and play it as a college football game. No more, no less. And I'm glad I did. But we'll talk about that later. Let's go to New Orleans and the Sugar Bowl.

Goodness knows our kids had earned the trip. They had caught pure hell our first spring and into the fall of 1981; and they learned how to win. Auburn hadn't been to the Sugar Bowl in 12 years.

We were going to play Michigan, a great name in college football. It wasn't a great Michigan team. But it was a durn good one. I would have loved to have been playing for the National Championship. Our team was good enough to play anybody. But we lost the game to Texas early in the season. Still, we were undisputed SEC champions. And to be truthful, that's a heck-of-a-lot more important to me than only concerning myself with the National Championship. All of us would love to win it. Every team in America would love to win it. But we've got 10, now 12, teams in the Southeastern Conference, and one of them is going to the Sugar Bowl *every year*. To me, that's a more realistic goal. If we get to the Sugar Bowl, or if we are in contention for it every year, then we are going to be successful at Auburn. And maybe one year we can go down there and play for the National Championship.

Bo Schembechler was the famous coach of the Michigan team. I didn't know him then. But I knew *of* him. I had studied his teams and admired him as a coach. I got to know him in New Orleans and afterward. He came down to Auburn to our coaching clinic. He was just like I thought he would be, just Bo. No pretense. A man who said what he believed. And his team played just as tough as I thought it would.

Our kids had a great time. And conducted themselves as gentlemen as they always do. Wherever we go, people that fly the planes and run the hotels and the restaurants always brag on our kids. They don't just represent Auburn on the playing field.

One thing I remember...it happened on Thursday, the day before the game. We went out to loosen up. I asked the seniors, I said, "This is your last time, men. Have you got anything you want to share with your teammates?" There was a bunch of leaders among those seniors. They'd seen the hard times. They were a hungry group. Each of them said something, what being in the football program, what Auburn had meant to them. And it came around to big Doug Smith. Doug was a smart guy; he stuttered, but he was a smart guy. He said, "I want to tell y'all, I had a big advantage over the rest of you, comin' to Auburn. A lot of you came to Auburn for different reasons. And I know one 'em was you *hoped* to win. When I came to Auburn, I *knew* we were gonna win. I played for Coach Dye and his coaches at East Carolina." I guess it doesn't read like so much on the page. But the way he said it went through me, and I'll never forget it.

I was looking at the film of that game a couple of weeks ago. Talk about a hard-hitting game. They played hard. We played hard. Al Del Greco kicked a 23-yard field goal with 23 seconds left. He'd kicked two others in the second half. We didn't score a touchdown, but we won the game, 9-7. And it was just that close. Bo ran for 130 yards. He was voted MVP. Our last drive went 60 yards in 16 plays.

We finished the season, 11-1. Miami upset Nebraska in the Orange Bowl, and was voted No. 1, with Nebraska No. 2. Both had lost a game, the same as us. The *New York Times* uses a computer to figure the No. 1 team. They take into account how tough the schedule was you played. They picked us No. 1. If we ever win a National Championship in the polls, I'm gonna be tempted to claim two, including that one from the *Times*. I think we could have played anybody by the end of the season.

Auburn was back. We've averaged winning 8.5 games each of the last 11 years, and seven times we've won nine games or more. Starting in 1982, we played in nine straight bowl games. Of course, in 1991, we had our second losing season in 11 years. But the most important year in football is always next year. Building the next team is what keeps me young as a coach. And we've got our work cut out for us in 1992. I'm looking forward to it, and so is my staff.

ON THE HIGH GROUND

The next two seasons were like bookends. Each year, we had success on one end and disappointment on the other. We won 17 games. But we lost the last one each year to Alabama. We beat Tennessee. We lost to Tennessee. We beat Georgia Tech, and Georgia, and Ole Miss, and Florida State, twice each; you have to be proud of that. Both Florida State games were wild ones, and the one in 1984 was the wildest I've ever coached in or even seen. Florida beat us twice. We won the Liberty Bowl. We lost the Cotton Bowl. Bo won the Heisman Trophy. We played a lot of big games in a lot of great arenas. I say again, I don't know why the losses stay in your mind so much longer than the wins.

We agreed to play Miami in the Kickoff Classic outside of New York. I think it was a good decision, even though we lost the game, 20-18. We got to play the defending National Champions. The school got nearly one million dollars. We were on national TV. Our players got a rare trip to New York. I hope they enjoyed it and remember it the way I remember going up there on the *Look* Magazine All-America trip.

We didn't play well on defense against Miami. And they had a pretty fair country passer, Bernie Kosar, now with the Cleveland Browns. He passed for 345 yards. We actually led the game, 15-14, in the second half. Pat Washington threw a touchdown pass to Clayton Beauford, and we kicked three field goals. We had the ball at their 46 with a chance to win in the last two minutes, but we fumbled a pitchout. Bo gained 90 yards, but he sprained his ankle.

That sprained ankle might have cost Bo a separated shoulder the next game against Texas. Their All-America safety Jerry Gray pulled him down from behind. I can't recall anybody else ever catching Bo from behind. He wasn't full speed. How tough was Bo? He carried the ball three more times, even scored a touchdown they called back before he told us his shoulder was separated. We turned the ball over three times and spotted them a 14-0 lead. They finally beat us in Austin, 35-27. We had been picked No. 1. And we were 0-2. But we'd played two strong teams on the road.

They always pick you according to how you finished the year before. We lost a lot of good football players from 1983: David Jordan, Pat Arrington, Ed West, Lionel James, Al Del Greco, not to mention quarterback Randy Campbell. And that was just on offense. We certainly missed Doug Smith, Quency Williams, Donnie Humphrey, and Dowe Aughtman on defense.

When you lose a great football player, you better get everybody playing together, everybody closing ranks and playing harder. You don't dwell on it. Your focus is on trying to give the other guys who aren't hurt a chance to win. In 1984, our kids went on to win the next six games after losing Bo, including games with Tennessee, at Florida State, at Georgia Tech, and at Ole Miss.

Tough little Kyle Collins stepped in and scored three touchdowns on Tennessee. Gerald Robinson knocked the ball loose in the end zone for a safety. We won, 29-10. Tennessee still hasn't beaten us in Auburn. Or did I mention that?

In 1985, I made the biggest mistake I've ever made as a head coach. I couldn't settle on a quarterback before the Tennessee game in Knoxville. It was an honest mistake. That's the only good thing I can say about my indecision.

Anytime you lose, the quarterback gets more criticism than he deserves. When you win, he gets too much credit. The truth lies in between. We struggled a bit in 1984. We struggled in 1985.

Here's what happened before the 1985 season. Pat Washington had hurt his arm or his shoulder, preparing for the bowl game. I wasn't aware of it. Pat went through the entire spring of 1985 with a hurt arm. Being the kind of person he is, Pat didn't say anything about it. And he struggled that spring; he wasn't very productive. We had two talented, enthusiastic young quarterbacks who were fighting for playing time. And they had good springs.

That fall I should have said: Pat Washington is our returning starter. He's our quarterback. Period. And taken all that pressure off Pat. Instead, I didn't start Pat in the first two games, and I didn't start him in Knoxville.

There are things you wish you could go back and undo. But you can't. The person I feel the most sorry for is Pat Washington's mother. When you make a mistake like I did, there are people involved other than the player himself. Sometimes it's harder for friends and family to accept an honest mistake than it is for a player. Pat, being the terrific person he is, got over it quicker than his mother did. I still hate it.

Of course, we made a terrible mess of the 1985 Tennessee game. We got behind, 24-0, and were totally embarrassed. Bo banged up his knee and came out of the game. And *Sports Illustrated* wrote a story I will never get over, and I've already said, I'm not a man to hold a grudge. Life is too short. But I can't forget what they wrote and implied about a young man who stood for all the right things in college football. But I'll talk about that in a minute.

We lost the game, 38-20. Their quarterback, Tony Robinson, had a tremendous day, passing for four touchdowns. When we got back home, I realized we were in such a damn mess, I didn't sleep Saturday night or Sunday night. I walked in Monday morning and told the coaches—the whole staff—that I had screwed it up. That Pat Washington was going to be our quarterback. We were going to sink or swim with him. We went on to lose the terrific game to Florida, and we lost, I think, the greatest game that has been played between Auburn and Alabama since I've been the head coach here. And we lost the Cotton Bowl. We won the rest of them. But the losses stick in your memory.

Let's talk about the press for a minute.

The writers and sportscasters might be surprised to hear me say it, especially with what I've been through in the past year, but I get a kick out of the press. I didn't get a kick out the way some newspapers gave Eric Ramsey and his publicity-hungry lawyer a platform to make a ridiculous circus out of ridiculous charges against me. But I've been a football coach for 27 years, and I've had a good, even fun relationship with the press over the years. Sometimes I speak with my heart and not my mind, and it gets me in trouble. If you know me, you know I don't think enough people are sticking up for the "little guys," the underdogs, be they athletes who

You may not believe it, but I get a kick out of the press.

grew up without stable home environments, trying to make something of themselves, or walk-on kids trying to *work* their way into scholarships. Or maybe I'm sticking up for the benefits of an athletic dorm at Auburn for kids who need a home environment. Funny thing, a couple of years ago, I stood up for the Prop 48 athlete; I didn't think eliminating the rule was fair to the black athlete and other underprivileged kids. And I got blasted by most of the newspapers in the South, as a coach who would "use" athletes. But when John Cheney, the basketball coach of Temple, criticized the rules change, and when John Thompson, the basketball coach of Georgetown, walked off the court before a game in protest of the rules change, the national press wrote them up as heroes. I don't necessarily agree with everything the two coaches said and did, but I agree Prop 48 was a fair and good rule.

Whatever gets written about me, I don't think I'm going to stop standing up for what I believe in. I'd rather you not like me for what I am than like me for something I'm not.

I enjoy most writers. I try to respect all of them who deserve it. They are human, have their own opinions; they are not going to write everything to please me, just as I'm not going to do or say everything to please them. There's a couple of writers out there I don't trust. The ones I don't trust can ask me a question, and I'll just give them a generic answer, the most predictable response I can think of. I've got some friends in the press in Alabama, and around the South, who I can talk to off the record...writers that I trust. There have been some I talked to off the record, and it didn't show up the next day, but it showed up sometime during the year. To me, if it's off the record, it's off the record. After practice a couple of years ago, we were shooting the breeze. And a guy goes back and writes a bunch of stuff, quoting me, uncomplimentary of a FSU player. I wouldn't hurt any player's feelings in the paper on purpose. And FSU is plenty tough enough without stirring 'em up. I try to answer "on the record" questions as directly and honestly as I can. If I don't want to answer a question, I just won't answer it. I'm not going to lie about it.

I respect the job the press has to do. I sure don't agree with everything they write. In a moment of frustration last fall, when I couldn't answer charges being made against me, I even suggested on my radio show that Auburn listeners might not want to do business with the Montgomery newspaper. I didn't use the word, boycott. But I would have been better served to ignore them. I think newspapers have a responsibility to the public to be fair in what they report. But the public has to be the ultimate judge of that quality of fairness. It's not my job. I'm a football coach with my own responsibilities. But I don't have to like unfair treatment. Nothing in my contract requires that. And over 27 years, most reporters and most newspapers have been fair to me and the teams I've coached.

Sometimes I wish the reporters writing about football knew a little more about the game. But they know the final score. They know who won. You are not going to fool them about that. They can have their own opinions about what happened and why and who's to blame. And if that bothers you, you ought to just get out of coaching because you are going to be miserable. I understand people. I understand the public. I've said before, some of your best friends are going to get upset when you lose. Don't expect the press to be unemotional about it. If we lose a game to Alabama, and they want to single me out as "fourth down and dumb," that's exactly the way I would prefer to have it. I can take the heat. It can be really unfair to a player, who may have done exactly what he was supposed to do on a certain play that backfired. You can even have a young assistant coach whose confidence can be hurt by criticism. It's not going to hurt me. That doesn't mean I'm going to agree with unfair remarks. But I try not to get excited about them. If I don't think what is written, or said, is honest, I may say so, or I may just prepare my pure "vanilla" answer if the reporter or sportscaster ever asks me another question. There's an old country saying, and it's a good one, too, and it expresses my relationship with the press: "You can clip a sheep every year, but you don't never skin him but once." I don't mind getting clipped now and then. I don't aim to get skinned but once. Even then, I'm not gonna get defensive and uptight about it and spoil my pleasure in the job I love. Even with all I've been through in the last year, I get up every morning excited about my job, about making a difference in the lives of the kids I coach.

I don't even mind a little "honest" controversy. Sometimes, I get a kick out of Paul Finebaum. He's the controversial columnist and radio talk show guy up in Birmingham. I respect this about Paul: if he interviews me, he quotes exactly what I say. You can't ask for more than that in an interview. Paul even drove a John Deere tractor from Birmingham to Auburn, like he said he would, if we beat Alabama in 1989. I sure don't agree with everything Paul writes about me, or about Auburn, or about Alabama, for that matter. I don't guess Sue agrees with *anything* he writes. But sometimes I get a kick out of Paul. And if our team plays poorly, I don't expect to read in Finebaum's column, or in anybody else's column, that we are coached by a genius. The media in Alabama have been good to college football. And I think college football has been good to them; it's their most exciting subject. The press comes with the territory. I'm lucky to have the best sports information director in the game, David Housel. The first thing David is with the press is honest. I hope I am, too. We may have our ups and downs on the field, but if we can be honest about it, we'll come out okay.

Now I'll say a word about the *Sports Illustrated* story in 1985 that I haven't entirely gotten over. And I'm not a guy to hold a grudge, and I hope I never will be. And *Sports Illustrated* published a feature about me in 1991 by a young writer, Tom Junod, who was more than fair. I'm sure Junod would have preferred I not go out and have my first losing season in ten years. So would I, Tom. But I remember the 1985 story, not because it hurt me, but because of what it said and implied about Bo Jackson.

Sports Illustrated sent a writer down to Auburn. He spent a week with us. We gave him every courtesy. Went out of our way to accommodate him. We welcomed the guy with open arms.

We go up to Knoxville ranked No. 1 and play Tennessee and get embarrassed. Beaten. Bo doesn't have a very good day. He gets hurt in the ball game and comes to the sidelines.

I sure didn't expect *Sports Illustrated* to write a phony story about how well we played, or how well Bo played. I expected them to give Tennessee all the credit in the world. This was supposed to be Bo's day, and it was Tennessee's day. I wouldn't try to tell the man how to write. But he comes out with a story that's all cynicism and ridicule. The kind of truly phony story that doesn't have a source, that the writer just makes up, thinking he's being funny, saying that we in the South just expected them to give Bo the Heisman Trophy before the season started. And then implying he was a coward for taking himself out when he hurt his knee. I looked the story up and read it again, but damned if I'll quote it.

If there has ever been a young man who was fearless, and who lived clean, and who stood as much for what America stands for as any kid, it was Bo Jackson. I don't think it's expecting too much to expect fairness and judgment from the country's leading sports magazine. The writer had every chance to visit with Bo and find out the kind of young man he is. The writer didn't mind making a hero out of the Tennessee quarterback—who had a terrific day—and his play deserved all the praise you could give it. But after the kid was injured, he was indicted on drug charges and ultimately sent to jail and his football career was destroyed. It was tragic. I hated it for the young man and for Tennessee. But Bo Jackson was an All-America kid if there has ever been one. He suffered a separated shoulder the year before and missed six games and did everything he could do to come back and play, which he did. He played one of the greatest games of his life against Alabama in 1985 with two broken ribs. There has never been a greater competitor in college football than Bo, or one who came closer to standing for all the right things.

You don't watch Mickey Mantle strike out three times in one baseball game and ridicule him as a ball player. You judge him by his career. Mantle struck out a lot, but if you go to the baseball Hall of Fame, you'll see jersey No. 7 hanging there. You also judge Bo or any football player by his career. And if you visit the college football Hall of Fame in a few years, you'll see jersey No. 34 hanging there. Bo, with the help of his teammates, went on to win the Heisman Trophy. Nobody gave it to him.

Bitterness is something I try to keep out of my life. I don't believe it hurts anybody but yourself. Maybe I'll forget that story one day. The world has forgotten it. The world hasn't forgotten Bo.

We had two tough games with Ole Miss in '84 and '85. We had

to come from behind the first year to win, 17-13. The next year, they caught us after the Tennessee game, and Bo ran for 240 yards. We set what may still be an NCAA record: our 39 first downs to their two. I hated that we scored 41 points. We didn't need that many. We played everybody. I respect Billy Brewer, the Ole Miss coach. I also like him. He does a heckuva job. He's also of the Old School, like Majors and myself. We Old School guys have got to hang in there together. Brewer's teams play hard on every down. He's lifted Ole Miss back among the top teams in the conference. We'll be playing them every year from now on with the new split schedule.

David Housel called it a "wild west shootout" when we beat Florida State in Auburn in 1985, 59-27. But it was "peaceful city" compared to the year before. In '85, we were tied at the half, 17-17. Bo ran 53 yards for one touchdown. Then he ran 35 yards for another in the second half. We got out front, 31-7. FSU can score in a hurry. They got back in it, 31-27. But we broke the game wide open with 28 points in the fourth quarter. I wouldn't be surprised if that isn't a record against a Bobby Bowden team. Freddy Weygand ran a reverse for a touchdown, Kevin Porter intercepted a pass for a touchdown, and tackle Ron Stallworth intercepted a pass for a touchdown after Brian Smith flattened quarterback Chip Ferguson.

That sounds pretty wild. But that game was tame compared to the shootout against Florida State in 1984. Tallahassee is the toughest place we've been to play. The noise is unbelievable. And you are going to be up against a great team and a great coach.

Remember, Bo was hurt. Collis Campbell played the game of his life at halfback. And Pat Washington played good, I mean, *good*. You got to picture it down there at night: the crowd's on top of you in that steel stadium. A wild Indian, painted all over, rares up on a horse and throws a flaming spear in the ground. Drums are beatin'. That damn chant is goin' in the stands. They got a huge flaming feather on the scoreboard that measures the noise level, and it's lit up like a world war. Now all you got to do is go out there and whip one of the best football teams in America.

Collis Campbell ran for 93 yards, and 69 came on one run for a touchdown. Brent Fullwood scored three times from in close. Ed Graham made the wildest play of the night, picking up a fumbled kickoff return by Fullwood and running it 60 yards for a touchdown. Pat hit eight passes for 199 yards. Freddy Weygand caught four of them for 147 yards. We led, 10-3, in the first quarter, 22-17, at the half. They led, 32-29, after three quarters. And we went ahead, 42-41, with 48 seconds to play. Florida State gained *691* yards. We gained 472. The game was wilder than the yardage or the points, with that Indian circling the field on his horse every time they scored, and the crowd going crazy, and the officials having their troubles. I can tell you it was a madhouse on the sidelines.

We used a split officiating crew, half SEC, half All-South Independents, I think they were called. There were always problems between the two crews. Not just in our games. Kentucky had problems with the split crew once when they played Tulane. The last two or three times we played FSU, we got a crew of Eastern Independent officials to come down and work the game.

Anyway, the score is raging back and forth, and, finally, we get in the third quarter. They run a reverse. The Florida State quarterback clips our defensive end. The official on our sideline was standing right on top of the play. And I'm close enough to talk to him. He said he saw the hit was a clip, but it wasn't his call to make. It was the referee's. And the referee—both these two officials were Independent officials—the referee said it was a clean block. I mean the quarterback hit our end, dead center, right in the back. They scored, and they went ahead.

So we took the ball, and we came right back down the field and scored. But the last 12 yards, Pat Washington ran a bootleg, or waggle, where we fake one way and pull both guards the other way, and Pat got outside. The strong safety came up and played the run, and our guard actually hit him right in the numbers on his chest, knocking him out of bounds; as he fell, the kid turned his back and might have ended up being pushed from behind.

Now the same official who couldn't call clipping on the other side of the ball, throws his flag: 15 yards. No touchdown.

I'm trying to get this official to explain to me why he could call clipping on our run and couldn't call it on Florida State's run. I get a 15-yard penalty. Well, that's 15 yards for the clip, and 15 yards for unsportsmanlike conduct on me. I'm still trying to get him to explain, and he calls the referee over there, and I'm trying to get *him* to explain, and he drops *his* flag, so that's another 15 yards. I look up at the scoreboard, and it reads: first down and 55 yards to go.

I turned to Jack Crowe, and I said, "You got a good first-and-55 call?"

Well, we didn't score. But we ended up winning the game.

We even got a break from one of the SEC officials, but it didn't help. Nate Anderson was the umpire. The umpire calls holding and stuff at the line of scrimmage. Nate's a great guy. He wasn't gonna call much on either side. But, finally, he called a holding penalty on Florida State. It was third down and eight. Nate called holding, and that made it third down and 25. They had run the draw play on third and eight. They ran the draw, the same play again, and made 25 yards and another first down. I had to laugh, and it's still funny. Even our "own" officials couldn't help us.

The Independent officials made one too many rulings, and it backfired on them. It might have cost FSU the game. We got the ball, behind, with two minutes to go. We were the length of the field from a winning touchdown. We completed a 35-yard pass, but the officials didn't stop the clock while they moved the chains, the way they are supposed to. I called the referee over. I said, "You need to put about 10 or 12 seconds back on the clock." I was wanting all the time we could have to get the ball in the end zone. The referee shook his head; he wouldn't do it; he left the seconds off the clock.

We scored with 48 seconds left to play. We kicked off. Gerald Robinson sacked their quarterback, Eric Thomas, two times for minus 27 yards. Thomas completed passes that night for 357 yards. And the last play of the game, he completed a long pass to about our 25 or 30 yard line. It put them in field goal range, and they were only one point behind, 42-41. But they had *no time left*. If the referee had put those 12 seconds back on the clock in the last two minutes, like he was supposed to, FSU might have beaten us.

I don't know if I could live through another game like it. In fact, I almost lost it four years later at a game we didn't win at Florida State. We won three straight games against them. And then we lost three straight. And, finally, we won the last one in the series in 1990, and it was as wild as any of them but the 1984 game. All of the games between us and FSU have been tough games.

Well, we lost down there in 1989. We got off to a rotten start. We were behind, 16-3, and finally lost, 22-14, with a chance to tie in the last seconds. We couldn't do it. And we were sitting on the bus, waiting on all our kids to load up. Exhausted. Beaten. Frustrated. Our ears ringing. We'd been hearing all that noise all night, drums beating, yelling, all that chanting. And here comes a drunk on our bus, painted up like a wild Indian, screaming: *eeeeeiiaaaaaiiiaaaiii!* I couldn't take it anymore. I got him off, I got him by the throat up against the side of the bus, and thank goodness my own kids, kids I'd spent years teaching that fighting was not the way to live, they pulled me off of him and kept me from doing something I'd have durn sure regretted. I should have ignored the SOB. It took me a long time to learn that growing up. I was raised in a tough deal, and I've fought in every kind of damn situation. But I long ago learned fighting is stupid and not the way to live, and not what you need to be teaching kids. We are not going to let our players do it, in games, in practice, anywhere. And the old coach ain't going to, either. If you want to fight, get up in the ring.

I feel the same way about jiving and taunting the other team. We are not going to do it at Auburn, if we lose 100 straight games. I like the new rule against it. An FSU kid, a terrific player, ran by our bench before the 1989 game, grabbing his genitals. He did it again in 1990. Now how do you look his mama in the eye after the game, when he does a thing like that? Coach Bowden doesn't believe in it. He's really from the Old School. I asked him once why he put up with some of his players' antics. He said he stopped all that celebrating a few years ago. And they were playing Miami, and getting beat, and showing no spirit. He got on his players after the game, and the players said he told them they couldn't show any spirit. So he decided to let them celebrate after a big play. Sometimes it gets out of hand. I don't mean just at FSU. I guess Miami was famous for it. But Coach Dennis Erickson has gotten it stopped. I like the new rule. There's no place for taunting in college football. I know Coach Bowden and Coach Erickson feel the same way.

Let me make this plain: we've won some great games and lost some great games against Florida State, and I think Bobby Bowden is one of the best coaches in the game, maybe the best offensive coach. I think Alabama screwed up when they didn't hire him to follow Coach Bryant. Nothing against the coaches who did follow him. You'd have to say Gene Stallings has done a helluva job. Ray Perkins and Bill Curry and Gene are all good coaches and all have done good jobs at Alabama. But Bobby Bowden is something special. He is one of the best, one of the all-time best.

We talked about our two losses to Florida. And how great their 1984 team was. I'm glad we don't have to play that team again.

We've never lost to Georgia Tech, but it hasn't been easy. We got ahead, 41-0, in 1984. Pat Washington was hurt. And Mike Mann came off the bench to quarterback us. I'm glad he had the chance to do it. Everybody on the team at Auburn is important, including the least scout team walk-on. When we win, we all win. When we lose, we all lose. You sit on the bench, you never know when your number is going to be called. Mike's was called when Pat went down. And he answered the call. It's hard to believe, but Tech outscored us in the second half, 34-7.

Next year's game wasn't as strange. But it was just as tough. They led us in Atlanta, 14-10, in the fourth quarter. Bo ran 76 yards for the touchdown that won the game. He gained 242 yards that day. There was a critical play that maybe saved the game. Shan Morris, whose daddy, Larry, was a great player at Tech, made a diving tackle on their star runner, Jerry Mayes, on a kickoff return. I think Mayes would have scored. In fact, he was injured on the play. Shan was your classic over-achiever, who played on desire and intelligence. Even after he hurt his knee, he was a winning player. I've said before, I'm not the kind of a coach who believes you have to have an All-America at every position to win. I think you can win with a kid who just won't lose, a kid like Shan Morris.

We also played Mississippi State without Bo or Pat in 1984. Tim Jessie scored twice for us. And we kicked a field goal with 0:00 left on the clock to win, 24-21. It was another example of how tying the game can help you win it. We tied it, 21-21, with just a few minutes left to play. They came out passing and we intercepted, letting us kick the winning goal. State jumped out ahead of us, 6-0, the next year. But we dominated the game. Lewis Colbert averaged 46 yards a punt, kept them backed up.

We stayed in the conference race—for one more game—in '84 by beating Georgia, 21-12. Tommie Agee had a big day. Two big runs for touchdowns, 34 and 56 yards. The next year I guess we got the Cotton Bowl bid by beating Georgia, 24-10. Bo broke it open with a 67-yard touchdown and scored again from in close. It was a big game for his Heisman Trophy chances. Tracy Rocker was a sophomore. He made 15 tackles.

Alabama. It always comes down to that if you play for Auburn. Let me say this about 1984: I thought it was the one time against Alabama when we didn't play hard. I felt we gave 'em the game. In 1990, we played hard; we didn't play smart. In 1991, we didn't take advantage of our opportunities against a strong Alabama team. I'm not faulting the kids. I'm faulting myself.

Let's get straight to the call on the goal line in 1984. Alabama is ahead, 17-15. Kevin Greene intercepts a pass, Pat Washington runs a quarterback keep, and we're on the one-yard line, fourth down. There are three minutes to play in the game. There were several reasons I went for the touchdown instead of a field goal. No. 1, they hadn't made a first down—maybe one first down—in the fourth quarter. If we don't make it, I figure we can hold 'em and get the ball back in time to kick a field goal. Which we did. They dang sure weren't going to get fancy with the ball on their one-yard line. No. 2, if we score the touchdown, a field goal won't beat us. No. 3, if we kick the field goal, they are going to get the ball back, and they'll have four downs all over the field to get in range for their own field goal. It's a lot easier to move the ball when you are behind and willing to risk all four downs. And they are sitting there with a great field goal kicker.

We make a mistake in our play selection. We go to the line of scrimmage in all that noise with an "audible" called. The quarterback can check off and run the play to either side. If we hear the call, there is no reason the play won't work.

Bo Jackson would be the last player in the world to go the wrong way. It wasn't Bo's fault. It was our fault for calling an automatic on the goal line with the noise like it was. The last thing that Bo heard in the huddle was "Combo 57." Bo couldn't hear the automatic at the line of scrimmage. The last number he heard was his number. He went with the number he last heard. You can't blame him. And Brent Fullwood had no lead blocker and was stopped on the sweep.

If I had it to do over, I would give it to Bo over the top, like we did when we beat 'em in 1982. Hindsight is 20-20.

But, we did hold 'em. We did get the ball back. And Pat Washington did a terrific job getting us into field goal range. We missed it. But we didn't play hard that day; we didn't play Auburn football. I regret that more than the fact we lost. It's my job to get 'em to play hard.

I think the most significant thing that's happened since I've been at Auburn happened the Monday after we lost that game to Alabama. I went before the board of trustees, and they voted unanimously to enlarge the stadium, double-deck the East Side and build luxury suites to help pay for it. A couple of trustees might have been against it, but they voted unanimously for it and all of 'em showed up to get their picture taken when it was finished. The stadium would be enlarged for the 1987 season. It would go from 72,169 seats to 85,214. Coach Jordan had led a similar campaign to add to the stadium in 1980. That raised it from 61,261 to over 72,000. Coach Jordan showed a lot of foresight, because the team hadn't been playing well and wasn't filling up the stadium they had. Our teams of the eighties soon filled it up. And we were ready for another expansion. I don't think there is any doubt that the 85,000-seat stadium has had a tremendous impact on our football program. I really believe that we need to start thinking about enclosing the South end zone, the way Georgia has done. I would like to see us do that. I really would like to see us tie the expansion in with academics—both students and faculty. Let a certain amount of that added revenue go to student academic scholarships, to student government, and some of it go to faculty enhancement programs. So everybody will benefit. I've tried to do that over my years at Auburn. We gave the faculty right at $400,000 a few years ago. We also pledged one million dollars to the expansion of the library, and we've now given the majority of that pledge.

We still weren't hitting on all cylinders when we played Arkansas in the Liberty Bowl after the 1984 season. They had the best option offense we've played against since we've been at Auburn. They recovered a fumble on our six-yard line and scored to go ahead. We were struggling. I was standing by Bo on the sidelines. I told him, "Bo, if we are gonna win this football game, you've got to win it." It wasn't long after that he ran 39 yards for a touchdown. We finally won it, 21-15. We were struggling, but we had won 29 games in the last three years.

In 1985, Auburn and Alabama played a great college football game. It was blood and guts the whole way. And the kid, Van Tiffin, kicked a 53-yard field goal on the last play of the game, with no time left, and won it.

We lost, even though we came from behind twice in the fourth quarter to take a lead. But they did the same thing. We scored more points in the fourth quarter and still lost the game. We went into the last quarter seven points behind; we scored 14, and they scored 10, which was enough to beat us. Only in 1981 and in 1990 has Alabama outscored us in the fourth quarter.

There was great talent on the field that day. Bo Jackson, Brent Fullwood, Ben Tamburello, young Tracy Rocker. Gene Jelks, for them, a freshman, running for 192 yards. He ran for a 74-yard touchdown in the fourth quarter. They had Cornelius Bennett and young Derrick Thomas on defense, two All-Pros. But it wasn't just the great athletes who made the game; it was all the not-so-great athletes playing at two or three levels above their own ability, guys like Yann Cowart and Jeff Lott for us and Joey Jones and Randy Rockwell for them; Rockwell always played so hard at linebacker against us.

Bo played the game with two broken ribs. He still gained 142 yards and scored twice. It was a heroic performance. There was some controversy over the fact the TV analyst, Frank Broyles, didn't tell the audience that Bo was playing with broken ribs until the last of the game. Frank is athletic director at Arkansas, and he was a great coach there. He didn't say Bo was hurt because I asked him not to until the game was about over. Frank is a man of honor and wouldn't go against his word. I didn't want the defense ganging up on Bo more than they already would be. Some people wrote that ABC didn't bring Frank back because of it. I hope that's not so. I hope Coach Broyles was just ready to quit TV. I thought he was one of the best analysts they had.

So, we lost both games to Alabama in 1984 and 1985. And a lot of Alabama folks thought they were headed for another long winning streak over Auburn. You couldn't blame them, with Gene Jelks and Bobby Humphrey and Cornelius Bennett and Derrick Thomas coming back. But it didn't work out that way.

I made a serious personal decision after the game with Alabama in 1985. I made up my mind I was not going to let that one game ruin my life for a year when we didn't win it.

If you are going to coach at Auburn—or if you are going to coach at Alabama—you have to live in this state with a big, big football game for both sides. Nobody has more respect for Alabama than I do, for its tradition, its players, its fans. And I know that our tradition, and our players, and our fans are equal to theirs. We may not win the game every year, but our coaches are just as good as their coaches, and our players are just as good as their players, our fans are just as loyal. We've got the most loyal fans in football. Everything being relative, we are going to win our share of these games, and Alabama is going to win its share.

Now, I had to figure out a way to live with the game. I could dwell on it, agonize over it, go into mourning when we lost. But I decided, from then on, I would keep it in perspective. Play the game. Play it to the best of our ability. Hope that we won. And if we did, it would be a great win for us. And if we lost, we would get ready to line up and play 'em again next year. I wasn't gonna have the hives any more over a football game.

It was one of the best decisions I ever made. And not just because we won the next four games. I think it took some pressure off me and off our football team. It helped us play better, harder. And I know it has made my job a lot easier. I can even look at a loss in 1990 and think that it might have been good for us. Maybe we had won to the point we thought we were better than Alabama, all we had to do was show up. That attitude won't work for either side.

Not even my new attitude helped us in the Cotton Bowl after the '85 season. We lost to Texas A&M, 36-16. I mentioned they went ahead and scored again with the clock running out. I remember that. We struggled. But Bo had a great day, running for 123 yards and catching passes for over 70 yards, and scoring two touchdowns. He was voted MVP. He was voted MVP of every bowl game he ever played in. Even Bo wasn't enough. But I was glad to see him go out with a great performance worthy of the Heisman Trophy that he won. Our fans got a look at a scrappy redhead at quarterback, Jeff Burger. He came in and completed some passes. But we turned the ball over too many times, and made too many mistakes on defense to stop an outstanding team like A&M.

We struggled in the game. We had been struggling for two years. I had already made up my mind we needed to make more changes in our program and in our staff.

A NEW BEGINNING

hange. It's part of life. It's part of football. It's always unsettling. The first big change we made was after the 1984 season. We gave up the wishbone. Talk about some soul searching. It's hard to lose your religion once you've got it. I'd been living with the wishbone since I was an assistant coach at Alabama in 1971. I'd never run any other offense as a head coach. We had won at Alabama. And we had won at East Carolina, and at Wyoming, and at Auburn. We'd won the conference championship in 1983.

Coach Bryant liked the wishbone because somebody hit somebody at every position. It made football players out of everybody.

I didn't change because we weren't winning. We *were* winning. But we weren't scoring many points. I looked at the defenses we were playing against, and I just thought we had to be able to throw the ball more effectively to win championships. We could still be winning at Auburn, running the wishbone. But I don't know if we could have won three straight conference championships.

I especially looked at our last three games. I don't know when I first started calling them "Amen Corner." You know I'm from Augusta, home of the Masters golf tournament. And they call holes No. 11, 12, and 13, "Amen Corner." Many a tournament has been won or lost on those three holes. Well, we had to finish our season every year with Florida, Georgia, and Alabama. If that's not the "Amen Corner," there ain't one. Three strong teams known for their strong defenses. I just didn't feel like we were going to be able to knock those three teams down and run over 'em every year.

And the new rule that lets the offense use its hands in blocking makes it easier to protect the passer. Makes it easier to pass the ball down the field. I loved the wishbone. It made your offense tougher. It made your defense tougher, working against it. And in the wishbone, you never had a game plan because you ran the same thing every week. You just waited until Saturday to see how your opponents were gonna line up, and how they were gonna handle the option. Then, you adjusted accordingly. As I said, I miss the wishbone from time to time. But I don't miss it when we need to pass.

I'll tell you something ironic. I think the run and shoot, that Houston University and some pro teams are making so famous, is the same as the wishbone, except in reverse. You wait and see how the defense is gonna line up. Then you run your pass routes accordingly, and the quarterback reads the defense. Most of the pass routes off the run and shoot are option routes. You may have somebody running a pre-determined clear-out pattern. But there is somebody running an option route nearly every down. That is, the receiver turns in if the defender turns out, and the quarterback reads him. It's tough to stop. But the trouble with the run and shoot is the opposite of the trouble with the wishbone. There are times when you need to line up and run the ball. It's third and one on the goal line. You look like a fish. You smell like a fish. You are a fish. But you got to swim it in the end zone, anyhow. You can't get in a running formation in the run and shoot. And you can't get in a passing formation in the wishbone.

I remember when Oklahoma was still killing everybody with the wishbone. They won some National Championships with it, as Alabama did, because in those years they didn't play anybody good enough on defense to stop it. Then Oklahoma started playing Miami. And never beat Miami. They couldn't throw the ball down the field.

Nebraska hasn't run the wishbone. But they've run the option. And they haven't been able to get the ball down the field fast enough against strong, fast, passing teams, like Florida State. And Nebraska, except when Bob Devaney was coaching there, and maybe in 1983, Nebraska hasn't had the speed on defense that Oklahoma has had. But Miami has dominated college football because Miami is strong enough and quick enough to play defense, and Miami can pass the ball down the field. Don't think they can't run it, too. You can say the same for Florida State.

So, in 1985, we went to the I formation. I wanted to be able to get in a passing formation. And I wanted to give the ball to Bo going left and right. We would be able to run play action passes. We would be able to do a lot of things that we are still doing today. But our offense of 1991, that's a story for later.

We moved the ball, but we still struggled in 1985.

I'd already made up my mind before we went out to the Cotton Bowl that I was going to make some changes in the coaching staff. It probably hurt the team to do it before the bowl game. But once I made up my mind what I was going to do, I wanted to get it done. I wanted to give the coaches plenty of time to decide what they would do, to find other jobs if they wanted them. Let me be clear about that: I didn't fire anybody. But I was going to change their responsibilities. When you make changes there is always pain.

I've never fired but one coach in my life. The straw that broke the camel's back with him...we were scrimmaging; we had an upper classman who was kind of a renegade guy; he hit a scout team player downfield late. The scout teamer jumped up off the ground just to try to defend his honor. And this coach really comes down on the scout team player. After that, I thought he didn't have enough judgment to coach for me. He should have been jumping on the upper classman, who's gonna play for you, and gonna get penalties because he's undisciplined. Instead, he jumps the weak guy.

I hadn't gotten concerned at Auburn after any one ball game, even the Cotton Bowl loss. It was a long process with me, not being entirely satisfied with what we were getting done. And it wasn't as if I hadn't discussed it. Our staff was very much aware that I was not completely satisfied with what we were getting done.

Our defensive coordinator, Frank Orgel, was the first guy I hired when I went to East Carolina. We were teammates at Georgia. We are still good friends. He's an excellent football coach. And he's doing a fine job at Georgia. Our offensive coordinator, Jack Crowe, was an exceptional teacher and coach. He's proven it with the jobs he's done at Clemson and Arkansas. He did so well at Arkansas as an assistant, that when Ken Hatfield moved to Clemson, Frank Broyles made Jack the Arkansas head coach. Jack and I remain good friends. And we'll be playing against each other in the SEC's new split schedule.

It wasn't a personal thing, the changes. I had to make a

decision: if I was satisfied with our being ordinary, or if we were going to make a run again at being a great defensive and offensive football team. Making changes can be a painful part of the job as head coach. And to be honest with you, if Coach Larry Blakeney hadn't gotten the head job at Troy—and I think he will be an outstanding head coach—I would have made a change in the offensive staff in 1991. I don't know what I would have done, but I would have made a change. As it turned out, we added Tommy Bowden as offensive coordinator in '91. But we'll get to that.

After the 1985 season, I promoted Wayne Hall to defensive coordinator. And we formed an unofficial "committee" to run the offense. It all worked pretty well. We won three straight championships and beat Alabama four straight times.

I tried to hire Wayne Hall when I first went to East Carolina. He went to Alabama as a graduate assistant and then to Virginia Tech with Jimmy Sharpe. And then they got fired. And Wayne came to East Carolina. I knew he was tough, and I knew he was a very, very smart football player. I mean he came out of the toughest high school program you could imagine; he played for Tommy Owens up at Huntsville, Alabama. Wayne was just as tough as a bone. I coached him for five years. He played on bad knees. He played, not because he could run fast, or had tremendous strength, or was a fluid athlete, he played the game because he was fundamentally and technically *perfect*. He never made a mistake. He never took a false step. He wasn't strong on pass defense, but he was always in the right place, so nobody threw in his area.

Wayne came to East Carolina and went to work, and he has been with us ever since. I've never had a coach, or anybody, that I was closer to than Wayne. He is one of the outstanding young coaches in the country. He would make a terrific head coach, and I hope he will get the chance. Until 1990, every lineman who had started on defense for Auburn since we'd been here had ultimately made all-conference. That will show you the kind of job Wayne has done. One year a bunch of our former defensive linemen, who had made it in the pros, got together and gave him a fine watch. Wayne demands everything. But the players know he does it for them. We don't have to worry about our defense falling into a lot of bad habits. Because Wayne and the defensive coaches just aren't gonna let 'em do it. If you are going to build a championship football team, you better start on defense.

A POWER EMERGES

I'll tell you about the year 1986. It was a big turning point in the state of Alabama in college football. At Auburn, we had already dropped the wishbone and put in the I formation after the 1984 season. A lot of people still don't realize it, but after 1986, we were committed to the forward pass. We still are. That year was also the start of the Jeff Burger era. You wouldn't call it dull. Sometimes it was as lively as a punch in the mouth.

We started a four-game winning streak against Alabama. In Tuscaloosa, Ray Perkins decided to leave college coaching and go back to pro ball. And I'd have to say it was a shock, a *total shock*, to me when Alabama hired Bill Curry as head coach. I don't mean I was shocked because they hired Bill himself. But because I was familiar with the old resentment that still existed between Georgia Tech and Alabama. I was surprised they went to Tech to get a coach. There were so many of their own people out there who were available, who would loved to have had the job, Gene Stallings being one of them. I'd have to say I was also surprised to see Bill Curry leave Georgia Tech. I don't know if he had a lifetime job, but there wasn't even close to as much pressure on him to win at Georgia Tech as there would be at Alabama. To be frank, knowing Bill, and having recruited against Bill, being familiar with the way he was selling Georgia Tech and its "higher education" as compared to most state universities, I mean a pretty hard academic sell, I was surprised that he went to a state university like Alabama. I mean Georgia Tech is also run by the state, but Bill really sold their academic standing. We'll talk about our relationship later.

Pat Sullivan came with us to coach the quarterbacks. Remember, I had tried to hire him back in 1981. After I came to Auburn, I got to know Pat even better. Nobody had more respect for him as a player than I did. He was a great one. He'd whipped our Alabama teams two years in a row. He was a quarterback, and I was an old guard. I needed somebody to coach the quarterbacks. I asked Pat to do one thing: "Put a winning quarterback on the field for Auburn." He's done that. And he's done a heckuva lot more than that. He's a fine coach. Kids like him and respond to him. He's a terrific recruiter. He has the makings of an outstanding head coach.

Pat took over the coaching of Jeff Burger. He improved his technique, and his ability to read defenses, and helped make a winner out of him. Jeff was already a fighter, as we'll see. Pat had done such a great job that it was awfully difficult for me to bring in an offensive coordinator from the outside in 1991. And I'm not just thinking of Pat, but of our line coach, Neil Callaway, who has done an outstanding job for many years, since he coached for me at East Carolina. But Pat and Neil took it like men. And to be exposed to other offensive systems has been a great experience for them both. But that's down the road. The year 1986 was exciting enough in its own right.

As far as our "offensive committee" was concerned, I pretty much let the coaches work it out for themselves. We visited several schools in the spring, as we always do, looking for ideas. This is the way it worked when the season opened and for the next several years: Larry Blakeney and Neil Callaway sat in the press box and called our plays. Larry, more or less, controlled the passing game and actually called down the plays. Neil made suggestions for the running plays. Then, of course, Pat Sullivan relayed the plays to the field. Bud Casey and James Daniel were on the phone hookup and monitored what was going on. Once in a while I'd stick my nose in and change a call. Not often.

The fact is, a football game plan is pretty much determined in practice, a long time before you get to the stadium. You go through down and distance, field position, all the different situations you may be faced with during the game, put it on a board and chart it, and determine this is what we want to run in this situation. You cut out 95 percent of the guess work. You have a pre-determined plan for what you are going to call. And you practice all week to make

Lawyer Tillman on the famous reverse in 1986; let's just say he didn't feel too welcome in Tuscaloosa.

those plays work in those situations:

I got involved enough so I could take the blame if what we were doing didn't work. If it was going to be "fourth down and dumb," it was going to be me. That's the way I wanted it. As I say somewhere else, criticism doesn't bother me. It's the nature of the game and comes with the job.

Back to 1986. Our program was stable at Auburn. It was built on a sound foundation. And other Southeastern Conference schools were in transition. Coaching transitions put teams, people, programs in a vulnerable, weakened state. Still, we had the two losses to Alabama hanging over us, and they were returning the core of their great players.

We whipped Chattanooga and my old school, East Carolina, pretty good. There ain't no miracles on the football field.

We embarrassed Tennessee on national television, the way they had embarrassed us the year before in Knoxville. The score was 34-8. Brent Fullwood had one of the greatest days running the football that any Auburn back has ever had. He gained 207 yards. Wayne Hall's defense stopped Tennessee 11 out of 11 times on third down. I think everybody remembers the big hit Carlo Cheattom put on Reggie Cobb, knocking him out of the game, setting the tone for the whole afternoon.

We beat Georgia Tech again. Fullwood ran for 183 yards. Lawyer Tillman, our sophomore end from Mobile, caught a 34-yard touchdown pass from Burger. Lawyer let us know early he was going to have a great career...and especially against Alabama.

Fullwood made a run of 88 yards against Mississippi State, the second longest touchdown run in Auburn history. Brent had one of the best seasons running the ball in Auburn history. He gained 1,401 yards. He was voted All-America. Nobody deserved it more. Brent played all those years behind Bo Jackson, and he didn't quit, when he could have started at tailback for any team in the United States. That's why I wasn't going to leave him at home when we went to the Citrus Bowl. I caught hell about it. I knew I would. We'll get to that.

Florida finally beat us, 18-17...third year in a row they'd whipped us. We talked about how Kerwin Bell came off the bench on one leg on the winning drive. I'm glad we got all those Florida losses over with early in the book. We did fumble the ball twice going in when we should have put the game away. You've got to tip your hat to the Florida kids, though.

Georgia ran over us. I mean, ran over us. They beat us in Auburn, 20-16. We just weren't ready to play. They lined up and handed the ball to big Lars Tate and kicked our butt. Their starting quarterback had to miss the game, and they just gave the ball to their big backs. It was Vince Dooley football at its best. They kept the ball from us all day. We only ran for 138 yards. We finally got something going. But it was too late. I don't guess anybody but maybe Nebraska has run on us in Auburn like Georgia did. Georgia whipped us. But they didn't whip Kurt Crain. He made 26 tackles, 19 by himself.

I said I think the 1985 game was the greatest game Auburn and Alabama have played since I've been the head coach here. You could make a case for the 1986 game. The outcome was sure a lot more fun for us. And maybe it was the best Alabama team we've beaten. We've beaten some good ones.

We had lost two straight Iron Bowls up in Birmingham. And we had a lot of respect for this Alabama defense. We thought we had to throw the football against them. We went in with the attitude that we were going to throw it regardless of what the score was, behind or ahead, and we were going to keep on throwing it. We did that. But as the game went along, we began to run it better, too. We ran it pretty good.

Remember Bobby Humphrey ran for over 170 yards in the *first half.* He gained 204 yards before it was over. Fullwood was something for us. He ran for 145 yards. Except for the interceptions Jeff threw as we were going in for scores, Burger also played a great game.

Every Auburn person remembers the fourth down pass on our last drive. There was 2:18 left in the game. We had three yards to go or give up the ball and the game. Burger threw a down and out pass for nine yards to Trey Gainous who made a gutsy catch. Thank goodness Frank Orgel and I once went to Americus, Georgia, to see a quarterback we never signed and came away liking this kid, Trey Gainous. Burger did a good job reading the defense on that pass play. In the Sugar Bowl, a year later, we called the same play on fourth down on our tying drive against Syracuse. That time Jeff hit Stacy Danley out of the backfield for a first down. Jeff Burger was a man among men when the game was on the line.

The famous reverse. No question Lawyer Tillman raised the level of his game every time we played Alabama. Circumstances around the rivalry...some things got said to Lawyer during recruiting season...the kind of thing no school intends to happen, but sometimes it happens anyway. Kids don't forget. No need to open up old wounds. But Lawyer didn't feel welcome in Tuscaloosa. Lawyer and Bo always played their best against Alabama.

Lawyer wasn't supposed to be in the game on that reverse. It was third and goal at the Alabama seven. He tried to signal for a time-out. He couldn't get the official's attention. Lawyer had the presence of mind to go on and run the play and made a helluva cutback to get in the end zone. It won the ball game.

I have to laugh. Two years before, when a kid makes an unfortunate decision on the goal line and we don't get it in, they write me up as "dumb." And when this kid makes a fortunate decision on the goal line, and we do get it in, they write me up as "dumb." I told you I got a kick out of the press. I got a kick out of the 1986 game, I can tell you that.

The play in that game that sticks out in my mind the sharpest wasn't any of the plays we've talked about. But it was the play that saved the game, and the play that captured everything I believe about the value of college football and about what makes a winning player and a winning team.

We had a little walk-on, Chip Powell, at defensive back. He was 5-10. Weighed 177 pounds. He didn't have much speed. He didn't have much natural talent. He didn't know it. All he did that year was lead the Southeastern Conference in interceptions. He had the heart and soul of a competitor.

We are trailing Alabama, 17-14, in the last quarter. Their great halfback, Gene Jelks, breaks through the line and runs half the length of the field for what looks like the touchdown that's gonna win the game. Chip Powell was the backside corner; he was the last guy who had a chance to catch Jelks before he scored. He took off after Jelks. Chip never ran the forty faster than maybe 4.7 in his life. But somehow he outran Alabama's Greg Richardson who was trying to block him, and Richardson was a true sprinter. There is no way Chip Powell can outrun Greg Richardson. But he did. And Richardson pushed him from behind. They called a clip. And they called back the touchdown. Alabama missed a field goal, got nothing from the play. We went on to win the game. And it was Chip Powell who knocked down their last desperation pass to end it. If you ever want to know what a winner looks like, get out a video tape of the 1986 Auburn-Alabama game and look at that one play by Chip Powell, when he ran faster than he possibly could.

We beat a tremendous team, with Cornelius Bennett, Curt Jarvis, Derrick Thomas on defense. Of course, they had Bobby Humphrey and Gene Jelks on offense. And a lot of other top players. Coming out of high school, Humphrey didn't surprise me. I knew he had the tools to be a great back. Jelks surprised me. I saw him play a lot in high school. I never thought he would be big enough to be the kind of back that he was. I was wrong. The next year, Alabama moved Jelks to defense. I can't second guess anybody for doing something like that. I've moved good offensive backs to defense. I have to say, though, we thought Jelks was a more dangerous runner than Humphrey. Don't get me wrong. We thought Humphrey was a great, great back, as he has proven to be in the pros. But we felt Jelks was even more dangerous until he was moved and got hurt on defense.

Let's put the score down, 21-17, Auburn. It was a game to remember.

Here came the controversy. Brent Fullwood had gotten behind in his classes and had quit going. A helluva lot of great football

Brent Fullwood: Bo was the only back in America who could have kept this fine football player on the bench.

players in the Southeastern Conference have done that in their last quarter, or semester, of eligibility. That doesn't excuse it. At Auburn, we don't play football players who don't go to class. It would have been easy for me to be a hero and leave Fullwood at home. I felt we could beat Southern California in the Citrus Bowl without him. I could have been wrong about that. But I don't think so. We had to come from behind to win. But we dominated the game. I didn't make the decision to let Brent go because we might win or lose. I did it because I felt Auburn owed Brent. He played all those years behind Bo. No other back in America could have kept him on the bench. But he didn't leave Auburn. Also, Brent came to Auburn with a poor academic background. He had to scratch and scramble to stay eligible. He could have dropped out. He didn't. I knew Fullwood had a chance to be drafted in the first round in the pros and make millions of dollars. A kid who had never had anything. I wasn't going to ruin that chance for him. He *was* drafted in the first round, and he *has made* millions of dollars. And when one of our black players in 1990, frustrated maybe by his own late spot in the draft and by his senior season, told the press that we ran a "racist program" at Auburn, who stood up and denied it and said he owed everything to Auburn? Many stood up and denied it, and Brent Fullwood was among them. He met all the NCAA rules of eligibility for the bowl game. No question about that. I let him play. I took the heat. And I got plenty of it. And I can understand honest objections to my decision. And no kid at Auburn who doesn't go to class is going to play for us. If that one decision was a contradiction, if I bent my own rules, so be it. Ain't none of us perfect, the kids we coach, the professors who teach them, the coaches who coach them, the fans who love them—when they win—or me, least of all. I said, sometimes I get in trouble speaking from the heart and not the head. Sometimes I get in trouble making decisions the same way. But I don't mean to stop doing what I believe to be the right thing so that I can be popular.

We beat Southern Cal, 16-7. Tracy Rocker and Aundray Bruce had big hits on their quarterback, Rodney Peete, who is having a good career with the Detroit Lions. Rocker caused a safety, and Bruce caused a fumble. Ed West caught a touchdown pass from Jeff. Our defense stacked 'em up. They only rushed for 41 yards. Looking back at that game, it occurs to me that our kids have beaten some great names in the history of college football: Southern Cal, Michigan, Ohio State, Texas, Florida State, Alabama, Georgia, Tennessee, all the rich names of our own conference. I don't think there is any doubt our tradition, our program, our kids belong among the great schools, the great traditions of the college game.

It was a good year, 1986. We won 10 games and lost the two. And we were pointed toward three championship seasons.

A Tie in New Orleans

You didn't get bored coaching Jeff Burger. You didn't rest easy, either. It was unusual, getting the team ready for the 1987 season. We didn't know if the quarterback was gonna be with us. A psychology professor had accused Jeff of plagiarism. You couldn't read anything else in the newspapers, or hear anything else on the television. How did I keep the team's attention on football? That was easy. If you work 'em hard enough, all they're thinking about is surviving. They aren't worried about who is gonna play quarterback.

The University has a committee to rule on such charges. I had nothing to say about it. I did read the paper Jeff wrote. He left off some quotation marks. But I looked up the meaning of the word, "plagiarism." The *American Heritage Dictionary* says, "To steal and use (the ideas or writings of another) as one's own." Jeff left off some quotation marks, but in the footnotes, he gave the book and the page number that each quotation came from. It didn't seem to me as if he was *stealing* the ideas as his own. I'm the last person to be an expert on plagiarism. But I do think you have to take into account a person's intent. I think it was blown out of proportion. Jeff messed up the punctuation in the paper, and ought to have been penalized for it, and he ultimately was, but do you ruin his life for leaving off punctuation marks, when the sources are identified? Well, the administration didn't think so. I didn't get a vote. But I didn't think so, either.

Of course, there was hell to pay from some people for letting him play. But that's okay. I think Auburn did the right thing. I don't mind catching hell as long as I'm catching it for doing what I believe to be the right thing.

What kind of guy was Jeff Burger? He had red hair. He was a country boy. He liked to hunt. He liked to go out and drink a beer. He was kind of a Huck Finn. Except he came from a tough environment in Cedartown, Georgia. He grew up a street fighter type. He was a throwback to the old times, to the kind of kids I played with and against. I hope we all grew up to be productive citizens. I don't think Jeff was a bad, malicious kind of a guy. But if he was in a place, and something got started, he wanted to be where the action was. If you jumped on him in a Krystal, as some guys—unfortunately for them—did, you better know who you were jumping on, or you might find yourself laying across the hood of a Ford truck looking for your front teeth.

I'll tell you the kind of competitor you had in Jeff Burger. Finally, he was eligible to open up the 1987 season. We were trying to get ready to play Texas. Remember they had whipped us out in Austin in 1984 when Bo separated his shoulder. We were working out in the stadium. Seems like we had on shoulder pads and headgear, maybe we just had on headgear, but a young, energetic defensive end came a little too hard on a pass rush and ran into Jeff. And Jeff just turned around and let fly with his fist. You can hardly stick your fingers through an iron face mask; you ain't gonna ram your fist through one. And Jeff rattled that face mask with his fist.

I got with him after practice. I said, "Jeff, I've always wanted to coach a quarterback who I felt could whip everybody in the huddle. But it takes a damn fool to hit somebody in the face mask with his bare fist. Particularly when you've been through everything you've been through to get eligible." I said, "How would I explain to the press, and to your mama and daddy, if you came up with a broken hand because you hit this guy on the practice field?" That was Jeff Burger.

You wouldn't say Jeff had great ability. But he was a competitive son-of-a-gun. He played to win. And I think the one thing about Jeff that stands out, he was at his best when the game was on the line.

We opened the season with Texas on national television. The stadium expansion came off without a hitch. It was beautiful. We

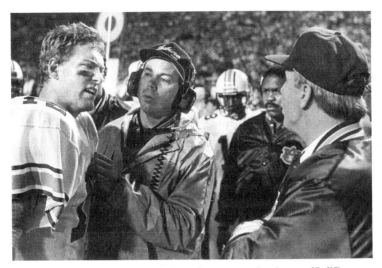

Coach Pat Sullivan helped make a fine quarterback out of Jeff Burger, who was a tough, tough competitor.

had the biggest crowd in the history of college football in the state of Alabama, more than 80,000 fans. You cannot overestimate the impact of the enlarged stadium on our program.

Texas was a good team. They were not a great team. We hurt 'em throwing the football. Since that game, we have been committed to the forward pass at Auburn. Jeff threw two touchdown passes, the last one to Alexander Wright for 49 yards. Wright came to Auburn as a track man. He'd played very little football. I didn't know if he would ever be a football player. But he stuck with it. Our coaches stuck with him. He came into his own his senior year. And he helped us beat Alabama in the biggest game ever played at Auburn. Kurt Crain made 15 tackles, and we forced four turnovers. It was a good start.

We needed a home game. We paid Kansas $400,000 to come to Auburn. It wasn't close.

Knoxville. We played to a 20-20 tie. It was a good football game. But I don't think either one of us was a real good team when we played. We had a hard time running the ball. So did they. We got out ahead, 20-10. Win Lyle kicked a couple of field goals. Jeff threw a short pass to James Joseph for one touchdown and Reggie Ware got in from the one. Reggie Cobb scored for them from inside the 10 to pull them within a point. I think Johnny did the right thing tying it up instead of going for two. He put the pressure on us. We moved it to the Tennessee 33. But we couldn't get the clock stopped to kick the field goal.

It seemed like old times going to Chapel Hill up in North Carolina. I said before the game, it was a great feeling to go in there with the same kind of talent they had after all those years of taking my East Carolina boys in to play more talented North Carolina teams. I say again, North Carolina outscored us some—but they never *beat* us.

They didn't beat us in 1987 or outscore us either. But they took it to us for a while. They blocked a punt and got ahead of us, 10-3. Kurt Crain wasn't gonna let us get beat. He intercepted two passes himself. We got four as a team. We really got after their quarterback, Mark Maye. Kurt sacked him twice. A funny thing. Their coach, Dick Crum, took the quarterback out of the game in the second half. Afterward, Crum said we were "trying to kill him." We were getting after him, all right. But we were never called for a late hit on their quarterback. They were called for *three* late hits on ours. Jeff Burger was not the kind of a guy you had to worry about taking out of a game. We won, 20-10.

Aundray Bruce tied a school record with three interceptions against Georgia Tech. He turned a close game into a 20-10 win. Jeff proved we were committed to the forward pass. He threw 46 times and completed 30, both school records. Lawyer made one of the great catches in the end zone to put us ahead 14-10 in the last minutes. On that drive, we threw 17 passes in a row. Of course, I'm known as a conservative, grind-it-out football coach. Tech played us tough, but we won again in Atlanta.

I should have known things were too peaceful. The football team had Sunday off and our center Jim Thompson and Jeff Burger got involved in a hunting trip. Jeff and Jim are both big, old, fun-loving guys, who especially love to hunt. A friend of Jim's was having a dove shoot. Actually, it was a guy who followed Alabama who flew through Auburn and picked up Jeff and Jim on Sunday afternoon. He took 'em to shoot some doves and dropped 'em back off. They didn't think anything about it.

I say again, I haven't been too smart in staying away from controversy. I make decisions with my guts instead of my brains sometimes. It may be a strong suit, but it can also get you in trouble. I don't expect I'll change. I'm going to go with what I think is right.

And that's what I did this time.

We held the boys out of the Mississippi State game the next week while we waited on a ruling from the NCAA. Reggie Slack played the whole game for us at quarterback. He did a first rate job, completing 11 of 17 passes for three touchdowns and no interceptions. We won 38-7.

We got the okay to play Jeff Burger and Jim Thompson against Florida. But we couldn't start them. I didn't want to get involved in a quarterback controversy. Burger was a senior. We were going to play him at quarterback in the Florida game and the rest of the year. It would not have been fair to Reggie to put him out there for one series. He could have made a mistake big enough to cost us the game, but he wouldn't have the whole four quarters to make up for it. I talked to Reggie. I said I wanted him to go in and take the first snap. Then we were going to send Jeff in to play the football game. Reggie didn't object, didn't say a word. He just did it. He had his time coming. There was no question he would be our quarterback the next two years—both championship years, as it turned out. Reggie knew it was Jeff's senior season, and Jeff had been the quarterback the year before. No question we could have won with Reggie. But he was a team player. He was willing to wait for his turn.

I caught some hell about that decision. Maybe you guessed that. If you did you guessed right. One thing we didn't have was a quarterback controversy. And Jeff was a white guy, and Reggie was a black guy. But they weren't white or black to me. They were just two fine competitors, two team players.

We whipped Florida, 29-6. I've said Florida Field was the toughest place to play in the SEC. Jordan-Hare Stadium hasn't been a joy ride for Florida, either. We drew 85,187 fans. Another state record. Stacy Danley ran for 93 yards and scored a touchdown, and so did the kid halfback, Harry Mose. Harry could have been a fine football player. But he hurt his neck, or he was born with a neck condition. We didn't know about it until after the Alabama game. And Harry had to give up playing. It was a shame. Win Lyle kicked three field goals against Florida. Jeff threw a touchdown to Lawyer. The defense held Emmitt Smith, a truly great back, to only 72 yards; he was averaging twice that.

Florida State was waiting for us. They'd lost to us three years in a row, and they had an open date to get ready. They were ready. And we had been fighting for survival. They came in and whacked us pretty good, 34-6. We went into the game leading the nation in turnover ratio, but we turned it over *six* times, leading directly to 17 points. We were never in the game.

But we were still in the Southeastern Conference race. We went to Athens. Jeff had a big day. He hit 22 passes. Stacy Danley ran for 73 yards. Stacy, for three years, had big games against Florida, Georgia, and Alabama, Amen Corner, and we won all three games all three years. I don't think a lot of schools have beaten those three teams three straight times. Little Duke Donaldson caught nine passes against Georgia. Lawyer caught a touchdown pass. Kurt Crain had a big game on defense.

Our defense got better and better as the 1987 season went along. We were a good defensive football team by the time we got to Alabama up in Birmingham. I guess we proved it when they blocked a punt and got the ball on our nine yard line and couldn't score. Bobby Humphrey, a great back, got it down to the one. But two of the four plays they ran were finesse plays, and they backfired. They faked a field goal on fourth down from the one, but we had pressure and the pass was incomplete. Bill Curry faked another field goal a couple of years later in Auburn but it didn't work, either.

We had a big pass play from Jeff to Lawyer off the goal line that set up our only touchdown just before the half. Lawyer, like Stacy Danley, always got up for Alabama. Harry Mose scored the touchdown from the five. As I said, it really hurt our program to lose Harry Mose to a neck condition. Stacy ran for 157 yards. Kurt had another big game, with two interceptions and 16 tackles, and he made a tremendous hit on an Alabama receiver at the end of the game that you could hear all over the field. The kid was knocked cold. I was glad he wasn't seriously hurt.

We finished with a 9-1-1 season. We were undisputed champions of the SEC, and we were back in the Sugar Bowl.

We had a great deal of respect for Coach Dick MacPherson and his Syracuse program. In fact, he and his coaches came down to Auburn the year before we played them in the Sugar Bowl. I think they came down to look at our defensive scheme. He's a good fellow, a lot of Irish enthusiasm. I got a kick out of seeing him coach his first pro game after he took the job with the New England Patriots in 1991. He was grabbing guys and huggin' 'em and hittin' 'em on the back like a college coach.

We had a lot of injuries going into the Sugar Bowl, and we lost kids as the game went along. Syracuse was undefeated, untied and ranked No. 4 in the country and had a good football team. We were ranked No. 6.

Jeff hit Lawyer, and we scored first. The lead swapped back and forth. Win Lyle kicked three field goals. Our kids played hard. Too damn hard to lose the football game. Syracuse got it down close to our goal, but decided to kick the field goal. They went ahead, 16-13, with a few minutes to play.

We were driving to win the game with a touchdown. I mentioned that Jeff called the same pass play on fourth down that he had thrown to Trey Gainous to keep us in the Alabama game the year before. This time he hit Stacy for a first down. We could have kicked a field goal on that play if we had wanted to settle for a tie. Finally, we got to their 13-yard line. It was fourth down. Our kids had played too hard to just throw the ball up for grabs in the end zone and lose. And I knew they wouldn't let Lawyer Tillman off the line of scrimmage. They'd been holding him all night, and we weren't getting a call. So I said to hell with it; we'll kick for the tie. Win Lyle kicked it through for the first tie, 16-16, in the 54-year history of the Sugar Bowl.

I caught hell from the writers. I'm still catching hell. And I still did the right thing. Some radio station up in Syracuse started a big campaign to send a load of the sorriest old neckties down to Auburn that they could round up. I came in the office one day, and here were these old ties. The nastiest looking ties you ever saw. I got the idea to put the score on 'em, and sign 'em, and sell 'em to our people for $100 apiece. We sold the ties to raise money for athletic scholarships. I have to smile every time I think about that load of old ties.

It was that kind of season. It was a hard season; it was a fun season; it was a championship season.

PEOPLE

Criticism doesn't change me, or what I believe in. I mean, I expect it. Because I know people. There is nobody who loves Auburn, who follows Auburn who is going to look at my job, or our situation, realistically. They can't do it. It's not humanly possible.

You know that those who believe in you are going to stay with you, be loyal to you, they trust your judgment, even though you make mistakes, here and there; they trust your judgment. But the most loyal one of them will want to know why you aren't playing so-and-so at wide receiver? Oh yes, it's human nature.

Truth Marches On

And the thing with Charlie Dare came up.

Vince Dooley said surviving as a coach is a question of surviving a string of crises. He was right. But that's everybody's life. Not just a coach's. I don't know anybody out here working, out here trying to make a go of it, who hasn't had his bad times. Some people may have more than others, but there is always a crisis somewhere in everybody's life. On a farm, it's every day.

The thing that I've learned—and I learned it before I ever got to be a football coach—is that you may have a drought today, but it's gonna rain some time. And if you get too much rain, it's gonna quit raining some time. You've got no control over it. In the times when you have a bad crop, you just have to be strong enough to survive it, and come back, and plant again next year, and hope you'll have a harvest in the fall.

I was down in Florida, and a friend called me and said, "Coach, you have a problem."

I said, "What kind of problem?"

He said, "I hear you are going to be investigated over the recruiting of Charlie Dare."

And I laughed. "For what?"

My friend said that Charlie's story was he had been promised by Auburn he would make his ACT score, that he could take his test in Florida where Bud Casey's brother-in-law monitored the test, and we were gonna set it up for him.

I said, that was news to me. And that I didn't believe it.

Well, I just laughed it off. The last thing in the world I was worried about was the recruiting of Charlie Dare of Enterprise, Alabama. The boy's name was Charlie. His old man's name was Robert. The boy was a big ol' lineman, highly ranked in the state. Bud Casey had met the family when they lived out in Colorado.

Our president, Dr. Jim Martin, and faculty chairman of athletics, Dr. Joe Boland, and Dr. Wilford Bailey, who had been the faculty chairman and who was now president of the NCAA, all three of them had known the Southeastern Conference was starting this investigation and not one of them had said a word to me about it. Nothing!

But I knew there was nothing to it and didn't worry about it. I laughed about it. So I went to Dallas, Texas, for the CFA meeting. I'm getting ready to leave there, and Joe Boland said, "Pat..." He said, "Er...I need to see you in my office Monday morning."

And I said, "Joe, is this about the Charlie Dare thing?"

Of course, when I said that, his eyes got big and his jaw dropped. He said, "Well, I can't discuss it."

When I got back to Auburn, I got a message from Joe that the meeting in his office had been cancelled.

The only thing that existed against me at the time was an accusation. They take the old man, Robert Dare, up to Montgomery and give him a lie detector test, with their own guy reading it. The result, *they say*, is "legitimate," he is "tellin' the truth." I understand when you take a big, old, fat guy and strap him in a lie detector machine, you can't tell often times whether he's lying or not. I don't know what they asked him. But when he accused me, he was lying. This was on a Wednesday.

Dr. Martin goes to see Bobby Lowder—remember, he's an Auburn trustee—on Thursday in Montgomery. Tells him they've got to see me on Friday. They call me and say they've got to see me Friday morning in Dr. Martin's office.

From what I understand, originally, Dr. Martin and Dr. Boland were going to let me walk into Boland's office on Monday, and they were going to confront me with the accusation and a lie detector test. Right there, before I had even *heard* of Dare's charges. When I found out about the accusation at the SEC meeting, there was a change of plans.

When they called me Thursday, I called Bobby Lowder. I said,

"Bobby, you need to be at that meeting Friday."

By this time, oh hell, yes, I knew I was looking at a potentially career-ending accusation. But one other thing I knew—it was a lie! Try defending yourself sometime against a lie. I guess I was hardened enough by the Dare experience for it to help me with the Eric Ramsey experience. Denying a lie is not easy. Following Dare's accusation, I took a lie detector test myself. I passed it. And I ain't a fat guy. I tell you it will make you sweat, even if you know the charge against you is a lie, and you are innocent. Lie detectors aren't admissible as evidence in court because they aren't always accurate. You have to worry about that when you take one.

I told Bobby, "I haven't done anything." I also said, "I've never been accused of cheating, and I've been in college football since 1965. I'm gonna do whatever's necessary to get my name cleared, and I don't even want a letter of reprimand to come out of it."

We met in Dr. Martin's office in Samford Hall on Friday morning. Myself and Dr. Martin and Joe Boland and Bobby Lowder.

Dr. Martin described the accusation against me.

I told Dr. Martin, "I don't care about the accusation. I ain't worried about that. I haven't done anything wrong. And I'm gonna hire the best lawyer I can find and make damn sure that I get my name cleared because I haven't done anything." I said, "I'm not really worried about the Charlie Dare thing. What I'm worried about is our problem right here in this room." I said, "If I had heard about something six weeks ago that might jeopardize your job as president, or hurt you, I'd have picked up the phone and called you immediately." I said, "Here this thing is, y'all have known about it for six weeks and nobody has contacted me, nobody's talked to me. Whenever the Southeastern Conference receives an accusation of an irregularity, it is supposed to go through the athletic director's office. None of this has come through my office."

I said, "I'm a helluva lot more concerned about what's going on on this campus, in this room, than I am about Charlie Dare." I said, "I resigned one job because of the president." I said, "I ain't resigning this one. I ain't leaving Auburn." I said, "When I leave Auburn, they are going to carry me out feet first. And there are going to be dead sons-a-bitches laying everywhere." As I remember, that's what I told them. And nobody said anything.

Let me say here, I liked Dr. Martin. I respected him. I think he did an outstanding job as president of Auburn. He supported our athletic program, the expansion of the stadium. I guess he presided over the biggest building boom in the history of the school. I got along with him. I helped support him every way I could, especially raising money for the library. As I said, I respected him. I still do. But I was fighting for my good name, and my life as a football coach.

Of course, the charge was a lie. A big lie. You know Hitler said, if you are gonna tell a lie, tell a big one, and keep telling it until people believe it. Turns out, we had never had even one football recruit take the ACT test at Lake Wales, Florida, where Bud Casey's brother-in-law was in charge of the testing. We signed Harry Mose from down in there, but he took the test somewhere else.

It was a painful time. The story stayed in the newspapers and on the radio and TV. But I knew I was going to come out of it from the beginning. Because I knew I hadn't done anything wrong. I realize there are times when innocent people are convicted of things they didn't do. But I didn't fear that.

So, the investigators came to me with their questions and accusations. The accusations were a bunch of lies. We caught the first lie with my calender. Robert Dare said I called at 8:30 on Saturday morning, January 8, when Charlie was in Oklahoma. Well, I didn't remember it. I knew I only called him *once*. I just didn't remember it being on a Saturday morning. I told my secretary, Jennifer, "Let's look at my schedule. Let's see where I was on Saturday morning at 8:30 on January the 8th." She checked my schedule, and I was speaking at the Fellowship of Christian Athletes meeting in Montgomery. I told the investigators, "Any business calls that I make, I either make them on the office phone, or I put it on a credit card. Occasionally, I call from my house and don't charge it to my credit card. So, I got all three records: from my house, my office, and my credit card. The only call I made to Enterprise, Alabama, was on a Tuesday at four o'clock in the afternoon. I remembered making the call. I just didn't remember exactly when I made it. But Bud Casey was down there recruiting Dare, and called me, and told me I needed to call him. I did. And I went down to Enterprise that night to a basketball game.

There was nothing to be proved against me...by the NCAA, by Auburn's internal investigation, by my own lawyer...they couldn't turn up anything. There wasn't anything to turn up.

I had no idea if a recruit of ours had ever taken the ACT at Lake Wales. I didn't even know that Mary Ann Casey's brother monitored the tests there until late June when we were having our football camp. And Bud said his son took it there. He's a bright kid. I understand he made 21. We've taken Prop 48 kids who could not pass the ACT. Some of them missed it by a fraction of a point. But we have *never cheated* to help any one of them pass the test. Nor have we been accused of it.

How did we come to be accused? I can only speculate. Maybe the old man, Robert Dare, or his son, Charlie—and the acorn didn't fall too far from the tree—shot off his mouth to Bill Curry after Charlie failed his ACT test and was ineligible to play at Alabama as a freshman. Did I forget to say? Charlie signed a football scholarship with Alabama. And Bill Curry took their accusation to the Southeastern Conference. If Bill didn't take it to 'em, he damn sure endorsed the investigation.

All Bill had to do was pick up the telephone and call me. The truth of the matter is, I never cared about Charlie Dare coming to Auburn. Charlie couldn't believe that because I did recruit him. But, remember, I only called him *once*. My lack of interest probably showed through in recruiting, because I don't think Charlie considered signing with us. He just wasn't going to fit in at Auburn. But our assistant coaches were in it, of course. They felt their personal pride at stake in being able to recruit the top kids in the state, and he was a top-ranked kid.

The problem I had with Bill Curry is that we had talked about potential problems between us, and if there was ever a problem in our recruiting, he could pick up the phone and call me. And I would do the same with him. And I did that on several occasions. If he had called, I could have told Bill I had no personal interest in our recruiting Charlie Dare. And I'm pretty active as a recruiter when I think a young man is right for our program. Bill would be in a position to know that. We've gone after the same kids enough times. I didn't want the boy; I damn sure didn't want to cheat to get him...or any other recruit. But Bill didn't call me. To be honest, I think the temptation was too great. It looked like they had me dead to rights. That I could be put out of business. And they went to the Commissioner of the SEC with it.

By doing that, Bill believed the Dares. And the old man's life was a pitiful record of failure and desperation and bankruptcy. Turns out, even during the investigation, Robert Dare was wanted by the Colorado State Police for not paying a bill he owed them.

Things haven't gone much better for him since. I take no satisfaction from the family's troubles. But I guess the old man doesn't follow the college game of football too closely. He was quoted as saying, "I don't hate Auburn just 48 minutes a year." I guess maybe he's since learned that the college game lasts 60 minutes. And maybe he's learned that lies and accusations aren't over until they are answered.

Let me say this about Bill Curry, because his side of the story isn't going to appear in this book, and the idea of this book is not to beat up on Bill Curry. If you visited with Bill, and asked him today, he would probably still think we did something wrong in recruiting Charlie Dare. It's easy for me to say Bill over-reacted. But I never had anybody throw a brick through my office window, either. There was a lot of pressure on Bill, his being from Georgia Tech and coaching at Alabama, and his never having beaten Auburn. I made every effort to stay out of that, to not put extra public pressure on Bill Curry. I still don't hold any grudges. Life is too damn short. When you carry a grudge, you don't hurt anybody but yourself. And, as I said, I like Bill and a lot of the things he stands for. Bill and I get along fine. So do Carolyn and Sue. We've got a great group of friends involved with NIKE shoes: Bill and Carolyn, and Johnny and Mary Lynn Majors, and Vince and Barbara Dooley, and there is a young group of coaches and their wives coming on.

Well, finally, August 24, 1989, the NCAA closed the Dare case, saying there was "insufficient information to support that additional violations occurred..." They accepted the findings of the university, which turned up several minor infractions. One, Charlie Dare's sister rode my horse, Lightning, or got up on him. And I was signing autographs at an Enterprise basketball game, and Charlie, who was playing in the game, came running up and spoke to me; he knew it was a violation. Bud was kept from recruiting for a year. Bud didn't deny that he might have said his son took the ACT test in Florida, but he denied telling the Dares he would fix it up for Charlie to take it there and pass it there.

I don't think it helped Charlie Dare's credibility a lot, *after* he had been interviewed by the NCAA, when he got up at a Huntsville church meeting, and told the congregation that Auburn had offered him "$70,000 and an automobile" to sign a grant-in-aid. Charlie had neglected to mention this "modest" accusation to the NCAA.

I can't say too much for the professional job done during the investigation by my lawyer and good friend, Sam Franklin, of Birmingham. The whole investigation cost Auburn $350,000.

You wouldn't believe the amount of publicity this false accusation was given over the months. And when it was finally thrown out, David Housel said, "It would be accurate to say I'm shocked that (the result) hasn't received any more media attention, that there's not as much interest in the findings as there was in the charges."

That's life. In the arena.

A CLASS OF WINNERS

W e've had four championship teams at Auburn since 1981. We've had only two losing teams. And that '81 crowd put the guts, the heart and soul in our program, and I hope no one ever forgets it. We've had two great teams at Auburn: the 1983 team and the 1988 team. With a break, here or there, either team could have played for the National Championship.

We were a special defensive team in 1988. There's no mystery why they were special. Look where those guys went on to play, at least for a while, and some are still playing: Craig Ogletree went with the Cincinnati Bengals, but he got hurt; Brian Smith with the Los Angeles Rams; Tracy Rocker with the Washington Redskins; Ron Stallworth with the New York Jets and then with Kansas City; Benji Roland with the Atlanta Falcons; Kurt Crain with Green Bay and then with Houston, and then he was hurt; Smokey Hodge played in the World Football League; Quentin Riggins played in Canada.

The secondary was one of the best we've had, even though we were playing three natural free safeties: Carlo Cheattom, Shan Morris, and John Wiley. Shan came back and played winning football after a terrible knee injury. Greg Staples was the strong safety, and he was tough.

We didn't play so well in our first game, but we got by Kentucky. Greg Staples made a big interception in our end zone to keep 'em from tying the game late.

Tennessee came to Jordan-Hare Stadium and ran into the Auburn "jinx." The jinx was a damn good football team playing at home. Carlo Cheattom set the tone for the whole game when he knocked the great running back, Reggie Cobb, cold. And we got the fumble and scored a touchdown.

We won the game, 38-6. We scored 21 points in the third quarter. Reggie Slack proved he would be an outstanding college quarterback. He completed 14 of 18 passes. One went 75 yards to Alexander Wright for a touchdown. Tracy Rocker made 14 tackles, played a great football game. Tennessee only ran for 35 yards.

North Carolina scored some points on us, but the game wasn't close.

You can't change the past. You can learn from it, but you can't change it. How much would we all give if we could go back and change something in our lives?

We go down to Baton Rouge and play LSU. If we keep LSU's offense off the field one more series, we win; we go undefeated; we play for the National Championship. Simple as that, and forever impossible.

We dominated the football game in Baton Rouge. They only rushed for 28 yards. We went into the game feeling we could throw the ball against them. We felt we could run it, too. But our plan was to beat them throwing it.

We had guys open. But something happened every time to stop us. We overthrow it, we drop it, our protection breaks down.

We had the lead, 6-0, in the fourth quarter. Win Lyle had kicked two field goals. We had the ball down around their 20-yard line. I remember it as if I were still standing on the sideline. It was third and three. We ran the ball for a first down. But there was a procedure penalty. Made it third and eight. We passed. They tipped the ball and intercepted it. We could have kicked a field goal for a 9-0 lead, and they were never gonna score 10 points.

We should have run the ball more all night. Tired their defense. Kept their offense off the field. Of course, they made a 12-play drive in the last minutes. And Tom Hodson hit a fourth-down pass for 11 yards to win the game, 7-6. You got to give them credit. It was a gutsy drive. Hodson was a heckuva quarterback. And I've still not had a team that won every game. The schedule we play, it won't ever be easy. But it's possible. You've got to have some luck. I remember Tennessee missing the point-blank field goal from the three-yard-line against our Alabama team in 1966. They had completed a halfback pass and another big pass down the middle. They went the length of the field in less than a minute. But they missed the field goal. It was our day. It was our year. You've got to have some luck to win 'em all.

We didn't get tested again until we went to Florida. Auburn hadn't won in Florida since 1972, 16 years.

We checked into the Ocala Hilton. Sue and I walked in our room, and there was a nice note: "Welcome to the Ocala Hilton. Let's start a new winning tradition on Florida Field." The young woman who wrote the note, I want to say her name was Dianne Robison. But it was Robison, I know. Auburn, class of '72. Well, I met her. And I introduced her to our squad. She was the sales manager for the hotel. And a great Auburn fan.

We were extremely ready to play. We had only lost the one game, to LSU. The afternoon of the Florida game, I didn't even give 'em a pep talk. Well, I never give a 'pep' talk anyway, but I didn't even have a pregame talk. I just walked in the dressing room and told 'em they were ready to play.

We wanted to throw the ball more that day. But we couldn't protect the quarterback. Reggie was running for his life. So we ran the football. And we ran it some more. Stacy Danley had a big day. He gained 131 yards and scored our only touchdown. Quentin Riggins had intercepted a pass and returned it to their nine. Quentin made 18 tackles in the game. He was one of the finest young men and greatest leaders ever to play for us at Auburn. If you want to know what's good about college football, just get to know Quentin Riggins.

Win Lyle kicked three field goals. We won the game, 16-3. Remember, we hadn't won at Florida Field in 16 years, since 1972. And our Ocala Hilton sales manager, Dianne Robison, had graduated in the class of '72. If you believe in omens, we were meant to win.

Georgia came to Auburn with one loss in the Southeastern Conference. They'd beaten Tennessee and Florida. Kentucky slipped up on 'em. If Georgia won, Georgia was the SEC champ and would go to the Sugar Bowl. We won the game, 20-10.

They scored first. But Reggie played one of his best games at Auburn. He completed 20 passes, two for touchdowns. And Brian Smith was all over the field. He made 14 tackles, knocked 'em loose from the ball, knocked down a couple of passes. Stacy Danley ran for 172 yards.

So we played Alabama. And we won the game, 15-10. If you remember anything from this book, remember: there are no miracles out there in college football.

We were a great defense. I believe we were ranked No. 1 in the country. Alabama was struggling on offense. They had a good football team. But they'd lost three games.

There was a big difference in this Auburn-Alabama game. It was the first time the ticket split at Legion Field was not 50-50. We had finally come to an agreement to move our future home games with Alabama to Auburn—after we played one more "home" game in Legion Field in 1991. Now that's a story we'll talk about in a minute. I think moving our home game with Alabama to Auburn was the second most important happening for our football program in my years as coach. I said before, to me, the expansion of our stadium was the most important thing to happen to Auburn football. The two events go together. We needed a big stadium to hold such a big game.

The new agreement between Auburn and Alabama meant the visiting team would get only 10,900 tickets, the same number all visiting teams are given in the SEC. So the crowd, for the first time since the series resumed in 1948, was, officially, mostly Alabama. Until the game started. The way the game went, our 10,900 fans made about as much noise as their 60,000. To tell the truth, I expect there were a lot more than 10,900 Auburn fans who managed to find a ticket. At least it sounded that way.

Reggie didn't throw a touchdown pass. But he passed for 220 yards. I didn't realize it until I was working on this book. But we didn't throw a touchdown pass against Alabama the first nine years we played them, even though we won six of the games. I guess it means we were able to knock it in when we got it down close, or we kicked a field goal. We didn't throw a touchdown pass against Alabama until 1990, and we lost that game. Maybe we better stick to the ground.

Win Lyle kicked three field goals in the '88 game. And we only made one touchdown. It was scored by fullback Vincent Harris. That's a name to remember. Vincent was never happy at Auburn. I guess he must have been happy, for a few seconds, when he dived in for a touchdown in all that noise, with the whole country watch-

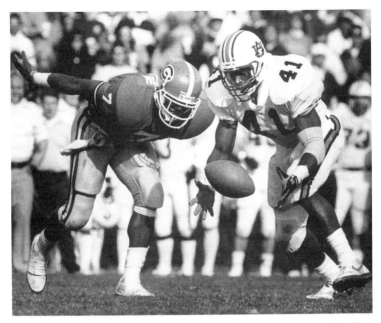

I don't know that we've ever had a finer leader than Quentin Riggins.

ing. Vincent might never have been happy at Auburn. But he did get his degree. I believe I have had a positive influence on 98 percent of the kids I've coached. I don't mean I've never made a poor decision or even an unfair decision. I'm not perfect, a long way from it, and I don't expect perfection in other people. But I try to make honest decisions when it comes to the lives of the young men who play for me. I believe the great majority of those who have been in our program at Auburn are better young men for having been in it. I believe they would tell you that. I never said I could reach 100 percent of the kids I coached. I wish I could. I wish I could have reached Vincent Harris.

Alabama, that day in Legion Field, only gained 12 yards rushing against us. Stacy Danley had another great game against them. He ran for 97 yards. Ron Stallworth sacked their quarterback in the end zone to give us the lead, 5-3. It was more like a baseball score. Stallworth had 13 tackles and four quarterback sacks.

Ron Stallworth came to Auburn a highly-recruited player from Pensacola, Florida. He wasn't ready to play big-time football. He was tall, and he only weighed about 220 pounds. He was highly recruited, but he wasn't spoiled. He came from a wonderful family. He took a redshirt year, and he still wasn't ready to play. He worked every day in practice. He had tremendous work habits. He was just a terrific young man, with as fine an attitude as any student-athlete we've ever had at Auburn. Working under Wayne Hall, Ron made himself a football player. When a young man like Ron Stallworth comes along, you know you haven't wasted your life coaching college football.

Give Alabama credit. They took the ball at the end of the game and went the length of the field and scored a touchdown. They tried an on-sides kick. But we got it. And ran out the clock.

We beat Alabama for the third straight year. That hadn't happened in 32 years. We finished the season, 10-1 and were champions of the Southeastern Conference for the second straight year.

There is no resting place in college football. When the noise dies down in the stadium after you win a big game, you better get ready to play another one. I think we got ready about four days too soon.

We were headed to the Sugar Bowl. We were going to play a great Florida State football team. We hadn't played them in the regular season. Our series started back up the next year.

We really wanted to play FSU. Emotionally, we were ready to play on Friday. If we had played on Friday, I think we would have won the football game. But we didn't play until Monday. We went inside the Super Dome, down in New Orleans, on Friday. Reggie Slack that day was awesome throwing the football. I never saw anybody throw it better. Everything we did, the entire football team, was perfection. That was on Friday afternoon.

Saturday morning, we started the other way. We lost our concentration. If you know me, you know I'm adamant about not getting a team emotionally ready to play until the kickoff. You can't win the game until it starts. In practice, you better just go about your business trying to improve, trying to get better. I knew Saturday's workout was nothing like Friday's. It scared me. We didn't practice, of course, on Sunday, the day before the game. And when the game started, we were struggling.

Oh, FSU had a great team—the big running back, Sammie Smith, Deion Sanders, the great cornerback now with the Atlanta

Falcons and the Atlanta Braves. They ran up and down the field on us the first half. We turned it over four times, but they only managed a touchdown and two field goals. Sammie Smith ran for 115 yards. He was the first back to run for over a hundred yards on us in two years. That's how tough we were on defense.

Reggie finally hit Walter Reeves, our great tight end and a fine young man, for a 20-yard touchdown. FSU led at the half, 13-7. Nobody scored a point in the second half, but we both had our chances. Smokey Hodge intercepted a pass, but we fumbled it back at the FSU 12. We stopped them inside our 20-yard line I don't remember how many times. FSU faked a field goal, and that didn't work, and they tried a couple of other gimmick plays, and they didn't work, either.

Finally, in the last minutes, we were driving. We converted three fourth down plays. We got it down close, and Reggie passed to Freddy Weygand on the goal line, and no question a defender came over Freddy's back, but we didn't get a call. That's life in the arena. On Reggie's last pass in the end zone, Sanders made a great interception. We lost the game, 13-7.

But our kids had shown all the heart and class you could hope for fighting back. I'll always believe if I hadn't taken the team to New Orleans so soon, we would have won the ball game. The loss gave us a 1-1-1 record in three Sugar Bowls. You know my theory: when you play teams as good as you are, you're gonna win about 50 percent of the time. Our bowl record is good at Auburn. We've won six, lost two, tied one. But most of the time we've had the best team. Nothing miraculous about it.

Do remember this: the 1988 Auburn team was a great one.

When you have a great football team, you can be sure of one thing: you had a great senior class. Up in Birmingham, at the senior banquet, we gave watches to some of the best defensive players ever to line up for Auburn: Tracy Rocker, who won the Lombardi Award and the Outland Trophy, one of the few players ever to win both, and Ron Stallworth, Benji Roland, Brian Smith, Carlo Cheattom, Greg Staples, Smokey Hodge, who in his fifth year was just outstanding. Smokey is proof, if you keep on workin', good things can happen to you. On offense, we were gonna miss tackle Jim Thompson, tight end Walter Reeves, guard Rodney Garner, who's now our recruiting coordinator. It's all right to lose good ones, as long as you have good ones taking their places. If you don't have good ones coming along, that's when you have problems. One of the things I like about college football is the changing personality of each year's team.

We missed those guys. But other guys stepped forward. We weren't a dominating football team on offense in 1989. But we became a fine defensive team. And we won a share of our third straight Southeastern Conference championship. We also beat Alabama for the fourth straight time. But the most important thing we did, the thing that will be remembered as long as Auburn plays football: we played Alabama *in Auburn* in front of *85,319* fans. The last brick was in place. The dream, begun so many years ago by Jeff Beard and Shug Jordan, was complete. Let me be sure and say this again: I didn't start the great tradition of football at Auburn. It was here a long time before I came. Hell, I played against it. I remember those blue jerseys across the line of scrimmage, guys who could play, guys who knew how to win. I'm just happy to have come along with a lot of great young men, and an outstanding staff of coaches, to keep alive the tradition and to take it to four championships and a lot of big wins in a lot of big arenas. Don't forget the defeats. No tradition has any staying power that can't absorb the defeats and learn from them and go on to other victories. I'm a people person. Auburn people have made Auburn football. I'm proud to be an Auburn man for the rest of my career and for the rest of my life.

In the opening game of 1989, we beat Pacific. First play of the game was a 78-yard touchdown pass from Reggie to Alexander Wright. Then we beat Southern Mississippi. We were gonna find out up the road we wouldn't always do that.

And there we were up in Knoxville playing Tennessee in a driving rain. We kept having trouble with the kicking game. Two snaps over the punter's head, one of 'em for a safety. Not the best way to beat Tennessee in Knoxville.

I remember looking over at Coach Paul Davis. We were in his hometown. He grew up in Knoxville. He'd been a great football coach for a long time; he helped coach the Georgia teams I played on. Johnny Majors, over across the field, used to coach for him at Mississippi State, owed a lot of his career to him. I don't know how old Coach Davis was, up in his sixties, I guess. He didn't have to coach. He was retired. He was a volunteer. I looked over and I felt sorry for him, coaching our kicking game. Here we were out gettin' beat, gettin' soakin' wet, snappin' the ball over the punter's head, I thought to myself, "I don't have a choice. I got to be here. And Coach Davis, you don't have to put up with this stuff." It wasn't any fun that day, that's for sure. Before the season was over, Coach Davis put together a winning kicking game.

They beat us, 21-14, and we were driving to their goal line if you can believe it when the game ended. I don't know how we stayed in it. It was a credit to Reggie Slack and a team that wasn't playing very well but wouldn't quit.

Reggie Cobb, who we'd knocked out a year before, came back like a great athlete does and ran for 225 yards, more than any back ever gained against one of my teams at Auburn. He was the first SEC back in three years to run for 100 yards against us. Craig Ogletree played a good game on defense, and so did Eltin Billingslea, who intercepted a pass.

Reggie hit Alexander Wright with an 83-yard touchdown pass to get us within three points, 14-11. Win Lyle kicked a field goal, and we were behind, 21-14. But a fourth down pass going in didn't get to Wright with just over a minute left. That was it for us. But Reggie showed that day the kind of leader and competitor he was. He passed for 285 yards in a rain that never stopped. We gave up 416 yards that day, most of them on the artificial turf. But before the year was over, we became a damn good defensive football team. And I guess it was the one year when we lost to Tennessee and still won a share of the SEC championship. When you get beat, you can't look back; you got to look ahead to the next game. Football teaches you that. And it's true every day the rest of your life.

We had to work to beat Kentucky up in Lexington. We never have an easy game with Kentucky. They scored one touchdown on us. The next seven weeks we didn't give up but one touchdown to an SEC team, Florida, and they recovered a fumble on our five-yard line.

Shayne Wasden, bless him, returned a punt 33 yards that let us score in the fourth quarter and beat LSU, 10-6. I don't know what we would have done that year without Shayne Wasden running back punts and catching passes. Stacy scored the winning touchdown. We only gave up 56 yards rushing. And we kept the heat on their fine quarterback, Tom Hodson, who had beaten us the year before in Baton Rouge. We've played LSU three times since I've been at

Auburn. We've won two and lost one. In the future, we'll play 'em every year instead of Tennessee.

Florida State beat us for the third straight year. I think only Florida has also beaten us three years in a row, in '84, '85, '86. Interesting question: what school has had the overall best teams of the schools we've played regularly? We've played seven FSU teams, and they've all been good, some of them were great. Florida's had one truly great team and many outstanding teams. Alabama has had outstanding teams almost every year, and so has Tennessee. In the early eighties, Georgia dominated the league. At Auburn, we're not short of outstanding teams to play against every year.

Our game with FSU in '89 was a lot like the Tennessee game. We went down there and got behind, 22-3, at the half. A 13-yard punt didn't help us. But we didn't give up. Frankie Stankunas intercepted a pass. James Joseph, one of the best leaders and toughest competitors ever to play for us, scored. And Reggie hit Stacy for two points and we were back in it, 22-14. They fumbled on our goal line. Reggie took it down the field. Time just ran out with us on their 18-yard line. So after six games, we stood 3-3 against FSU. But they had won the last three. One thing I wanted very much to do in 1990. I wanted us to beat FSU.

Our offense had been stalled. I was determined we were going back to basics. All the next week, we just practiced three plays: the sweep, the sprint draw, and the counter. That was it. That was about all we ran against Mississippi State. We won the game, 14-0. We only passed for 37 yards. We ran for 241. James Joseph ran for 172 yards. We ran 59 running plays, 35 of 'em by James, who was a man in every sense of the word.

Like I said, Florida was the first SEC team since Kentucky to score a touchdown on us, but only after they recovered a fumble on our five yard line. We held the great Emmitt Smith to 86 yards, half his average. They scored and held the lead until the last 26 seconds of the game. Reggie stood in there and found Shayne Wasden— thank goodness again for Shayne—in the end zone for the winning touchdown. The pass was thrown on fourth down and eleven. Quentin Riggins made 23 tackles. Like James Joseph, Quentin was one of the great competitors we've had at Auburn. I don't know that we've had a finer leader.

We beat Georgia for the third straight year. Craig made 11 tackles. John Wiley intercepted two passes. We held their great back, Rodney Hampton, a first-round draft choice by the Giants, to 29 yards. And Darrell "Lectron" Williams had his first big impact on a game. He ran for 128 yards and scored once.

Here came Alabama. To Auburn.

Before we talk about the game, let's talk about how we got it moved from Birmingham to Auburn. How we did it. And why.

ALABAMA AT AUBURN

When I first got to Auburn, I wasn't thinking about the size of the stadium, or where we played Alabama. I was trying to build a football team, trying to survive. We had a contract with Alabama to play every year in Birmingham. I wasn't even sure when it ran out. I didn't have time to think about it. There was no use making any noise until it was time for a new contract to be written. But as time passed, and we had success, and certainly, with the new addition to our stadium, it was *inevitable* that we would play our home games with Alabama in Auburn.

I got to know Auburn people. Speaking to 'em, visiting with 'em. It wasn't a matter of direct pressure, from Auburn people or from the board of trustees. It's just there was an obvious consensus among all the Auburn family that our home game with Alabama ought to be played in Auburn.

No question from a financial standpoint it would make a great deal of difference to both schools. Tickets to the game had always been split 50-50. It was pretty obvious if we started splitting the tickets like a regular home game, giving Alabama 10,900 tickets as visitors, we would be able to sell thousands more season tickets. And we've done that. You have to keep your season tickets up every year to see us play Alabama in Auburn every other year. The reverse is true for Alabama ticket holders.

Don't think the idea of changing the ticket split didn't appeal to Alabama. We were already selling more season tickets than they were. You know, Coach Bryant never pushed season tickets—it didn't bother him if they didn't sell a lot of season tickets, they were gonna sell out all the games anyway. And they really didn't have a fund-raising, priority seating system, tied to season ticket sales, like we did. They do now.

Changing that ticket split was as important to Alabama as it was to Auburn, maybe more important as they had to establish their priority ticket system. They call it "Tide Pride." It wouldn't work as well without a guaranteed ticket every other year to the Auburn game.

When did I first make up my mind we would move the game to Auburn, and that we would change the ticket split? I crossed that bridge before I proposed that we enlarge Jordan-Hare Stadium. By then I *knew* we *would move* the football game. Remember, the Monday after we lost to Alabama in 1984, the board of trustees gave us unanimous approval to enlarge the stadium and build the sky boxes. I had already discussed with them the reasons for moving the Alabama game to Auburn. Of course, they were for it. And the two boards of trustees of the two schools ended up settling the issue between them. Their lawyers actually worked out the details, but the two boards finally agreed to it.

The first time we sat down and met with the Alabama athletic department about moving the game was in 1987. We met in Atlanta. I can't remember the hotel, but it was downtown. We were playing the Southeastern Conference basketball tournament at the Omni in Atlanta. We met during the tournament.

There was Hindman Wall, and our attorney Tommy Thagard, and myself. We met with their athletic director, Steve Sloan, and Jim Goosetree, and their lawyers.

What were their first feelings about it? Well, they made it plain they didn't want to move the game out of Birmingham. I didn't blame them. Birmingham was a second home field for Alabama. I never minded actually playing the game in Legion Field. I like Birmingham. I like Legion Field. I coached at Alabama nine seasons. We won a lot of great games in Legion Field. A road game doesn't necessarily hurt the play of the visiting team. But it *helps* the play of the home team. I realize the tickets were split, 50-50, in the Iron Bowl, but the artificial playing surface, the familiar stadium itself, the people who work in the stadium and who work outside it, all of that together makes up a home field for Alabama three or four times a season. Playing there is an advantage for them. It's simple: we have a better chance of winning our home game in Auburn. Not to mention the financial benefits to us and to them.

Realistically, Alabama knew where we played our home game was our choice. What was their alternative? They could have appealed to the Southeastern Conference. But if they took it to a conference vote, I had no doubt we would be allowed to play our home game in Auburn. They could get out of the conference. They didn't want to do that. But we never had to take it that far.

What was Steve Sloan's personal feeling about moving the game? Well, he was concerned about it. He knew Alabama people wanted to play the game in Birmingham. But he also knew what it came down to was we were going to play our home game where we wanted to play it. As an Alabama administrator, he was deeply concerned about it. But as a man, he knew we ought to have the right to play where we wanted to play.

There was a contract extending the series in Birmingham. Bryant had signed it; Auburn hadn't. We didn't believe it was a legal contract. Nobody wanted to go to court about it.

Alabama was resigned to the fact we would move the game...eventually. And don't forget, a new ticket split was important to their new priority seating plans.

The compromise was worked out between our lawyers, and Alabama's lawyers, and the City of Birmingham's lawyers. And the City of Birmingham is the reason we ended up playing our home game in Legion Field one last time, in 1991. By all rights, that game should have been played in Auburn.

Well, everybody had to prove a point, everybody had to win something. Birmingham felt we were obligated to play the game there every year. Alabama didn't want us to move it at all. We intended to move the game. So we compromised. We moved the 1989 game to Jordan-Hare Stadium and all our home games that will come after it...except, we agreed to play one more home game in Legion Field in 1991. It was a fair compromise.

I was speaking to the Auburn alumni in Birmingham before the 1989 season, and I just made an off-hand remark that we were "throwing Alabama a bone, playing in their sandbox one more time." I wasn't being ugly. I was just having fun, talking to an Auburn crowd. The expression got written up big in the Birmingham newspapers. I'm afraid it hurt Steve Sloan. I have great respect

Reggie Slack: We told him to get the ball in the hands of Alexander Wright. And he did.

for Steve. I remember what a gutty competitor he was for Alabama. I remember how much he meant to us in 1965 when Coach Bryant built a football team in the middle of the season. I remember Steve gutting out those fourth down plays in the last drive against Ole Miss. Alabama never had a greater competitor or a finer gentleman.

It was unfair. Alabama fans blamed Steve for moving the game to Auburn. Steve took the blame and the criticism, but the game would have been moved if Ray Perkins had been there, or Hootie Ingram, or even Coach Bryant. We had the right to move it, simple as that.

We moved it. We still had to play it.

I can remember talking with my offensive coaches toward the end of the '89 season. I said, "I don't give a damn how you do it, but get the ball in the hands of Alexander Wright." He was one of the fastest athletes who had ever played for Auburn. But he had played very little football in high school in Albany, Georgia. He mostly ran track. We signed him only because of his speed. When I first saw him on the practice field, I honestly doubted he'd ever be able to play. He was just so far behind. We tried him on defense. It didn't work out. And we put him back on offense. Coach Blakeney did a terrific job with Alex, never gave up on him, and the kid never quit. It paid off for him. He became a top draft choice of the Dallas Cowboys, and it looks like he'll have a long NFL career. This spring he won the title as the fastest player in the NFL.

I can't tell you how big the Alabama game was for Auburn in 1989. Of course, it was the first one to be played in Jordan-Hare Stadium. I made up my mind after the 1985 season that I would treat the Alabama game as any other game, win or lose. And I had done that. But moving the game to Auburn, in my opinion, was bigger than the game itself. I said, 50 years from now, nobody will remember the score, but they will remember this was the first year the game was played in Auburn. It was just unthinkable to our fans that we would lose it.

I got up one morning and here in the paper was a story that the Alabama players had gotten death threats, that Bill Curry had called in the FBI. I guess he called them; he said he did; but the FBI never called me. Bill certainly didn't call me about it. I had never gotten any death threats. But I talked to our players, and they laughed about it; they said they had been "living with that crap for years," that it didn't worry 'em. Well, the commotion about it in the papers and on TV also didn't bother them, and it didn't bother me. I can tell you, a lot of people were not too happy about Curry's calling the FBI, including a lot of Alabama people. They were embarrassed. We just went about our regular stadium security in our regular way.

Then Curry went on TV and said how much it helped Alabama win the game with LSU when a lot of their fans, who didn't have tickets, went to Baton Rouge and stood around the stadium. He urged the Alabama fans without tickets to do the same thing at Auburn. We were a little concerned about the idea of several thousand people without tickets milling around. So, the university set up a big TV screen in the coliseum and invited people without tickets to watch the game in there. I don't know what happened to Bill's appeal, but not many Alabama fans showed up without tickets.

Looking at film of Alabama's games, I thought their coaches did a helluva job getting 10 straight wins with a team that, to me, was not a great football team. I give a lot of credit to the offensive coordinator, Homer Smith, who is now back at UCLA. He started out as an old wishbone guy. Coached at Army. I didn't know him then, but I knew about him. We were also running the wishbone. Let me say this, and I believe it: Homer Smith is a genius...when it comes to football. I understand he has a Ph.D. in Divinity from the Ivy League. It doesn't surprise me. He's smart enough to have any degree he wants. I don't think there is any question that his mind works in such a manner that he is out there beyond everybody else coaching offensive football. It's that tough to defend against his schemes. Homer got the shotgun started. I mean today's version, running the ball from the shotgun.

After all the commotion, it was finally time to play. As Coach Jordan used to say, "The talk had about dried up." Our campus was so excited, I took our team out of town to spend the night before the game. There was a feeling about that game on our sidelines. After we had walked down the street through the tens of thousands of fans to the stadium—we call it the Tiger Walk—there was a feeling among our players so strong, I knew Alabama didn't have a chance, they just didn't know it. Especially after what happened when we began to warm up. Their players came out of the tunnel and split up and some of them high-stepped down our sideline, behind our bench. I don't know what they thought they were doing. I guess they were trying to intimidate us. We just stood back out of the way and watched 'em come by. No scuffles. Notre Dame and Southern Cal fought before a game, and FSU and Miami players fought going on the field. I don't believe in that stuff. It's got no place in college football. We just watched 'em. But we weren't going to be intimi-dated. I knew that. Our crowd, from the start, picked our players up, and I knew it was going to be very difficult for Alabama to win the

The Tiger Walk set the tone for the showdown: Alabama AT Auburn.

football game. Alabama was hoping to go undefeated, and they would be playing Miami in the Sugar Bowl for the National Championship. We intended to win our third straight share of the Southeastern Conference championship.

Our coaches didn't take long to throw the ball down the field to Alexander Wright. When you have an outstanding talent, you've got to get the ball down the field to him. Sometimes you have to force it. Just like we did throwing deep, on third and five, on the third play of the ball game. Reggie Slack got good protection; he had it all day long. He stood in there and hit Wright about their five-yard line. Alex caught it over their best defensive back, Efrum Thomas. It didn't make any difference how good he was, he wasn't good enough that day against Alex. James Joseph scored. We led, 7-0.

Their great field goal kicker, Philip Doyle, hit one and then Gary Hollingsworth, an awkward athlete but a sharp quarterback, hit a touchdown pass. We were behind at the half, 10-7. They had made the one field goal, and faked a second one, but the play never had a chance. I knew by then we were the stronger team, that we would win the football game.

They had a drive going to start the second half. They tried a 48-yard field goal, into the wind. It was short. Reggie passed to Shayne Wasden, and he ran for 59 yards. James Joseph scored. We were never behind again.

And we still meant to throw the ball to Wright. He was shoved out of bounds on a sideline route—holding was actually called on

The 1989 Alabama game: You've never seen fans like these. They wouldn't let us lose.

the play and, of course, declined—and Wright kept his balance and came back in bounds to catch a 60-yard pass. It's hard to believe that the Alexander Wright who first showed up on our practice field knowing so little about football could have grown up enough to make that play. Win Lyle kicked a field goal. Then 'Lectron scored a touchdown. We were leading, 27-10.

Give Alabama credit. Hollingsworth got 'em moving for 10 points. Then they tried an on-sides kick, but our backup quarterback, Frank McIntosh, fell on it. I wouldn't take anything for that—Frank making a big play in the biggest game ever played in Auburn. Frank was one of those kids who loved the game, who never missed a practice, even when he didn't expect to play on Saturday. He had all the intangibles that are more important to winning football games than All-Americas. We tried a pass that had my heart in my throat. They nearly picked it off for a touchdown. Then Lyle kicked another field goal. We led, 30-20. I went ahead and kicked it. It put the game out of reach. I didn't want to be defending the goal in the last seconds. Even a tie would have knocked us out of a share of the championship.

We'll play Alabama many times in Auburn. Sooner or later,

they'll beat us in Auburn. Life will go on, as it always has. The sun will come up. And we'll get ready to play 'em again the next year. But in the year 1989, Auburn won the biggest game Auburn ever played.

The Hall of Fame Bowl game was fun. Down in Tampa. We played another big name team, Ohio State. It was our fifth straight bowl game on New Year's Day. We won it, 31-14. It wasn't easy. They got out ahead, 14-3. I think the play that turned it around was when they knocked out Stacy Danley. I rarely go out on the field. I leave it to the trainers and the doctors when somebody's hurt. They know what to do. But I knew how tough Stacy was. I went out there to see about him. His bell was rung. But I told him, not to walk off, to run off. Not to let those Ohio State boys know they'd hurt him. He ran off. It fired up our players. Shayne Wasden got us back in it just before the half with a punt return. It set up a touchdown. Shayne did it all year.

Reggie passed for over 300 yards. And Stacy came back to run 20 times for 85 yards.

We won 10 games for the second straight year. Our seniors won 39 games in their careers, an Auburn record. And they beat Alabama four straight times and won or shared the Southeastern Conference championship three straight times. No Auburn kids ever had greater careers.

THE WINNING ZONE

To win, you've got to rise to that upper level of effort, a higher zone, and be confident and not tight.

When I was coaching at Wyoming, I was up late one night watching a TV talk show with Billy Jean King and Chris Evert and Martina Navratilova. All three of them said that what set them apart from average professional tennis players was their mental toughness...their ability to rise up in this winning zone and hold it.

SEASON OF STRUGGLE

Struggle was our middle name in 1990. I think I said that about our 1965 team at Alabama. But we never got it turned around with the '90 team. We had our moments. We came from 19 points behind to tie an outstanding Tennessee team. We came from behind to beat Florida State, maybe the best team in the country. They went undefeated after losing to us, destroyed an outstanding Florida team. We had lost three straight times to them. I don't know if I have ever been as happy as I was the night we beat FSU in Auburn. But two weeks later, when we were manhandled at Florida, I couldn't remember one thing about the win over FSU. I doubt I could have told you the score. That's the way the game is. The losses stay with you 10 times longer than the wins. We only lost three games in 1990. And we beat a tough Indiana team in the rain in the Peach Bowl. But it was not a team that improved, and that's been our tradition at Auburn, to improve every Saturday. We had our moments, but we never truly came together as a football team. For the first time in four seasons, we lost to Alabama. We played hard in that game. We didn't play smart. And by the end of the season, I knew I had to make some changes, and as we've already seen, changes can be painful for a coaching staff.

One thing I didn't expect to do during the season, I didn't expect to wind up in the hospital. I'd never spent the night in a hospital in my life. Until 1990. It was that kind of year. And maybe I had better talk about what happened to me first. Then we'll talk about the season.

I had never been sick in my life. I mean, seriously ill. But in the spring of 1990, I had some minor trouble with my stomach. I felt hunger pains at times, or what I thought were hunger pains. I suspected I might have passed some blood in my stool. I told my doctor, Jim Matthews, about it. I started taking Zytac, and the feeling went away. Of course, when I didn't feel any pain anymore, I quit taking it, and the hunger-like pains came back. So I started taking Zytac again. But I had no other signs of illness.

Sunday night, after we tied Tennessee, I was resting, relaxing, getting ready for the next week's work. I felt a little weak, or tired. About 8:30, I told Sue I was going to bed. I got to the bedroom, and I felt a little nauseated. I looked for some Alka-Seltzer or something to settle my stomach. I couldn't find any. So, I went on to bed.

The minute I lay down I got nauseated again. I went to the bathroom and threw up. And it was solid blood.

Of course, I called Sue. And Brett was home. They took me to the hospital immediately. As soon as we got there, they started running all kinds of tests. Made all kinds of examinations. Checked my blood.

When they ran a tube down into my stomach, they saw this irritation, in the lower part of the stomach. I had x-rays, CAT scans, everything. They found that my spleen was abnormally large. At first, they thought something was wrong with my spleen. Anyway, to make a long story short, we ended up going to Birmingham to get a second opinion.

They found the trouble was with my liver. And then as the tests began to come back, they found I had an overload of iron in my system. I can't remember just how long it was before they knew the condition...it's called hemochromatosis. But they knew before the season was over what the trouble was.

The condition is hereditary. You've got to inherit a certain kind of gene from both your mother and your father to develop the disease.

Where my system retains iron, yours passes it on in waste. It takes a long time to build up an overload of iron. Nearly a lifetime. It's a gradual thing. But in the process, the overload of iron that is deposited in the liver damages it. This damage, or cirrhosis, to the liver caused by the excess iron impedes the flow of blood through the liver.

The back up of blood caused my spleen to be enlarged, and my stomach and my esophagus to develop varicose veins. The abnormally large veins in my stomach had something to do with the bleeding I had experienced. What gave the doctors so much concern was the size of these veins in my stomach and esophagus. And the possibility that if one of them ruptured, I could bleed to death before it could be stopped.

I mentioned my own doctor in Auburn is Jim Matthews. In Birmingham, I saw Dr. Christopher Truss and Dr. Albert LoBuglio. Both of them are supposed to be as good in their fields as you can find. They diagnosed my condition as hemochromatosis. And without exception, they said Emory University Hospital in Atlanta was the best place to go to treat it.

Well, after the season, I went over to Emory. They had forwarded all of my medical records from Birmingham. But the Emory doctors wanted to run their own tests. Which they did. My doctors at Emory were J. Michael Henderson and John R. Galloway.

They confirmed I had hemochromatosis. There was a question of how much damage had been done over the years to my liver by deposits of excess iron. The liver is a pretty tough organ. It can function on less than half its normal self. But if it is damaged too severely, you are talking about a liver transplant. And I came to realize that a liver transplant is far more complicated than even a heart transplant. They say the most advanced liver transplant hospital is up in Pittsburgh. They say it's like a slaughter house with livers and people waiting for them laying everywhere.

Tests showed my liver was working fine, but they'd have to get inside and see it to know just how much damage had been sustained.

I sat down with Dr. Henderson and Dr. Galloway and talked. I didn't have many options. One was to inject my varicose veins with a drug that reduces the size of them and the danger of hemorrhaging. I still would have had the back up of blood and the probability of bleeding. The injections wouldn't address the real problem, just the symptoms of the problem. Whatever option I chose, I would have to give a pint of blood, now and then, the rest of my life. When your system generates new blood, it pulls out any overload of iron. Women who inherit the condition don't develop it until after menopause, when they no longer are losing blood on a regular basis. I began to give blood, and I'll have to continue doing it.

Another alternative was major surgery.

Old Dr. Dean Warren, who is now dead, developed an operation at Emory in the 1960s to treat hemochromatosis. It is called a splenorenal shunt.

They take a vein that runs from your spleen to your liver and hook it to a vein that runs from your kidney to your heart. It's major surgery. It can take up to eight hours. In my case, it only took three.

Any treatment other than the surgery seemed to me just sticking my finger in the dike. Nothing else was a long-term solution. I decided on the operation.

I checked into the hospital on May 23, 1990. I had the operation the next day. Hospital officials told me they would treat me just like everybody else. And they did. Emory is a great hospital. They couldn't have taken better care of me. They couldn't have been more helpful to my family. And when I checked in, I slipped in the back door and missed the press.

I guess I should have been more afraid. I wasn't. I just made up my mind I would leave it to the doctors. I wouldn't fear it. If I didn't make it...well, I'd spent most of my life trying to help kids. I guess I hadn't done the wrong things too many times. Maybe the good outweighed the bad, and I would be all right in the next life. Anyway, I wasn't afraid.

Dr. Henderson had come over from Scotland to study under Dr. Warren, who perfected this operation. Dr. Henderson liked it at Emory, and they liked him, so he has stayed all of his career. Dr. Galloway went to the University of Georgia, which made us fellow alumni.

The best thing about the operation was that Dr. Henderson and Dr. Galloway were on the other ends of the scalpels. While they were performing the operation, they didn't have to use any blood, other than my own. They vacuumed up two units of blood where they were working, cleaned it, and stuck it right back in me. No need for a transfusion.

The thing about the operation, it was an immediate relief of pressure. When they hooked up the vein from my spleen to my liver, to the vein running from my kidney to my heart, the doctors said that they could see my spleen go down like a balloon. Instantly. I don't say it's a normal size, but it's much closer to normal than it was. I hope it has relieved the pressure on the veins in my stomach and esophagus, where I won't have the threat of hemorrhaging.

There is another reality for people with hemochromatosis: they suffer a higher percentage of cancer. It tends to occur in those parts of the body where the iron settles. So, I will have to be checked for that, from time to time. I'm lucky that there are no such symptoms to date.

All my tests these five months since the operation have been terrific. My liver is functioning at 75 percent, and they say you can live a healthy life if your liver functions at only 25 percent. There are no signs of any complications. I have all my old strength and energy. I feel great. Except when my football team gets beat. I don't think they have an operation for that.

I was up and around the hospital in a few days. They let me out in seven days. When I got home, I took it easy, but I stayed relatively active. I think you would say I had a normal recovery, with normal problems after an operation of this magnitude—they cut me from side to side. At first, I was uncomfortable, had difficulty sleeping, that sort of thing. But the pain of the operation, the recuperation was no big deal to me. It wasn't long before I'd get somebody to drive me to the farm or to Lake Martin where we have a lot and keep a boat. I took part in all of my summer football camps.

One of the great benefits to this recovery period had nothing to do with getting over the operation. I think the rest and recuperation that I went through was as good for me mentally as it was physically. I really hadn't had that much time off in 10 years. I'd take a week here or a day or two there. But I never had this amount of time to myself.

I was operated on the last of May, and cancelled all my speaking engagements, all my public appearances, until after the middle of July. I had a couple of things I went to in June. But the rest of it was cancelled. How did the operation, and the time off to think, affect me? I guess most importantly, the operation gave me the confidence that I could coach football as long as I wanted to coach. And I realized it's the thing I really want to do. And I'm at peace with myself, with my life. Auburn is my home, and where I hope to spend the rest of my years.

When you look up at the scoreboard, and you are behind, 19-3, at the half, to a tremendous football team, you might expect to be blown out. That was the score at the half of the Tennessee game. But it wasn't a true picture of what had happened. We'd had the ball nearly twice as many plays as Tennessee had had it. We kept shooting ourselves in the foot. I told Johnny Majors after the game that when I saw how many snaps his defense had been on the field in the first half that I thought we had a chance to get back in the game. It turned out his defensive coordinator, Larry Lacewell, was telling Johnny the same thing at the half. That they had to move the ball and keep their defense off the field.

Instead, we moved the ball. Our freshman quarterback, Stan White, had to grow up in a hurry. We scored 17 points in the fourth quarter. Stan hit touchdown passes on fourth down to both Dale Overton and Greg Taylor. The last one tied the game, 26-26. Stan completed 30 of 58 passes for 338 yards. We kicked off deep, hoping to hold them and get the ball back with a chance to win. But they drove it the length of the field and missed a field goal. So it ended in a tie.

I also told Johnny, "We could never have made the comeback without the lift the home crowd gave up. They wouldn't let us lose." Tennessee still hasn't beaten us in Auburn.

We had a fight on our hands the next week against Louisiana Tech. I got out of the hospital in time for the game. I wasn't sure what was wrong with me at the time. But I couldn't just stand by and watch us get beat. I don't know if I was helping us or hurting us, but I let it be known what I thought about the way we were playing.

We were behind, 14-13, with 2:02 left to play. We drove the ball the length of the field and Jim Von Wyl kicked a field goal to win. Stan hit eight of 10 passes. We wouldn't have won the game without Walter Tate. He made 13 tackles. He was in my doghouse at the time. He needed to make 13 tackles.

I told the players the next Monday what a sorry job we had done. I told them what it would have been like to lose that game. I said it would have been like coming home 15 years from now, to a wife and three children, who needed food on the table, and a mortgage to be paid on the house, and having to tell them that you had just been fired from your job, that you were just a complete, total failure. You can fail. But you don't have to accept failure. You can get up and do something about it. If football can teach you anything, it can teach you that.

We struggled as a team. We struggled as a family. All year.

We ran over Vanderbilt. They weren't good. But we played harder.

We needed to beat Florida State. The same way they needed to beat us when we had won three straight games from them. It wasn't going to be easy. By the end of the year, maybe they had the best team in the country. Maybe it was the best team we have beaten since I've been at Auburn. It was a damn good one.

We actually scored first. Tony Richardson carried it in from the six-yard line. But they put Casey Weldon in at quarterback. And he started every game the next two years. He took them to 17 points the second quarter. Here we were again, down 10 points at the half.

Our home crowd lifted us up. I don't know if I have ever experienced a greater home crowd advantage. Maybe in the Alabama game the year before.

Stan looked like a five-year senior, standing in there, hitting his passes. Stacy Danley scored to tie the game, 17-17. They had tried a "fumblerooskie" play on our end of the field. FSU put the ball on the ground behind a guard who was supposed to pick it up and run for a touchdown. Walter Tate fell on it instead.

Ricky Sutton made the biggest play of the game. FSU decided to pass on fourth-and-five, at our 37-yard line with 1:16 to play. Ricky broke through and hit Weldon and knocked him backward, and by the time he fell, he lost 22 yards.

Stan hit Herbert Casey who jumped higher than the secondary to catch the ball on fourth-and-eight at the FSU 18. Von Wyl kicked the field goal. We won the game, 20-17. It was a huge win.

I was in the little coach's room, just off our locker room, getting ready to do my post-game radio show. I was changing into my street shoes. I remember saying, "The good Lord wants us all to be happy. But it's a sin to be as happy as I am right now."

I guess the truth is that was our high water mark. We never again played with that much emotion. We outlasted Mississippi State, 17-16. They probably should have won the game.

And we took a tired, beat-up football team to Florida Field. We were massacred, 48-7. Florida gained nearly 500 yards on us. We couldn't run the ball a foot. We didn't pick up the blitz, and Stan was running for his life. It was the worst loss I've had as a head coach. Give Steve Spurrier and his team credit. They took it to us. Also realize, they'd had two weeks to get ready for us, not counting a soft week of preparation for Akron before their week off. We've finally gotten a week off of our own at mid-season. You need it to heal up. The modern game is so strong and fast, you have so many people banged up after five or six games. Florida has been waiting for us with an open date for years. But they have paid the price the week after our game, losing so often to Georgia.

We could have still felt pretty good about our season, I think. But we lost to Southern Mississippi at home the next week, 13-12. We were ahead at the half, 12-0. I made the decision to keep it on the ground. To win it on defense. We don't make first down with a yard to go several times. We keep giving them the ball, and finally their great quarterback, Brett Favre, throws the winning touchdown pass with 46 seconds left to play. We made a key pass interference on third down to keep their drive going. Southern Miss was not a poor football team. They beat Alabama and missed beating Georgia by inches on a last-second field goal. But we didn't play with the old Auburn intensity that won us four championships.

We gained some confidence against Georgia. We won, 33-10. I guess it was the fourth year in a row we had beaten them. We led by as much as 26-0. Stan played a solid game. Stacy ran for 88 yards. He played so many outstanding games against Georgia.

With all our disappointments, we could have shared our fourth straight SEC championship if we had beaten Alabama. We didn't do it. We lost, 16-7.

I said we played hard. We didn't play smart. We threw an interception on the third play of the game. Deep in our territory. They scored a touchdown, and then kicked a field goal in each of the next three quarters.

Stan hit Fred Baxter for our first touchdown pass in 10 years of playing Alabama. That's hard to realize, since we have won six of the games. Alex Smith broke a long run which would have been a touchdown if we hadn't failed to block the safety. We held them to 194 yards. But they held us to 237. James Willis played an outstanding game for us. He made 21 tackles. If James can stay well, he can be a great player.

We didn't play the game with the confidence and the intensity of an Auburn team. Gene Stallings did a fine job with the Alabama team after they lost the first three games of the season. I like Gene. I respect him. He was always one of Coach Bryant's favorites.

All year, we never did anything the easy way. We got behind a surprisingly strong Indiana team, 20-23, in the Peach Bowl. There were only minutes to play on a wet, slick field. Stan passed us down the field and scored the winning touchdown on a bootleg at the goal line. He completed 31 passes for 351 yards. That broke Pat Sullivan's school record in the 1970 Gator Bowl. Of course, Stan had the advantage of having Pat to coach him.

It was an 8-3-1 year, with a bowl victory. A helluva lot of schools would love to have won that many. But it was a disappointing year. Not so much the won-loss record. We never had the unity, we never played with the single heartbeat of other Auburn teams. Sometimes on a football team, your leaders are not your best players. Then, you had better be sure your team is following your leaders and not your best players. And that's the head coach's job.

Before the season was over I had already made up my mind that I was going to make some changes on the staff. I hadn't decided what changes. Larry Blakeney took the head coaching job at Troy. Larry did an excellent job at Auburn, and I think he will be a winning head coach. Larry had coached our receivers. I decided to fill that opening with an offensive coordinator. I also decided to bring him in from outside our own staff.

That was a hard decision. Pat Sullivan and Neil Callaway are outstanding coaches. I would have preferred to promote one of them. But, in my opinion, I felt we would be a better, stronger staff if we brought someone in who had had success with another offensive system. I hired Tommy Bowden.

I really didn't know Tommy. I had watched his receivers play at Alabama, and I had seen his offense play at Kentucky. I saw Kentucky take the ball the length of the field against Georgia and win the game, running the ball. His kids threw it and caught it and did everything but beat Tennessee. Except for an odd penalty, they might have beaten Tennessee. And Kentucky didn't have the athletes Tennessee did.

I met with Neil before I hired Tommy. And I wanted to meet with Pat, face to face, but he was with his family in Birmingham after the Alabama game. I spoke with him on the telephone. Both of them were disappointed. But they are both good, solid, quality men and quality coaches. Of course, after the 1991 season, Texas Christian University hired Pat Sullivan as its head football coach. They couldn't have made a better choice. In just a few years, Pat has proven himself as an outstanding football coach. I will be pulling for Pat and his staff every game they play, and I know all Auburn people feel exactly the same way.

I had my eye on two or three coaches, but Tommy Bowden was my first choice. Funny thing, I met his daddy, I believe at the Atlanta airport, some months before. I told him, "One day I'd like to hire your boy, Tommy." Bobby said, "He's a good one." He said he had three sons coaching, and they were all good ones. I had no idea at the time I would be hiring Tommy that soon.

Tommy's a fine coach. He's strong, and he's firm, and he's persistent. Just like Pat and Neil, he has great rapport with the players. No football team learns a new system overnight. We struggled on offense in the first half of the 1991 season. We moved the football. We had a balanced attack, running and passing. But we struggled in the four-down zone. We had trouble making the big play on the critical downs.

HILLS TO CLIMB

W hen I think about the 1991 season, I know I've never been through a year anywhere close to it. I guess you could call it a tremendous education. And I hope that I learned from it. Looking back, I think we had a chance to be a pretty decent football team.

Here I was lying in the bed—and I had never even spent the night in a hospital—reading that one of my former players is calling me a racist. It's not a great way to start the new year. Your health and your good name are two things you don't want to lose. To be honest with you, I'd give up my good name last.

Eric Ramsey's charges that we were running a racist program at Auburn would have been tragic—except they were ridiculous. His teammates and dozens of former black players in our program laughed at the charges. I couldn't laugh. I had too many stitches in my gut. At the time I also heard rumors that Eric had some kind of tape recordings he had made at Auburn, but I didn't think there was anything to it.

We had a lot of injuries in the spring; a lot of kids missed work, but those who were there showed good spirit. We worked putting in a new offense. I wasn't surprised that our new offensive coordinator, Tommy Bowden, was a good teacher; our kids responded to him, but you don't build a new offense in a day. As I've said before, we've been throwing the football around here since 1986.

We didn't set the world on fire when we started the season

against Georgia Southern, a good little team that's won several 1-AA National Championships. We got behind, 17-0. And did what we had to do to win, 32-17.

The next week we beat Ole Miss, 23-13, and when we played them, they were a pretty good football team. Thomas Bailey returned a punt 83 yards for a touchdown to break the game open. By the end of the season, Thomas had gained over 1,000 yards returning punts and kickoffs. Nobody in the SEC had ever done it before. Thomas also has a great future as a pass receiver. He didn't get to work much during the week on his pass routes last year because of a case of shin splints. We're expecting a lot out of him in 1992.

And then we go to Texas in Austin. I thought we played an inspired football game, even though we were struggling offensively. Texas had been to the Cotton Bowl the year before. Most of their players were back. But they had opened the season losing at Mississippi State. At that time, the "experts" didn't know how good Mississippi State was. We knew. We remembered them from 1990 when they could have beaten us. I also knew Texas would be angry and ready and playing in front of their own people. And they were all of those things. But we out-fought 'em, 14-10. I thought we played the hardest we'd played in several years. I don't know how many of their backs had to leave the game, including one quarterback. We kept stopping ourselves with penalties. And we dropped a long pass. Both mistakes plagued us all year.

I worried about the Tennessee game. To be honest, a team can't peak 11 times in a season. And we'd worked hard and played hard in an emotional game in Austin. Now we had to go to Tennessee. I could see we were a tired football team. If I had it to do over again, I wouldn't have put on pads a single day all week. We were not the same quick football team that played Texas.

And then the first Ramsey story hit the papers on Friday before the game. I'm not looking for excuses for why we lost. I never do. I only look for reasons. But the Ramsey story and the continuation of the Ramsey accusations throughout the '91 season just gutted our football team—and our staff, our students, our fans, even our administration. From week to week, our people weren't talking about getting ready to play Florida or Tennessee or Mississippi State. They were talking about what was coming out next in the newspaper. I guess I heard on Tuesday or Wednesday before the Tennessee game that the Ramsey accusation was going to be

I love a player who doesn't want to come out of the game.

published, and it came out on Friday. I called our president, Dr. Martin, when I first heard of the story and warned him to expect it. I knew from the start the university would take an impartial look into the accusations. It had an obligation to do that. I also felt the university would support me until there was evidence I had done something wrong, and I knew damn well I hadn't.

I guess the way I was raised, I've always been for the underdog, which probably led to my compassion, my feelings for black kids who I know have had a tough time. It's why I always supported the NCAA's Proposition 48. A kid who had grown up without much support at home, who didn't have a strong academic background, could go to college for a year and not play or practice but have a chance to prove in the classroom that he belonged. And then he could play college ball. It was a perfect compromise. I believe it's the American way to be given a chance. And then for me to be accused of mistreating black players on the one hand, and of doing too much for them on the other, was painful and ridiculous. Our kids couldn't understand why Eric was doing this; they were angry and frustrated. Still, we had Tennessee to play up in Knoxville.

I don't know if any of you reading this book have ever dealt with anything like that experience...of playing under those circumstances. I never had. I didn't know how to overcome it. The one thing I do know...over the course of the year, I gained tremendous respect for our players, the way they stuck together. And continued to pull together. And made an effort every week to win. Not once did they give up, or blame me or each other or even Eric Ramsey. Our seniors had a disappointing last season, but they had great careers, winning 33 games and two championships. I don't know what our 1991 record would have been without the controversy. Something hurt us, because we lost a couple of close games we could have won, which would have made a tremendous difference in our season.

If we had beaten Southern Mississippi and Mississippi State, we would have been in a bowl somewhere. We also would have had more confidence going into our last game with Alabama.

Could we have beaten Tennessee if the Ramsey story hadn't broken the night before the game? I don't know. They had a strong team and the home field. I do know you've got to have your mind absolutely on the game in front of 97,000 people. We jumped ahead. We had our chances. We were going in for a possible score before the half and had the ball taken away from us. We could have gone into the half with a 10-3 or 14-3 lead. Instead they scored and had the halftime lead. We gave up two long pass plays that we were in position to knock down. It was that kind of day.

Tennessee had a good team. They won, 30-21. And they deserved to win. Tennessee was a much, much stronger offensive football team than Texas. We never got to their senior quarterback, Andy Kelly. We didn't get the pressure on him we needed to force him into making mistakes. And we had too many missed tackles. We weren't the same quick outfit on defense we had been against Texas. I also know there wasn't an Auburn person in Knoxville— player, coach, or fan—who didn't feel sick to his stomach before the game ever started.

I'm not going into Ramsey's accusations in this book, except those against me personally, which I've already talked about. The truth will come out in our own investigation, and I can't wait until it does.

One good thing happened to me the week after the Tennessee

game. The doctors got all my blood work back, and my blood was as normal as you could expect it to be. I started giving a pint of blood once a month, which I'll have to do the rest of my life to keep my iron count down.

Two years in a row Southern Mississippi has whipped us in our own stadium. You have to tip your hat to them. Both losses hurt us and hurt our season.

We lost the game, 10-9. Seems like every offensive series some mistake would stop us: a lineman missing a block, a receiver dropping a pass, a back not picking up a blocking assignment. We let a punt hit us, and Southern Miss recovers and drives for what was a winning field goal. I thought our defense improved a bit over the Tennessee game. Our kids came back and practiced hard the next week. They didn't point any fingers. They just went to work.

Vanderbilt was no pushover football team. I didn't expect 'em to be. After our game, they went on to beat Georgia, 27-25. We were still erratic on offense. It's frustrating to the defense to stop them, get the ball back and take it down there and miss a field goal. We had to go back out and stop 'em again. I don't know what we would have done without Thomas Bailey returning punts. He brought one back 44 yards to put us in position for a last field goal attempt. This time Jim Von Wyl didn't miss. It put us ahead, 24-22, and we had to stop 'em one more time. Again, we moved the ball, but in the four-down zone, we couldn't get it in the end zone. Maybe we put too much pressure on our young quarterback, Stan White, and maybe, unconsciously, he put a lot of pressure on himself. We didn't help by dropping passes and missing blocks.

We had every chance to beat a good Mississippi State team. But we lost at our own homecoming. We haven't done that too often. They intercepted a pass for a touchdown, and we got behind, 17-3. Our defense held 'em to two first downs until their last possession. We are six points behind and block a punt but get nothing and, finally, recover a fumble on their 11-yard line and Reid McMilion scores. Of course, we get a high snap and a missed extra point. That leaves the score tied, 17-17. And four plays later, they take a pitchout 61 yards for the winning touchdown.

I told our kids, "I've been here before, and a lot of you never have, and I know how to get back up, and I hope you'll learn." We're still learning. But we'll get back up at Auburn. You can believe it.

If there was one great football team in the Southeastern Conference last year, it was Florida. At least until they played Notre Dame in the Sugar Bowl. They killed us in 1990. We were more competitive last year. We had our chances. We had the ball on their side of the 50 a half dozen times in the first half, but came away with only three points. We just didn't have the muscle to get the ball across the goal line. We began to do something about that this winter, in our off-season program, and we meant to keep doing something about it in spring training, and in summer workouts, and in fall practice. We are not going to be a football team that can't knock it in the end zone.

We got back in the Florida game at 17-10. We even made a first down after that, coming off our own goal line, but we had a penalty. I think that was late in the third quarter. Florida took control of the game in the fourth quarter. Our kids thought Eric Rhett was the best runner we played against all year. What was the score, 31-10? As I said after the game, "People don't hire you to do an easy job. They hire you for times like this." We built this program at Auburn 11 years ago, and we will build it back.

We scored 50 points on little Southwest Louisiana, and our confidence needed it. I thought we had a chance to win our last two ball games against Georgia and Alabama. I knew Georgia could run it and throw it and that bothered me. Alabama was more one dimensional, a running team. But they had the top-ranked defense in the conference. I thought we had a chance in both games. And we did. But we lost them both.

Georgia beat us for the first time in five years, 37-27. Their young quarterback, Eric Zeier, had a big day. He's a good one. We got behind 18 points, and our kids came back and scored 17. But we had to settle for a field goal again when we had good field position. After we pulled within four points, 28-24, they won the fourth quarter. That's something that hasn't happened to us often the last 11 years. But it happened too many times last year. They also controlled the ball running it, not throwing it.

We played our last "home" game in Legion Field against Alabama. I won't dwell on the game. We felt going in that we had to run the ball to have any chance to beat them. I thought we ran it effectively against them. And we protected the passer against their strong pass rush. Stan White did a good job throwing the ball. We dropped one or two that really hurt. We moved the ball well enough on Alabama to have scored more points. We missed a couple of field goals, and we fumbled the snap from center on the one-yard line. One thing we did do: we won the fourth quarter. I hope we can build on that. They were a good defensive football team. Gene Stallings and his staff have done a good job the last two years, including beating us.

That's about all of 1991 I want to think about. The first thing I want to do for 1992 is put the character and guts back in our football team. That has been the trademark of our teams in the past, character and guts. It seems to me the last two years, we have been searching for our identity. It doesn't do any good to talk about it. You've got to get it done. We mean to get it done in the off-season, in the weight room, in our conditioning, in winter workouts, in spring training, in summer workouts, in fall practice.

In the past around here, we've had hungry kids who worked hard, were willing to make those sacrifices, and as a result we won championships. I'm not being critical of the players we have now. Maybe we haven't asked them to do enough. Or maybe it's the WAY we went about asking them to do it. So, we are going to change up some things to try to create an atmosphere for our players to be as physical as they have been in the past.

We won't change a great deal. We are going to do a few things differently. Wayne Hall's still going to be in charge of our defense, and nobody is better at it. But he is going to coach the linebackers instead of the defensive line. If you know Wayne, you know the linebackers are going to get after it in 1992. James Daniels will move across the line of scrimmage and coach the defensive line. I've always believed a good coach could coach on either side of the ball, and James is a good coach.

I've promoted Tommy Raye as a full-time assistant coach. He did a terrific job last year with our special teams, and he'll handle them again this year and work with our defense.

Of course, Randy Campbell, the quarterback on our first championship team, will replace Pat Sullivan and coach our quarterbacks. Randy knows something about competing and winning. Stacy Searels, who had a great career at Auburn, will be a graduate assistant working with Neil Callaway and the offensive line. And Trey Gainous, who played with as much heart as anybody who ever loved the game, will help Offensive Coordinator Tommy Bowden with the wide receivers. Of course, Bud Casey will coach the running backs, and he'll have more speed back there to work with.

And Joe Witt will do the outstanding job he's been doing with the outside linebackers, and Steve Dennis will coach our secondary, which will be young but talented; Steve has a way of getting the best out of them.

I like our staff. It has a good blend of youth and experience. I can tell, after our first losing season in 11 years, we are a hungry bunch. I can guarantee you the head coach is hungry.

And I can tell you one thing we are going to do in spring training. We are going to run the ball into the end zone. I may practice 15 straight days in the wishbone to see who is tough enough to play the game. We better be tough enough. We play the hardest schedule we've played since I have been at Auburn.

We've got Ole Miss; Samford, a game we should win; LSU, an improved team; Southern Miss, which has whipped us two years in a row; Vanderbilt, now a competitive team; Mississippi State, that will be even stronger; Florida, and we have to go to Gainesville; Southwestern Louisiana; Arkansas, our new rival and a worthy one; Georgia; and Alabama. We better be tough. If you are going to be a good football player, sooner or later you've got to be a mean, tough sonofabitch. It's that kind of game. The greatest game ever invented to tell you all you want to know about yourself.

We'll get some help from kids we held out last year. And from kids who didn't qualify in 1991. And I think we just had one of the best recruiting classes since I've been here. The "experts" don't agree with me. The "experts" can be glad they won't have to play against them. No question Eric Ramsey's long-running charges hurt Auburn's image. But they didn't hurt our best recruiting resource: the kids who play for us. They know the truth about our program better than anybody because they are the heart of that program. It's important to us, as I have said, that any recruits get to know our players and that our players get to know them. We want young men at Auburn who respond to honest discipline and hard work, on the field and in the classroom, that dedication being the very guts of our program. Young men who spend the weekend with our players quickly learn our players work hard, but they are not abused, and they love Auburn.

I deliberately chose the Sunday night that "60 Minutes" was going to air its Eric Ramsey segment to visit with a high school running back, Steve Davis, of Spartanburg, South Carolina. I believe even the "experts" rated Davis as an outstanding player. Even "experts" can find an acorn sometime. I guess the fact that Steve is 6-2, weighs 217, and won the U.S. 100-meter dash his junior year of high school gave them some idea he was a prospect. He also rushed for 2,448 yards and scored 32 touchdowns. Steve may be a half-step faster than Bo Jackson.

Despite what the lawyer Donald Watkins said publicly—that what was on the tapes would discredit me—I knew I hadn't said or done anything wrong. I couldn't remember exactly what all was said by several people in my office two years ago; I'm not even sure I heard everything that was said because part of the time I had the Ramseys' baby in my lap; but I knew I hadn't done anything or said anything against NCAA rules. I wanted to be sitting with Steve Davis and his teammate Demond Fields, a tight end we were also pleased to sign, and with their families when "60 Minutes" came on the air.

What did Mr. Shakespeare say? A lot of sound and fury signifying nothing? Something like that. It was a dud, as far as anything I had to say. I'd told investigators long before—just as I said at the beginning of this book—that I called the bank and told them not to give the Ramseys any special consideration, to treat them like any other customers, but not to be prejudiced against them either. I don't believe in special help for any athlete, but it's not the American way to be prejudiced against anybody either.

Steve Davis and Demond Fields didn't think the accusations against me amounted to anything and neither did their families. I believe my willingness to come into the middle of their own families and take whatever "60 Minutes" had to dish out, which wasn't a damn thing, didn't hurt my credibility any. I believe Steve said, "By doing that, it showed me just how much he cared."

And I do care. I care about kids. And I care about honesty in our program. And to tell you the truth, I care about Eric Ramsey and what happens to him and his family over the course of their lives.

Where were we? 1992. We'll have more speed at running back this fall. We'll have more speed at receiver.

I'm going to be more involved in our game preparation. It's not going to be somebody else's defense and somebody else's offense. I intend to have the last say about what we do on both sides of the ball. I have confidence our coaches and our players and our fans will respond to the challenge.

We'll face the truth of our own investigation, and we'll get on with the job of putting Auburn football back where it ought to be.

I learned something when I was facing an operation. I learned I wasn't afraid to die. And I learned how much I wanted to live, how much I loved my family, my friends, Auburn people and Auburn football. I wouldn't change lives with any man. And when I make the last mile down the road, I want to be climbing some hill.

At Wanda's wedding: Brett, Sue, Wanda, me, Missy, Pat, Jr.

AUBURN FOOTBALL

Play defense, run the football, knock
the hell out of folks.